"What is man that you are mindful of him? You made him a little lower than the heavenly beings and crowned him with glory and honor. You made him ruler over the works of your hands; you put everything under his feet" Ps. 8:6-9

Author: *Dr. Bill Oswalt*

Foreword: *Dr. Earl Radmacher*

CrossBooks™
A Division of LifeWay
1663 Liberty Drive
Bloomington, IN 47403
www.crossbooks.com
Phone: 1-866-879-0502

First published by CrossBooks 12/13/2011

ISBN: 978-1-4627-1179-6 (e)
ISBN: 978-1-4627-1180-2 (sc)

Library of Congress Control Number: 2011960256

Printed in the United States of America

This book is printed on acid-free paper.

Certain stock imagery © Thinkstock.
Any people depicted in stock imagery provided by Thinkstock are models, and such images are being used for illustrative purposes only.

TABLE OF CONTENTS

FOREWORD

This book is designed to be a practical application of the process of discipleship demonstrated by Christ the Master Disciplemaker. It is not an exegetical development of Mat. 5:1-16. In theological terms, this is a progressive process that will take one from unbelief to regeneration (justification), from immaturity as a believer to maturity (sanctification), and from mortality to immortality with Him in glory (glorification).

Help I'm Hurting is a practical guide for anyone who wants to experience God's best in their life. It is the result of many years of study, years of development in his life and helping others in troubling situations. Bill has also used this book as a text for training Biblical counselors to help people not only restore and improve their life and marriages but to become true disciples of our risen Savior (Jn. 8:31). Dr. Oswalt's counseling and teaching has blessed many, many people who have been suffering because of a lack of understanding of these Biblical principles. Peace and happiness are promised as a result of following these principles.

The book is based upon the beatitudes as a guide to discipleship. This portion of Scripture is an introduction to the Sermon on the Mount which is Christ's first recorded sermon. Many other books have been written about the beatitudes and many have been helpful but none that I have seen equal this one for readability, practicality, and Biblical content. Dr. Oswalt has a genuine love for people and a real desire to help them to grow and learn—to live life in the rich fullness that flows from Christian maturity. This book truly accomplishes Dr. Oswalt's goal of providing a roadmap from new birth to maturity as God really desires for us.

Wherever a person is along the scale of Christian maturity, this book will be of great benefit. The beatitudes present a progressive process of spiritual growth for the citizen of the Kingdom of Heaven. It helps to really understand what happens at the point of regeneration and how God continually keeps us in his presence through his great power (1 Pet. 1:3-5).

Help I'm Hurting not only helps us understand the concept of sanctification but will help us discern what Jesus meant when He said, "Repent for the kingdom of heaven is at hand" (Mat. 4:17), "Theirs is the kingdom of heaven" (Mat. 5:3), "They shall inherit the earth" (Mat. 5:5), and "Your reward is in heaven" (Mat. 5:10). Jesus said, "… great is your reward in heaven" (Mat. 5:12). The last chapter will develop a Biblical concept of rewards and crowns leaving us with the question of what are we doing here on earth with what he has given us. This is all about our training now for reigning with him in the future Kingdom here on earth.

Dr. Oswalt has been my student for many years. First as a new seminary student fresh out of the U. S. Air Force, and finally as a candidate for a doctorate, earning his degree in 1996. This book was first written as his doctoral dissertation which I reviewed as his faculty advisor at Western Conservative Baptist Seminary. But this was not the first time I had seen the writings of Dr. Oswalt. As the material in this book was developed over the years, I had many opportunities to assist him and to see the benefits and blessings which flowed from these Biblical, truths as Dr. Oswalt and his staff assisted those seeking their help in finding God's direction for their lives.

I heartily recommend this book to anyone who wants to become a growing Christian—to anyone who wants to receive all the benefits and blessings, the peace and joy that always result from being closer to our loving God and more like his Son.

Dr. Earl Radmacher

ENDORSEMENTS

What a practical book!   Dr. Oswalt's down to earth, but totally Biblical approach to solving life's problems shows the reader how to gain true peace and joy here on Earth, and to gain rewards in heaven." After helping us get our life in order, this book shows us how to help others achieve that same peace and joy. What better way can we spend our time than doing these things? This book takes us by the hand and leads us to real happiness.

Terry George, Lawyer

So many of us struggle with identity in Christ, and then watch our relationship descend into a pit of mediocrity and confusion. Jesus knows this, and provides answers in His Matthew five discourse. Dr. Bill's beautiful amplification is practical, concrete and reveals with depth the hope and healing contained in Christ's message. Dr. Bill has taken a passage that is often read quickly and with little thought, and uncovers the power that Christ was all about.   Dr. Kurt Frederick M.D. Physician

The vast majority of Christians seeking psychiatric help do not need medication but every Christian benefits by growing in the grace and knowledge of Christ and in applying the beatitudes. It is my prayer that God would enable all of us to follow the principles Jesus introduces in Mat. 5:1-16. Dr. Oswalt has done a wonderful job in pointing us to a meaningful walk with Christ that guarantees us inner joy and peace.

Dr. Frank Minirth M.D. Psychiatrist

Help I'm Hurting is an incredible book that has truly improved my life and made it more meaningful. It did so by sharing a biblical discipleship model based on the beatitudes in Mathew 5 that provides me the opportunity to renew my mind. Progressing through being poor in spirit, mourning, meekness, hunger and thirst, merciful, pure in heart, and peacemaker my mind and heart are opened anew to the Gospel and the opportunity to be remade into the image of our Savior and Lord - Jesus Christ. More importantly, it provides me the tools to come along side other believers and disciple them. While the Bible can stand alone, fully defending its truth, we, on the other hand, are at the mercy of our understanding of its truth to defend God's word and lead others to a better place because we can only share what we possess. Reading and studying Dr. Bill Oswalt's book improved my understanding of much of the biblical truth I already knew and unwrapped my spiritual gift which I can now better share with others as God so leads.

Brad McMurray B.S., M.S. Businessman

The following is a result of Brad's changes. The biggest change I have seen in my husband since he began his study with Dr. Bill is twofold: his focus has changed and that has changed the way he responds to the world. His focus has become more eternal and less worldly. He seeks to make wise decisions based on what the Lord desires for him rather than what the world expects from him. He has a great desire to reign with Christ and wants to live a life worthy of that honor. When he instructs or disciplines our daughters, he uses truth from the Bible to help guide them toward godly living and wisdom. He seeks knowledge and wisdom from God's word to give him the discernment he needs as a husband, father and leader in our church. This new focus has reduced his stress and anger - he responds to challenges with more peace and trust. His compassion for others has greatly increased and he seeks to be available to be a witness for Christ in all aspects of his life. I see more humility in him as he leads our family and interacts with the people around him. His deeper love for the Lord has given him a new love for the people around him.

Lou Ann McMurray, BSF Teaching Leader

THEOLOGICAL TERMS USED IN THIS BOOK

ADMONISH — To put into the mind, sometimes to counsel, to correct wrong doing.

APOSTLE — One sent from. In Scripture there are two categories, first are those sent personally by Jesus (Acts 1:21-22, 2 Cor. 12:11-13) and second those sent by the Church (Phil. 2:25).

AUTHORITY — Liberty, freedom, power or rights, used of Jesus (Mat. 28:18), of people (1 Cor. 8:9), and of demons (Eph. 6:1-3).

CONFESS — To speak the same thing, to agree with, to admit guilt.

CONSCIENCE — To act with knowledge; that is, the mind, emotions, and will acting with knowledge from God or from the world

DEFERENCE — To defer one's opinion, to yield personal rights and take on responsibility (Phil. 2:1-4)

DISCIPLE — One who follows a teacher; a learner, involves thought and action, learning and doing.

EVANGELIST — A called man (Eph. 4:11-12), one who teaches church members how to share the Good News with their contemporaries.

EXHORTATION — A spiritual gift of one who comes along side a person, to admonish.

FORGIVENESS — An accounting term meaning to remove from the record or removing the penalty.

GODLINESS — To be conformed to the image of Christ, to be devout (2 Pet. 1:3-7)

JUSTIFICATION — To be declared righteous by faith alone, a one time event that occurs when you believe in Christ for eternal life (Rom. 4:25, 5:18-21).

PARTAKER — Sharing in His kingdom; one who is participating in His kingdom in this present age and training to reign with Him in the future (2 Tim. 2:11-13, Heb. 3:12-15).

PREDESTINATE — The predetermination of one's destiny; to a predetermined place in heaven.

REPENTANCE — To change the mind; to rethink; a paradigm shift

SANCTIFICATION — Set apart for God; to be conformed to the image of Christ; one participating (partaker) in His kingdom now is being sanctified. It is related to the process of discipleship. As we are being sanctified (a life time process) we are laying up treasures in heaven.

CHAPTER 1 - INTRODUCTION

"At that time Jesus answered and said, 'I thank You, Father, Lord of heaven and earth, that You have hidden these things from the wise and prudent and have revealed them to babes. Even so, Father, for so it seemed good in Your sight" Mt. 11:25.

God's Desire for His Children

Do you think you really desire God's best in your life? If you do, that makes you a very special person to God. He tells us that "those who seek shall find" (Mt. 7:7). My next question is, "Do you think you will be willing to do the things necessary to get His best?" Before reading this material, please consider the following exhortation from Jesus Christ the King of Kings and Lord of Lords. He came to establish His Kingdom on earth as it is in heaven (Lk. 1:32-33, 67-79, Mt. 2:1-6, 6:9-13, Mk. 1:14) and the religious leaders rejected Him. He now turns to those who will listen. That is you and I! If you have questions about your salvation and whether you are going to heaven, note appendix page 154. This book is designed to give you positive assurance of your eternal security. Because Jesus says;

"All things have been delivered to Me by My Father, and no one knows the Son except the Father. Nor does anyone know the Father except the Son, and *the one* to whom the Son wills to reveal *Him* Come to Me, all *you* who labor and are heavy laden, and I will give you rest. Take My yoke upon you and learn from Me, for I am gentle and lowly in heart, and you will find rest for your souls. For My yoke *is* easy and My burden is light" (Mt. 11:27-30).

Jesus had announced three woes on the cities He had just preached to and they did not repent (Mt. 11:20-24). Now He speaks to those Jews who were physically tired from laboring to pay the Roman taxes and temple taxes and providing for their families. Does that sound familiar? They were psychologically drained by all the religious responsibilities placed on them by the rabbis, priests, scribes and Pharisees. They were, in a sense, crying out "Help I'm Hurting." Then Jesus gives them the proper source for help. "Come to Me"—the One who has been given all authority in heaven and on earth—and He will give you rest.

That really sounds good! But how can I experience that rest today? What this process is all about is to demonstrate how we can experience His peace today. It involves first getting in the yoke with Him, that is believing in Him (continuous action, go on believing); coming to Him, becoming a citizen of the Kingdom of Heaven for eternal life. Secondly is learning; "learn of Me," understanding the nature of Christ and His Kingdom, which involves discipleship or knowing more and more about Him. We will develop this more as we proceed in the process. Remember the King has come and He is in the process of calling out those who will be partakers in His Kingdom when He returns again. Those who are partakers in His Kingdom now will become co-rulers with Him in His future Kingdom. James (the half brother of Jesus) states the same concept in different words.

Pastor of the First Church in Jerusalem

James was the pastor of the first Church in Jerusalem. He amplifies the first three beatitudes or what it means to "come to Him and learn of Him" when he says:

"But He gives more grace. Therefore He says, 'God resists the proud, but gives grace to the humble.' Therefore submit to God. Resist the devil and he will flee from you. Draw near to God and He will draw near to you [Poor in Spirit]. Cleanse your hands, you sinners; and purify your hearts, you double-minded. Lament and mourn and weep! Let your laughter be turned to mourning and your joy to gloom [Mourn]. Humble yourselves in the sight of the Lord, and He will lift you up (Meek)" (Ja. 4:6-10).

We must approach this process with our future destiny in mind (note Ps. 8:1-6), that is, the ultimate coming of Christ for His bride. Where and how do we want to spend eternity? We know the unbeliever will spend eternity in hell but as believers we know where we are going.   What will be your status when you meet Jesus at the judgment seat? We do have a choice to make in this lifetime (1 Cor. 3:10-15, Heb. Ch. 3-4). One choice is, I have my ticket and I'll just do my own thing (wood, hay, straw) while waiting for the bus (the rapture). If this is your choice, there will be no rest or rewards in this lifetime. You will go to heaven but with a loss of rewards (2 Tim. 2:11-13). The other choice is to get involved in His Body here and now, as a partaker or participator in His ministry in this life time (gold silver precious stones). The idea here is as you serve Him now you will be laying up treasures or crowns in glory and will become a co-heir and reign with Him in His Kingdom here on earth in the future (Heb. 3:12-15).

This is difficult to understand and that is what this book is all about. What you do now with all that He has given you will determine what you will be in the future. This is a Biblical Truth that has not been taught in some churches as it should be. We will try to help you understand what the Bible has to say about your responsibility in this lifetime and how you can develop all the skills needed to become a partaker in His Kingdom now. Note Paul's exhortation:

> "Now he who plants and he who waters are one, and each one will receive his own reward according to his own labor. For we are God's fellow workers; you are God's field, you are God's building. According to the grace of God which was given to me, as a wise master builder I have laid the foundation, and another builds on it. But let each one take heed how he builds on it. For no other foundation can anyone lay than that which is laid, which is Jesus Christ" (1 Cor. 3:8-11).

THE KING OF KINGS IS HERALDING HIS CALL TO HIS ROYAL FAMILY TO BECOME PARTAKERS IN HIS KINGDOM IN THIS LIFETIME

In other words God has done it all, "how majestic is His name". God is the one who plants (justification is salvation: #1 those who are born again) and waters (sanctification is salvation: #2 (those who are being discipled or partakers). When we were a grain of sand in the depths of the earth, He knew us, He formed us in our mother's womb. He brings about the circumstances that cause us to believe (Ps. 139:1-6, Eph. 2:4-5).   Not only that, He will nurture and keep us until we are taken up to be with Him (glorification is salvation: #3 - those to be taken up to be with Him, 1 Thes. 4:16-18). When we believe, we accept this all by His grace through faith not by anything we do or have done (1 Pet. 1:3-5, Eph. 2:8-9). He has already laid a solid foundation and we had nothing to do with that but to build upon that foundation, we have much to do. Note Paul's continued exhortation:

> "Now if anyone builds on this foundation with gold, silver, *precious stones, wood, hay, straw, each one's work will* become manifest: for the Day will declare it, because it will be revealed by fire, each one's work, of what sort it is. If anyone's work which he has built on it endures, he will receive a reward. If anyone's work is burned, he will suffer loss; but he himself will be saved, so as through fire" (1 Cor. 3:12-15).

Briefly, all who believe must go through a process of sanctification—that is being conformed to the image of Christ by faith and obedience (we were created in His image but that image has been marred). 'According to our works, whether wood, hay, or straw (disobedience) or gold, silver, or precious stone (obedience)' will determine our reward here and now, plus rewards in the future. All believers will be taken up at the end of the church age, to be with Him and receive rewards. Whether we receive rewards or loss, all will go to heaven. The dead in Christ will rise first, then those who are still alive will be taken up to join them in the air and all believers shall forever be with Him (1 Thes. 4:16-18).

We will develop all this later but in the meantime we must continue working through the process of being conformed to His image or discipleship. What we need to understand now is that a **true disciple** is an active participator in His Kingdom now (Jn. 8:30-33). A disciple is simply a follower of the teacher; a seeker— one who is training for reigning and anxious to learn from the teacher. In the case of an unbeliever, what he learns by following may compel him to receive Christ as Savior. But a **true disciple** is one who is committed as a partaker in His ministry now, in attitude and actions, abiding in His Word (Jn. 8:32), one who is consistently being sanctified (Heb. 3:14), although all believers will go to heaven. We must realize a **true disciple** is always growing and learning, laying up treasures in heaven (Mat. 6:19-21, 2 Tim. 2:15). God's desire for you as a believer is to become a partaker (Heb. 3:14, 2 Cor. 1:7)!

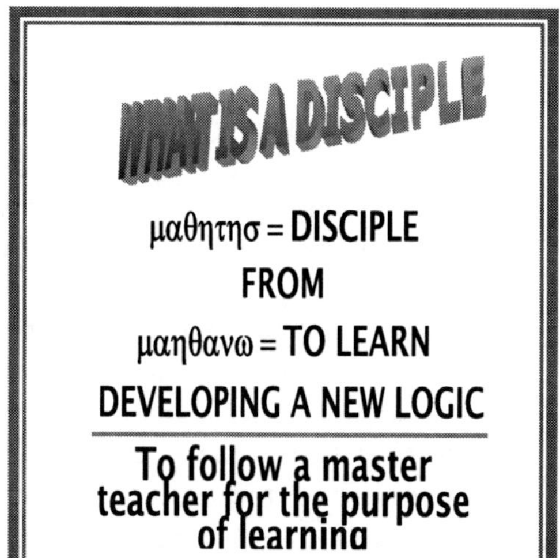

Training for reigning demands agonizing effort in all areas of our life (1 Cor. 9:25-27). Remember, Jesus set the example of perseverance and suffering even to His death on the cross (1 Pet. 2:21-24). To follow Him (**true disciple**) then, would indicate we must be willing to persevere and if necessary, to suffer with Him as a partaker until he comes and receives us to Himself (1 Pet. 4:12:16). Note Radmacher's comments:

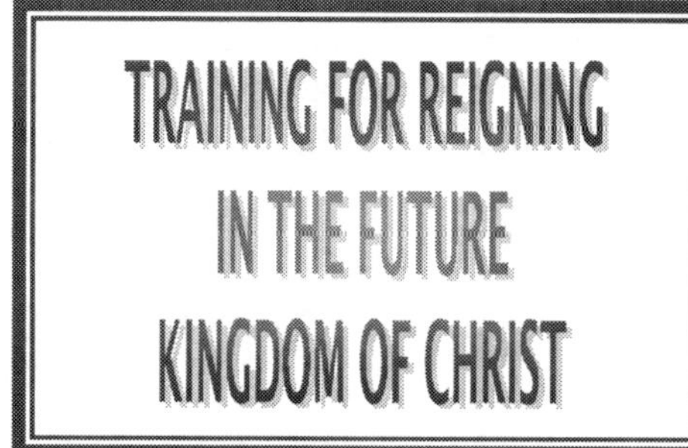

"After His ascension and exaltation to the right hand of the Father, Jesus made a magnificent offer to believers: 'To him who overcomes I will grant to sit with Me on My throne, as I also overcame and sat down with My Father on His throne. He who has an ear let him hear what the Spirit says to the churches' (Rev. 3:21-22). And in His last words in the final chapter in the Bible He reminded us, "… and behold, I am coming quickly, and My reward is with me, to give to everyone according to his work' (Rev. 22:12)." Radmacher, *Salvation*, p. 36.

Our ultimate goal is to become a partaker in this life and to reign with Him in the future Kingdom when the Church and Israel will experience oneness with Him.

I have been in discipleship ministry for over thirty years and have seen the damage done by non-Biblical people helpers, whether from the psychological world or Christians who try to integrate psychology and theology. I will not dwell on the negative; but in a positive way I will demonstrate that Biblical Theology (a study of God) is psychology (a study of the human soul) and has special powers to penetrate the human heart (Heb. 4:12).

The purpose then, of this book, is to present through research and development, a Biblical process of discipleship or spiritual growth that empowers a believer to become a partaker in the earthly Kingdom of the King of Kings and Lord of Lords, Jesus Christ. We will discuss where the King was born, how He developed, how the King introduced the New Covenant for His Kingdom, how He was rejected, persecuted, suffered and was ultimately crucified by the very ones He came to deliver. By doing this He paid the penalty for our sins and invites us to be citizens of the Kingdom of heaven and also the potential to earn the privilege of becoming a co-heir with Him in this future Kingdom.

I know this is a big undertaking, if not the greatest undertaking you will ever experience. It is a lifetime of growing in the grace and knowledge of our Lord Jesus Christ (2 Pet. 3:18). Note the contrast between God's wisdom and the world's wisdom. Paul alludes to this in his first letter to the Corinthians:

> "However, we speak wisdom among those who are mature, yet not the wisdom of this age, nor of the rulers of this age, who are coming to nothing. But we speak the wisdom of God in a mystery, the hidden wisdom which God ordained before the ages for our glory, which none of the rulers of this age knew; for had they known, they would not have crucified the Lord of glory. But as it is written, 'Eye has not seen, nor ear heard, nor have entered into the heart of man the things which God has prepared for those who love Him.' But God has revealed them to us through His Spirit. For the Spirit searches all things, yes, the deep things of God. For what man knows the things of a man except the spirit of the man which is in him? Even so no one knows the things of God except the Spirit of God. Now we have received not the spirit of the world, but the Spirit who is from God, that we might know the things that have been freely given to us by God. These things we also speak, not in words which man's wisdom teaches but which the Holy Spirit teaches, comparing spiritual things with spiritual. But the natural man does not receive the things of the Spirit of God, for they are foolishness to him; nor can he know them, because they are spiritually discerned. But he who is spiritual judges all things, yet he himself is rightly judged by no one. For 'who has known the mind of the LORD that he may instruct Him?' But we have the mind of Christ" 1 Cor. 2:6-16.

**What we do with what He has given us will determine
what we will be in His future Kingdom.**

The Birth of Jesus, the King of the Jews

The Magi came to Jerusalem asking, "Where is He that is born King of the Jews?" God had revealed to them that the King of the Jews was born and they saw His star in the East. When they came to Jerusalem they asked, "Where was the King born?" (Mat. 2:1-6). Herod called together the priest and scribes and they determined from prophecy that He would be born in Bethlehem. Herod, the puppet king, was enraged that there was another king and he arranged to have all children aged two and under to be killed. This Scripture also indicates the Magi went to Bethlehem to worship the King. He grew up in Nazareth and by all indications He obeyed and honored His father and mother in those development years (Lk. 32:39-40). The rulers in Jerusalem proceeded in their plans to kill Him (Mat. 12:14, 26:64-68).

This is the King that will one day rule the Universe. What an awesome truth! We who believe actually know Him in a personal way. God authenticates the King after He is baptized by John the Baptist. The King begins heralding the message of His Kingdom. Then the King reveals His Kingdom message in a strong imperative—"repent, for the Kingdom of Heaven is at hand Mat. 4:12-17." This is the same message John the Baptist (the forerunner of Jesus) had introduced in Mat. 3:2. The King in all His splendor is here, the Messiah is here, the prophecy of the Old Testament is fulfilled even to the forerunner, John the Baptist and the approval of the trinity in the voice from heaven descending as a dove resting on the King of Kings. The Kingdom of Heaven is near at hand. Note Joseph Dillow's comments:

> "The coming Kingdom of Heaven announced here is none other than the predicted Kingdom-Salvation of the Old Testament. It is the time of the restoration of the Kingdom to Israel (Acts 1:6). The miracles that confirmed it are powers of the coming age" (Heb. 2:4-6).

… Such salvation, joint participation with Christ in the coming Kingdom rule, is contingent upon our faithful participation and obedience. That is why He says, "Although He was a Son, He learned obedience from what He suffered and, once made perfect, He became the source of eternal salvation (soteria) for all **who will obey** Him" (Heb. 5:8-9). Dillow, *Reign of The Servant Kings, p.131-132.*

This is the announcement of the message and the messenger of the New Covenant and was promised in the Old Covenant that was given to Moses. We have been grafted into the olive tree (Israel, Rom. 11:16-18). The Israelites totally rejected their Messiah King. They even cried out to Pilate, the Roman governor, "Let Him be crucified" (Mat. 27:22). The Jews were not cut off from going to heaven but from the covenants and promises, and are under discipline until the fullness of the Gentiles. Then all Israel will be rescued or turn to their Messiah Jesus Christ and be saved. They will be restored to the covenants and promises. When the Gentile Christians are cut off or being disciplined by the Lord, they are not cut off from going to heaven but experience the loss of fellowship in this life and loss of rewards in glory (1 Cor. 3:12-15; 2 Tim. 2:11-13, Rom. 11:19-24).

When Jesus spoke these words, *"repent for the kingdom of heaven is at hand"* (Mat. 4:17), He was referring to the changing of the mind about God and the future kingdom. The Jewish people—from Isaiah, Ezekiel and other prophets—had been prophesying the coming of a King that would deliver them from their oppressors. He did come to His own and His own did not receive Him. "But as many as received Him, to them He gave the right to become children of God, to those who believe in His name" (Jn. 1:11-12).

They were expecting an earthly king, one who would deliver them from Roman control. Christ offered Himself as Israel's Messiah and King but they rejected Him (Mat. 12:22-37). Therefore, they are still looking for that deliverance, but it never has been realized because they will not repent and follow Him. This will not happen until the completion of the times of the Gentiles, which is the Church Age.

Both the Old and New Testaments say that the Messiah will not set up His Kingdom until the nation of Israel has come to faith in the Messiah and turned from its wicked ways (Heb. 3:6-4:10). While individuals are guaranteed participation in the coming kingdom just by believing in Christ, the national participation of Israel in that kingdom requires both faith and repentance. Jesus told the nation, "Repent, and believe in the gospel (Mk. 1:15). Jesus called for more than believing the gospel. If believing the gospel is sufficient for justification, and it is, then the Lord was clearly speaking for more than justification here. He was calling for justification and sanctification, faith and repentance for the Jewish Nation (Rom. 9-11).

After the Church Age, during the great tribulation, God will once again deal with the Nation of Israel (known as the seventieth week of Daniel—Dan. 9:20-27). He will appeal to them again and as a result of the overwhelming persecution and the ministry of 144,000 believing Jews, multitudes will turn to Christ as their promised Messiah (seven years of tribulation). At the end of the seven years of tribulation, Christ will return the second time to Earth (partakers—will return with him). At this time He will establish again the Davidic Kingdom and reign with a rod of iron for one thousand years. Satan and his forces will be bound during that period. It is during this period the partakers will reign with Him.

Our thrust in this book has to do with the Church Age. Why are we here? What should we be doing? Like the nation of Israel, when we, as believers, sin, our fellowship with God suffers. In order for us (believers) to restore that fellowship we must repent. For the unbeliever, the only condition for justification is by grace through faith in Christ alone (Eph. 2:8).

In Mat. 5:1-16, Jesus is giving an outline for basic training of His servant kings. If we are going to reign with Him in the future, then there are certain things we must do. This basic training is called discipleship. Those believers who faithfully participate in His Kingdom now and are obedient to His Word, will jointly participate with Christ in His position as King of Kings and the partakers will co-reign with Him in that future Kingdom. Those who do not faithfully participate will go to heaven, but will not reign with him in the future.

In this passage (Mat. 5:1-16), Jesus is unveiling the character of a citizen of His Kingdom. This is the new logic of the Kingdom. He had already been baptized by John the Baptizer, identified by the voice of God from heaven, had victory over Satan in the wilderness, and was followed by John's disciples. He went about Galilee announcing the message of the Kingdom predicted in the Old Testament. This message involves the changing of the mind from a kingdom based on the Mosaic Law to an eternal Kingdom based on God's ,grace; from a natural kingdom to a supernatural Kingdom. This repentance demands a change of mind about the kingdom from law to grace, that is, to believe the Messiah has come. The King is here.

Jesus began selecting His future kings and anointing them as His disciples in training. True disciples are His future kings. Many of them were John the Baptist's disciples. He called them saying: "follow Me and I will make you fishers of men" (Mat. 4:17-22).

After calling them, He immediately led them up the mountain and began teaching them the new logic of the Kingdom. The logic of the Old Covenant was being fulfilled in His coming. It was not that the logic of the Old Covenant was wrong or in conflict. It was the faulty understanding by the Jewish leaders that failed. The new logic teaches how to change "old man" thought patterns into Christ-like attitudes and actions. Jesus, in the Sermon on the Mount, proceeds to unfold a systematic process of discipleship (Mat. 4:19).

I am not saying His disciples understood all that Jesus was doing in this masterful plan for discipleship. Even with all the many discoveries in modern science, technology and theology, we still have difficulty understanding the complexity of His plan. However, He has given us the Sermon on the Mount, introduced by the Beatitudes and the entirety of the Gospels, so that all those who believe in Christ for eternal life can understand. In addition, He has, by His Holy Spirit, given us the Epistles to explain the disciplines that offer happiness, even in suffering (1 Pet. 4:12-14).

These great promises are found in Mat. 5:1-16, and are addressed to all believers who have responded to His invitation, "follow me." However, the plan of salvation is not explained in the Beatitudes. Many who followed Him had not received Him as Savior but were interested in what He had to say. Since the Old Covenant was still in effect, the focus here was on the Jews who were presently citizens of the Kingdom of Israel, still under the law. They only became true disciples when they obeyed His command, to repent and "follow Me" (Mat. 4:18-22).

Since the true disciples have already experienced the new birth, Jesus will guide them through three levels of spiritual development. First, the Emptying Process, which involves renewing the mind or repenting by changing the mind about God, self, and about relationships. The focus is on emptying of self or self-righteousness. Second, the Filling Process involves replacing our self-righteousness with His righteousness. This includes discovering and developing the things He did and said when He was here and building a life ministry around the gifts He has given. Third, the functional process, involving the actual doing of the things He called and gifted the believer to do, that is, to become salt and light in a bitter and dark world.

Jesus then summarizes with the introduction of rewards for the disciples' humility and obedience in actively participating in the divine nature (amplified in 2 Pet. 1:3-4) in this lifetime. The Lord promises that each believer who partakes in His kingdom now will experience overwhelming blessings in this lifetime, but will also have the privilege of participating in the future kingdom of David, with Christ Himself as the King of Kings on the throne and we shall reign with Him. Peter ensures each believer that he will not neglect to remind us of these things. Note the following parallels:

BEATITUDES Mat. 5	VIRTUE 1 Pet. 1:5-7
POOR IN SPIRIT v3	FAITH v5a
MOURN v4	GOODNESS v5b
MEEK v5	KNOWLEDGE v6a
HUNGER AND THIRST v6	SELF-C0NTROL v6b
MERCIFUL v7	PATIENCE v6c
PURE IN HEART v8	GODLINESS v6d
PEACEMAKER v9	BROTHERLY LOVE v7a
PERSECUTED v10	AGAPE – LOVE v7b

These things are necessary character qualities for members of His royal family that desire to please Him. We will guide you through each level of the Emptying Process, the Filling and the Functional Process which guarantees us inner peace or as Jesus states it "blessed." This diagram a picture of Christ's model for discipleship..

This is the basic training or process of discipleship given by the Lord Jesus. It is the process of sanctification described in Rom. 6-8. It is introduced here by the King of Kings which will be described in detail later. Note the beatitude model.

From Rags to Riches

This process involves discipleship or sanctification that is designed by God for the purpose of conforming us to the image of Christ, the King of Kings. This is your life and God desires that you live it for His glory. This process of being conformed to the image of Christ will challenge you to answer questions and perform certain responsibilities that will set you free from the bondage of the old thought patterns you have developed. My desire is that you will understand these things not because I said them but you have affirmed that God said them and you want to please Him.

This is an amazing process, given by the King of Kings and Lord of Lords. It is called the sanctifying process, moving from darkness (rags) to light (riches). It is amazing grace to ones who deserve the opposite. Here in the context of Matthew 5:1-16 are imbedded some of the greatest promises regarding those who persevere in service to Christ. We were created to co-reign with Him, crowned with glory and honor. Dr. Ron Allen's (in his book <u>The Majesty of Man,</u> a must read) gives us practical insight as to why human beings have such difficulty in understanding our purpose for life. Humans were created to rule. Note his clarification or a literal translation of Ps. 8:5:

"For you have caused Him to lack but little of God; and with glorious honor you have crowned him. You made him ruler over the works of your hands; you put everything under his feet: all flocks and herds, and the beast of the field, the birds of the air, and the fish of the sea, and all that swim the paths of the sea. O Lord, our Lord how majestic is your name in all the earth." Ps. 8:5-9, Dr. Ron Allen, Literal translation, *The Majesty of Man*, p. 70-71

He further explains why the word "elohim" was translated "angels." Note the following;

"The rendering "angels" for the Hebrew term "elohim" seems to have been a desperate attempt on the part of the translators of the Septuagint to avoid what they determined to be a difficulty in their own culture. Had they translated "a little lower than God," would not their pagan neighbors accuse them of worshiping demigods? Where would their great Jewish declaration of monotheism go if they admitted to this high view of man? Yet in our culture, we need the bold pronouncement of the text to be given clearly. In our day it is the nature of man that needs to be clarified." *The Majesty of Man*, p.71

However, because of the fall of Adam, he was removed from the garden and did not glorify God. Therefore God gave him over to a depraved mind (Rom. 1:24). Now, that is the way all humans come into the world. Yet the image of God is still present in man. He still has the potential (faith) to believe in God and be redeemed. This is God's plan, available to all who will believe. And when one believes in Christ for eternal life, not only is the image of God redeemed, but then one begins the process of being conformed to His likeness. Yes, humans are God's crown of creation, His masterpiece. Note Paul's comment;

"For we are His workmanship (masterpiece), created in Christ Jesus for good works, which God prepared beforehand that we should walk in them" Eph. 2:10.

However, being born again is just the first part of our salvation. That is what we call justification and all who believe have eternal life. There is more to it. We must be sanctified and that is the process of being conformed to His image. By our good works we are sanctified by becoming partakers in service to Him in this lifetime. These are the works He has prepared beforehand that we should walk in them. This is what this book is all about, not just your regeneration but helping you to develop the skills of a partaker (Heb. 3:1-6).

CHAPTER 2 - RIGHT THINKING ABOUT REPENTANCE

**"From that time Jesus began to preach and to say,
'Repent for the kingdom of heaven is at hand.'" Mat. 4:17**

The disciples were excited about what he had said! They were ready to not only follow Him, they were anxious to be taught His new logic. They were conditioned to the logic of the old covenant but they were already born again or justified. These men were anxious to learn more about this new-found Savior and the new logic of the King.

The Need for Change

Sometime ago, Larry came to our Center for help. He was about 29 years old, was outgoing, athletic, a school teacher in a very good Christian school and was involved in his church. He was never involved in drugs or alcohol and stayed clear of trouble. His parents were Christians who were very active in their church. When he came to the Center, he was ready to give up. He had no idea about why he was here, or what he was to be doing, much less that he should be in training for reigning with Christ. His root problem was that he did not know God well enough to trust Him; although he was a believer he had never been discipled. He had no concept of the coming Kingdom much less a partaker or a king in training (note 2 Pet. 1:3-7).

Even though he was clean and well dressed, he was broken. His eyes were red from crying and lack of sleep. He was slumped over with his hands over his face when I asked him to come into my office. Once inside he started crying, overcome with grief. He could barely talk. Finally he got control of himself and said, "My wife has had an affair and wants a divorce. What am I going to do? What has happened to me, Bill? What can I do?" He continued to sob. I felt deep empathy for him as I could sense his spirit was immobilized. He was emotionally out of control. I knew in my spirit there was hope for him, but how could I penetrate his deep sorrow? I realized this was no different than most human problems. This difficulty was not too big for God! Why would it be a problem for this man who believes in God and has the Holy Spirit living in him? Like with Larry, something is missing in our approach to discipleship.

In my recent studies, I have discovered a number of unanswered questions concerning the concept of discipleship. Since the mission of the Church is to make disciples, I would think we should understand what that means and what is expected of us. Larry should have been a competent spiritual leader, equipped with the resources necessary to lead his family (Note: Heb.5:12-6:12). However, he was trapped in religious traditions and an individualistic lifestyle. Too many believers are missing the basic training to become a partaker with Christ in His kingdom now (2 Tim. 2:1-13).

The more I think about this incident and others like it, the more I realize we must do something in the Church to head off this landslide of sensuality and individualism. I believe there must be more to the concept of making disciples than we have discovered. Consider the impact the disciples had on the day of Pentecost as they left the upper room filled with the Holy Spirit. They began to speak in their own language and the people heard them in their language (Acts 2:1-13).

There was an evangelistic explosion that took place and thousands became disciples. They immediately became involved in the teaching of the Apostles' Doctrine, fellowship, breaking bread together and praying (Acts 2:40-47). As the apostles and disciples functioned in their spiritual gifts, the people were in awe at what was taking place around them. There was a unity that had never been seen before. They actually cared for each other by selling their property to meet the needs that arose in the body. There were no independent spirits as we see in churches today. They were committed to each other in the power and giftedness of the Holy Spirit. They were partakers demonstrating God's purpose for His children. Even when they sinned openly they were disciplined (Acts 8:14-25).

These people had something most of us do not have. I have not seen this kind of unity in the churches in which I have been involved. The possibilities of disunity were present, but they processed it properly. They discovered and implemented God's plan, and it worked. Larry did not get it, because he did not see this in his church! This phenomenon did not stop in Jerusalem but began to spread elsewhere. It infiltrated Galatia, Macedonia, Rome, and the known world. Disciples were being made in the midst of persecution. Men and women were laying down their lives for their faith.

Something happened between the time the Jerusalem church was exploding and the time the Gospel had spread throughout the Roman Empire. Luke identifies this phenomenon:

"And with many other words he (Peter) testified and exhorted them, saying, "Be saved from this perverse generation." Then those who gladly received his word were baptized; and that day about three thousand souls were added to them" *(Acts 2:40-41).*

We must realize the apostolic church was doing something different than we are now. They had stability and a way to reach through the humanistic layers of fear people had built around themselves. The church was able to meet the needs of the people, even those of which they were not aware. God knew their needs and through the disciples' gifts they were met. They were turning the world upside down in Acts 17:6-8, because the church was willing to suffer and committed to making disciples.

Larry's church had various programs available, but somehow his psychological and spiritual needs were not being met. There was something missing in his spiritual growth process. He had a lot of knowledge about the Bible and the Church, but he was unable to discern or function in his basic responsibilities as a husband. He was bankrupt in his spiritual life. What was the secret of the early church? They were committed to "equipping the saints for the work of ministry." They gathered for edification and scattered for evangelization. They had a balanced view of discipleship and evangelism. They were doing "the work of ministry" by stirring up the believers and meeting the needs of the Body. They were committed to a lifetime process of repentance, or putting off the old, being renewed in their minds and putting on the new (Eph. 4:20-32). You see discipleship is more than Bible study, memorizing Scripture, having a quiet time and going to church. It demands a constant rethinking and evaluating past attitudes and actions with the motive to keep a clear conscience. It also requires a consistent understanding and yielding of all self-righteousness.

The early disciples' keen sensitivity to the psychological, physical and spiritual needs of the new believers enabled them through their giftedness to meet those needs. God chooses to work through His people! The members of that early church were deeply concerned about others needs and did their part to meet them (1 Cor. 12:12-26). Note Heb. 10:24-25 and notice the warning the writer gives. The Church, even at that early date, was suffering because some of the members were neglecting their responsibilities or not doing their part at all.

Present Need

This responsibility cannot be taken lightly. In Larry's case, the church had failed to realize—intellectually and emotionally—his basic needs. They were functioning more from a psychological model than from a Biblical model. They failed to recognize the deep inner conflicts, broken relationships, and deep hurts he had experienced in his childhood and young adult years. Nor did they consider the need to stimulate him to love and to good works as described in Heb. 10:24. Dr. Radmacher says:

"Despite these high privileges, these believers are in need of exhortation. They are not worshipping because they have lost their confidence; they are renouncing and abandoning the assembly—the local church—itself. The writer reminds them, however, that it is their duty to keep on considering one another to provoke them unto love and good works. And there was one particular way in which they could do this—'by not forsaking the assembling of ourselves together, as the manner of some is; but exhorting one another." Radmacher, *Nature of the Church*, p. 343.

Paul strongly admonishes the evangelist, pastor, and teacher to equip the saints for the performing of this very task, the edification or building up of the Body in order that there might be unity in the Body. The unity of the Body is accomplished as each member does their part (Eph. 4:13-16). This was the immediate need in the case of Larry and his wife. They are no longer to act like children and find themselves caught up in arguments, division, carried away by ignorance and the trickery and craftiness of men (Col. 2:16-19).

When we received Christ, we were regenerated, or born again. We were spiritually joined as parts (*ek meros*) of His Body with a mandate to follow Him, having been freed from the penalty of sin with the ability to become free from the power of sin. We became His agents, doing His business, at His pace, with His people. We are a part of the body function. We are the functional parts that people see, the body of Christ, and members individually of it (1 Cor. 12:27). What in the world is His business? He has revealed His purpose, and it has to do with right thinking about Christ the King, His Kingdom, and His people. We have been called out of the world into the Kingdom of Heaven. We are also living stones in His building (1 Pet. 2:4-8).

The Demand for a Paradigm Shift

This demands a paradigm shift (repentance) in the realm of discipleship. The word paradigm has its roots in the Greek word *paradeigmatizo* (Mat. 1:19), meaning example or model. It is a compound word from *para*, indicating along side and *deigma*, meaning a pattern or a change of the mind from wrong thinking to right thinking about a situation or thing.

In recent years *paradigm* has come to mean "a perception, a model, a way of thinking" or "a pattern for understanding and explaining present reality." A paradigm shift is a distinct, new way of thinking about old ideas. It does not mean the old idea was bad. It just means we look at a thing or process from many new perspectives. This is accomplished by taking the knowledge we have and looking at it from all directions, upside down, right side up, inside out, from a distance and microscopically. We will have gathered a storehouse of knowledge, much of it not usable, but we will be exposed to knowledge we would never have discovered. A prime example of this is space exploration. Many new ideas and products have been discovered as a result of a search for knowledge beyond the old limits. It is the idea the Bible talks about "renewing the mind, repentance or discipleship" as in Rom. 12:2-6, or when Jesus says to repent in constantly changing or renewing the mind about His Kingdom (Mat. 4:17).

An example of a paradigm shift is the Biblical concept of repentance. Repentance means that we are equipped with additional knowledge and are able to look at it from another perspective (God's way). Allowing for a better understanding of the idea, the pattern changes resulting in a paradigm shift. I must admit there has been great effort in recent years to modify the traditional view of discipleship. However, it seems that most of the efforts are exerted in an attempt to make changes within the old paradigm.

What I am beginning to see is something different, something I failed to see in the past. Could it be that these principles have been there all along and have even been used by some in different ways? Have we failed to see them because of the old way we look at them? Have we been caught up in traditions for so long we just have a difficult time discerning between God's way and our natural human responses? We are often further confused because these traditions, from a human perspective, seem to work. But they are not God's best for His people. To demonstrate how conditioned we are to old paradigms, I want you to do an experiment. Read the following statement for 15 seconds and determine how many "F's" you see. Then check the number below. If you have seen this before don't take it.

FINISHED FILES ARE THE
RESULT OF YEARS OF SCIENTIFIC
STUDY COMBINED WITH THE
EXPERIENCE OF MANY YEARS.

If you have never seen this exercise before you probably missed several F's because your present paradigm would not let you see the big picture. Most people who take this test see only three F's because they have been conditioned to pronounce the word "of" as "ov" in the traditional sense, thus they are not looking for an F. There are 6 F's in the statement. Could it be that in many other areas, even in the spiritual realm, we are so conditioned to traditional ways of looking at things that we cannot see something new? One thing is certain; you will never miss the F's again. You have changed your mind about the number of F's; you have repented. You have had a paradigm shift. Is it possible you could be negligent in other areas?

Larry was not aware of his need for a paradigm change when he came into my office. "What have I done wrong? God knows I've tried." He could not see where he had failed because those areas were blind spots like the F's. He was conditioned to respond a certain way, the way he always responded, defending himself. He was still an infant in a lot of areas and needed to be confronted. He was blinded by old paradigms (thought patterns) that would not let him see the dangers he was facing. He could not see it from God's point of view. The guilt from past broken relationships, deep hurts, and conflicts stimulated his defense system and he was out of control. He needed to be accountable, to re-think his past attitudes and actions, especially with his wife.

> "Only a minority of churches are focusing on what they should be doing, which seems incredible in light of such a direct strategy ordered by our spiritual Commander in Chief Himself. The Church at large has ignored her marching orders. It is not that Christians are deliberately avoiding God's plan for the Church; rather, we have our focus in the wrong place." Hull, *Jesus Christ Disciple-Maker*, p. 10.

When we exposed this circumstance to Scriptural principles he was able to rise above the circumstance and look at it from God's point of view and this huge problem becomes a project that he could work through. We will develop this concept more in Chapters 4 and 5. Note Dr. Pentecost's comments on discipleship:

> "Throughout His ministry Jesus Christ was occupied with making disciples. His ministry was devoted to teaching and training men that these men might be His disciples. From among those who called themselves disciples of the Pharisees and from among others who called themselves disciples of John, and from those who called themselves disciples of Moses, our Lord called men to be disciples of Jesus Christ. His earthly life was invested in these men that they might be His disciples and that they might do the work of a disciple." Pentecost, *Design for Discipleship,* p. 13.

Our spiritual dysfunction reveals weaknesses in our churches. These are concepts we need to wrestle with in our effort to change old paradigms. Where do you start? The answer to that question will give the answers to all the others. We must start with the Master Discipler. We must conform our thinking to His thoughts, and make our ways His ways (Isa. 5:8). The subject of discipleship is frequently discussed today but few are doing it. Men are called to become disciples without any definition of the concept and without any clarification of the requirements the Lord makes of those who are just disciples, to become a true disciple (Jn. 8:31-32). Discipleship is frequently equated with justification and often erroneously made a condition for being born again. Thus many are confused about it.

For Larry to succeed, he needed to change his mind about many things he had developed as a child and through his young adult life. He was conditioned to certain responses. He needed a church that was equipped with discipling; a church where all the gifts were functional. That way he could get an accurate picture of the divine nature of Christ and help him conform his thinking to the new logic Jesus came to teach. He needed to change his natural thinking to eternal thoughts. Many people in churches today are stuck in this same area. We need to return to the Biblical teaching in regard to humility or deference that is accurately taught by Jesus in the Sermon on the Mount. This is an almost forgotten concept. The Bible has a lot to say about deference. Paul amplifies the concept:

> "*Let* nothing *be done* through selfish ambition or conceit, but in lowliness of mind let each esteem others better than himself. Let each of you look out not only for his own interests, but also for the interests of others" (Phil. 2:3-4).

This is a challenge for Larry since his godly images were distorted in those early years. Not that we should blame his parents as they probably did the best they knew how under the circumstances. However, they were not perfect; they were also products of imperfect parents, and as a result they had a distorted image of God. The thesis of this book is to help people see the need to work through a process of transformation, which comes through the Biblical concept of discipleship. This is why Jesus came—to be show us the way to be true disciples in an ungodly world.

> "The term disciple is used in several different ways. Until we are able to distinguish these, we will not comprehend what is involved in discipleship. First of all, the word disciple means a learner, a pupil, a scholar, one who comes to be taught. The idea of teaching and learning is preeminent in the word disciple." Pentecost, *Design for Discipleship*, p.14.

I am not suggesting that we change Christ's principles, but rather that we look at them from a different angle, a different perspective (His way). We must take what Christ said about discipleship and transpose it into a relevant process for the church today. We need to rethink this whole idea of making disciples. We need to ask ourselves some critical questions. The answers may surprise you. In most books and articles I have read, the emphasis has been switched from discipleship to evangelism. In most circumstances we are struggling with the wrong goal, a goal resulting in inadequate discipleship. In a Spiritual Gifts Conference, Dr. Radmacher related this concept.

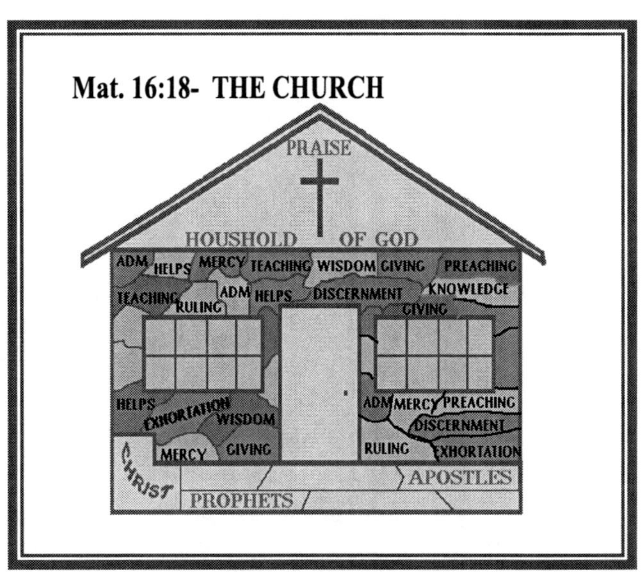

> "The church is a place where all of the members come together, they gather together to minister to each other. That's discipling. Somebody says, 'Who were you discipled by?' and they're expecting me to answer some particular person. You don't find that in the New Testament. Paul says, 'The things that I have committed to you among many witnesses, the same commit to others who shall be able to teach others also' (2 Tim. 2:2). Not the sole,

solitary kind of relationship, but many people building on other people. So when people ask me, 'who discipled you?' I ask them to sit down and listen to a list of about 50,000 people, for I am being discipled regularly. God does not develop us in isolation but in relation. The monastery is a mistake and the individualism and privatism of our society is an illness." Radmacher, Video series on Spiritual Gifts.

The following questions are significant to your growth process. Read Mat. 28:18-20, Jn. 8:31-32, and Acts 2:41-42. Answer the following questions.

PROJECT

1. Define discipleship in your own words.

2. What institution in the world is responsible for discipleship?

3. Define the concept of justification.

4. Define the concept of sanctification.

5. Define glorification.

6. Describe how we lay up treasures in heaven

CHAPTER 3 - RIGHT THINKING ABOUT DISCIPLESHIP

**"Go therefore and make disciples of all nations, baptizing them in the name of
the Father and of the Son and of the Holy Spirit." Mat. 28:19**

Larry's situation is typical of many young men and women in the Church who get stuck in the old way of thinking or the old man thought patterns. That is, the way we have been conditioned to respond to circumstances, habits, and conditioning from our childhood. They have reached an adult age physically, but have not been discipled psychologically or spiritually. Many adults never reach that maturity. When we are born again, we are spiritual infants and unless we are discipled, we become malnourished or stunted spiritually and never grow to maturity.

The writer of Hebrews supports this concept: "For though by this time you ought to be teachers, you need someone to teach you again the first principles of the oracles of God and you have come to need milk and not solid food" (Heb. 5:12-14). We tend to take

> **WE OUGHT TO BE TEACHERS, BUT
> WE ARE IN NEED OF
> BEING TAUGHT THE BASICS**

seriously the physical and psychological training of a child, but when it comes to spiritual training, we leave it to the Church. The writer of Proverbs says, "train up a child in the way" (Prov. 22:6 also note Eph. 6:4). God has given the parents this responsibility. This is talking about the aspect of training God has given to parents. God has given the Church the responsibility of discipleship of all its members. If Christians would take this responsibility more seriously, we would not have the wide spread ignorance that we have in the Church today. We should not allow any other authority to take this responsibility from us!

The same is true when we lead a person to receive Christ for eternal life; they become spiritual babies. They are infants and need constant care, nurturing, feeding, exercising, and discipline. We will talk more about what a disciple is later. This discipling needs to start immediately after salvation occurs or they will continue developing naturally or worldly.

Debate Concerning Salvation

The debate is whether we are saved or justified by faith alone or faith plus something else. Some theologians would lead us to believe that when we are saved, all those old man thought patterns have been erased. They fail to see that Justification begins the process of sanctification which is putting off the old man thought patterns and putting on the new man created according to God's righteousness (Eph. 4:22-24). Scripture reveals three tenses in regard to our salvation.

Salvation #1—Saved from the Penalty of Sin

This is the past tense—when we were saved from the penalty of sin. We were born of the Spirit; our spirit that died in Adam was regenerated. Our spirit was made alive. Jesus implants His Spirit in all those who believe. Our old spirit was dead in trespasses and sin. This new birth produces a spiritually immature baby in Christ. This process is called justification.

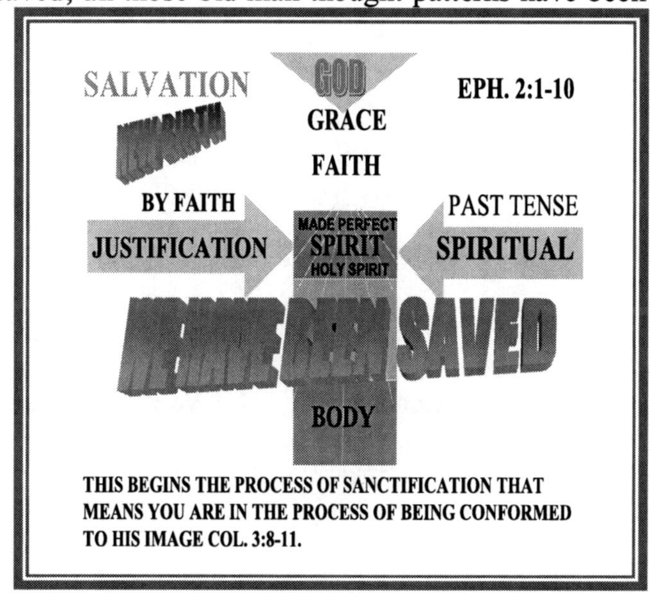

Salvation #2—Saved From the Power of Sin

This is a present tense of our salvation, in which we are being saved from the power of sin. This process is called sanctification. This is salvation of our souls in Mat. 16:24-28. This is a growth process that comes by faith plus obedience, the stage of being conformed to His image (Col. 3:8-11). We must move from the stage (being born again), to the adult stage in which we are being conformed to the image of Christ. This process is called sanctification or discipleship. It is the process of putting off the old man thought patterns and putting on the new (Eph. 4: 21-24), which is a lifetime process. There is more.

Salvation #3—Saved from the presence of sin

There is a future tense of our salvation, which pertains to the time when we will be saved from the presence of sin at the Rapture of the Church. This event is called glorification. It is a salvation of the body. Those believers who have physically died will be raised first, then those who believe and are alive will be changed in the twinkle of the eye and will be taken up to meet Him in the air to be forever with Him. (1 Thes. 4:13-18) After being taken up, all believers will appear at the judgment seat of Christ where their works will be judged. The righteous works will receive rewards and the unrighteous works will be burned and they will suffer loss, though they will be saved themselves (1 Cor. 3:12-15).

We will develop all three of these areas of salvation in the coming chapters. Those who believe are in this process of Salvation #2, called sanctification or discipleship. The writer of Hebrews demands that we reach out and encourage one another to love and do good works (Heb. 10:24). This is part of our responsibility as partakers. Paul directs us to confront, convince, rebuke, and exhort disciples with utmost patience and education (2 Tim. 4:2). Note Radmacher's comment:

> "Several years ago I spoke at the Annual Pastors' Conference at Moody Bible Institute. I had the good fortune of being preceded by two of my favorite speakers, Dr. Howard Hendricks and Dr. Warren Wiersbe. Having been edified by their messages, when it was my turn to speak, I said, 'I want to praise God because I got saved this morning while Dr. Hendricks was speaking.' And then I got saved again while Dr. Wiersbe was speaking." Radmacher, *Salvation*, p. 144.

What he's implying is that he was being saved in the sense of a present tense salvation, which is sanctification. He went on to talk about how he had been saved (justification—past tense, or was born

again), which started the process of sanctification. Sanctification is the present tense of salvation or being saved now. Glorification—or when we are taken up to be with Him (rapture)—is future salvation. Our problem in churches today is that we tend to always let salvation refer only to the new birth. As a result, we miss two thirds of what the Bible has to say about salvation or our preparation to reign, as a partaker, with Him in the future.

Paul said in Phil. 2:5, "Let this mind be in you which was also in Christ Jesus." Jesus is our example. "For this reason you were called, because Christ also suffered for us, leaving us an example, that you should follow in His steps" (1 Pet. 2:21). This idea of discipleship was Christ's idea, it is His plan. Most of our brain's memory banks are filled with our own ideas or the influence of others during our personality development. We must reprogram our thinking regarding who we are and what we should be doing with what He has given us. We desperately need a paradigm shift in the area of training for reigning in the future. The spiritual leaders of the Church have the responsibility of perfecting the saints for the work of the ministry. We can only take a person as far as we have been ourselves. Dr. Bing confronts this issue:

> "For decades a chorus of voices has been calling for a more precise definition of the biblical concept of discipleship while the Church goes on grappling with fulfilling her great commission to 'make disciples.' Christians have not lacked resources on how to be a disciple or how to make disciples of others. Too often these books are based on assumptions about what a disciple is while they take the meaning of discipleship for granted. Yet our understanding of biblical discipleship shapes our practice of evangelism, church growth, missions, and personal life-style." Bing, *Journal of the Grace Evangelical Society,* Vol. 5:1.

Discipleship Is Not Natural

Discipleship does not come naturally. It is a spiritual growth process, and Jesus is the disciple-maker. To be disciples, we must be participators with Christ. A disciple is always identified with a disciple-maker. The disciples of Socrates and Plato were among the first to be called disciples (*mathetes*) but they were natural men. They followed the teachings or philosophies of their teacher or disciple-maker. What we are talking about is a supernatural task—a new spiritual philosophy—which can only be accomplished by the power of the Holy Spirit. Jesus said, "Feed My lambs, tend My sheep, feed My sheep" (Jn. 21:15-17). These three imperatives demand urgency. They thrive on control of the Spirit. They require teaching and involve suffering.

Doing What Comes Naturally

One of the reasons discipleship has not been accomplished is because we have tried to do it naturally. This usually turns out to be wrong! As stated in 2 Pet. 1:3, the Holy Spirit "has given us everything we need for life and godliness." However, this does not mean we have been instantly sanctified. He goes on to say, "But also for this very reason, giving all diligence add to your faith virtue, to virtue knowledge, to knowledge self-control, to self-control perseverance, to perseverance godliness, to godliness brotherly kindness, and to brotherly kindness, love" (Gal.5:22-23). This is the mandate for a true disciple. There is a process of being conformed through growing and learning. Paul states it this way, "Be diligent to present yourselves approved to God-----" (2 Tim. 2:15). This process is called discipleship, renewing the mind, or repentance.

Problems in the Process

In the study of discipleship, I have found some areas of weakness. First, most instruction for discipling—written or verbal—is only encouragement to study or memorize Scripture. Disciplors study the Bible with them, pray with them, or guide them in a quiet time with the Lord. That is not enough! The fact is that God doesn't want our prayers without obedience as stated in James 1:22-25. Often we neglect confronting the disciple in areas of weakness, teaching them how to deal with guilt, bitterness, anger, depression, and un-forgiveness. Bible study and prayer are important, but just as important is the need to be free from inner conflicts and turmoil. Wrong attitudes and actions can void or hinder our prayers (1 Pet. 3:7, Job 42:8). Secondly, believers as disciple-makers are not fully equipped to accomplish this task because they do not possess all the gifts. Think back on your own spiritual growth. Who has had an impact on your life spiritually? If you're like me, you would have to say many people. Discipleship is a joint effort of the Church. It demands all the gifts functioning together.

This idea is foreign to most churches and Christian organizations, and will require us to rethink the whole idea of discipleship. Although the influence of outside church organizations was influential in initiating the concept of one-on-one discipleship, this is a task that can only be accomplished by the Church. Some even misquote 2 Tim. 2:2 and leave out the phrase "among many witnesses." These men and women were well-meaning but misguided in their hermeneutics. Discipleship is a shared load, and apart from the unity and diversity of the body as stated in 1 Cor. 12:14-27, it will not be done properly and will result in divisions, conflicts, hurts, and broken relationships within the body. Discipleship is a local church function. We must change our thinking and reproduce in the church, a discipleship process demonstrated by the Master Disciplemaker. Jesus presents His model for discipleship in Matthew, Chapters 5-7. It is not a psychological process but a Biblical model. Note chart:

Doing As the Israelites

The Israelites are God's chosen people. Those individuals who came out of Egypt who believed will go to heaven (1 Cor. 10:1-13) but those who rebelled will lose rewards at the judgment seat of Christ. In other words, even though they were justified, they were not exercising faith. Therefore, they will have no rewards nor will they reign with Christ in the future. When Jesus came on the scene, the Israeli leadership was corrupt. They were in rebellion against God and still are today (note 1 Cor. 10:1-6, Heb. 3:16-19). They placed their faith in Christ for eternal life, but were not obedient to His commands, they were carnal. Therefore, God was not well pleased with most of them and they died in the wilderness (1 Cor. 10:1-5). All who believed were saved and will go to heaven, but will not co-reign with Christ. It is not much different in the church today. We are somewhat like the Corinthian Church. Paul pleaded with them:

> "Moreover, brethren, I do not want you to be unaware that all our fathers were under the cloud, all passed through the sea, all were baptized into Moses in the cloud and in the sea, all ate the same spiritual food, and all drank the same spiritual drink. For they drank of that Spiritual Rock that followed them, and that Rock was Christ. But with most of them God was not well pleased, for their bodies were scattered in the wilderness" (1 Cor. 10:1-5).

We are doing the same things Israel did. This shift in paradigm was not for Israel alone. Granted, Israel is God's chosen people but His Kingdom will also include other nations. If this new Kingdom demanded a shift in paradigm for the Jews who are God's chosen people, how much more for the Gentiles who were separated from Christ, excluded from the citizenship of Israel without hope and without God (Eph. 4:12-13).

The Church is God's Agent for Discipleship

Although it was unknown to the Jews at the time, this paradigm shift would involve the Church. The Church is God's agent for discipleship and His message is *repentance*. The verb to *repent* (metanoeo) is not used by John in his gospel to the unbelievers, but it is used in the three other gospels and the Epistles of John. However, John does use the word regularly to the churches in Revelation 2-3 as an example. Repentance is the inner working of sanctification which involves discipleship and it is a life-long process. Note James' comments about changing the mind:

> "Who is wise and understanding among you? Let him show by good conduct that his works are done in the meekness of wisdom. But if you have bitter envy and self-seeking in your hearts, do not boast and lie against the truth. This wisdom does not descend from above, but is earthly, sensual, and demonic. For where envy and self-seeking exist, confusion and every evil thing are there. But the wisdom that is from above is first pure, then peaceable, gentle, willing to yield, full of mercy and good fruits, without partiality and without hypocrisy. Now the fruit of righteousness is sown in peace by those who make peace" (Ja. 3:13-18).

The Spiritual Dangers

Since our initial response is usually physical and natural, it will often be wrong. However, to rethink something gets us beyond the brain into the mind which gives us access to the psychological realm (the brain is physical the mind is psychological or immaterial). This is a dangerous move since there are many spirits, in the psychological or immaterial realm desiring to change or manipulate our mind. The evil forces are constantly appealing to man's heart or the soul (Acts 5:3-4, 2 Cor. 4:3-4, Ja. 3:13-16). If Satan and his demons can, in some way, confuse the believer into wrong thinking, he has control of that person. The evil forces of the world are always searching or appealing to those who are thinking wrongly and are controlled by their emotions. God's desire is to work through our spirit activating the mind by His Word. The demonic forces work through our emotions (Jer.

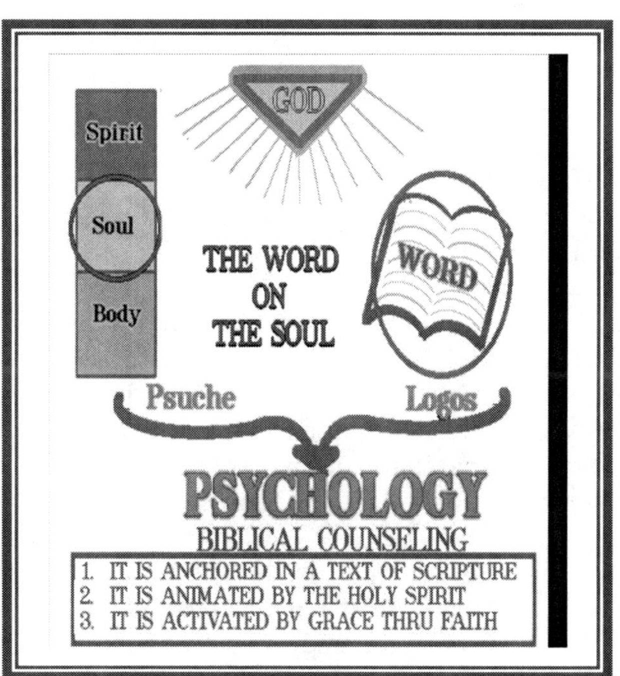

17:9, 2 Cor. 11:13-15, Rev. 12:9). Through subtle appeals, they neutralize our mind and we revert to the old thought patterns. The Word is God's answer to man's psychological needs.

The demonic world manipulates us to feel sorry without having a change of mind. That is what happened to Judas. He was remorseful, but did not change his mind. He went out and hanged himself as stated in Matthew 27:3-5. This incident exemplifies why the decisions we make in our lives should be tested against Scripture to determine whether or not we are acting according to the will of God. Repentance moves our thought process from the brain to the mind under the control of the Holy Spirit. The idea is not just to be sorry or turn from something, but simply to change our mind which will result in a turning from sin.

Larry, my client, was ready for a mind change. He was repentant. He had an identity crisis in that he was not sure who he was in Christ. He understood about justification and what it meant to be saved or "born again." In fact, he knew they were both believers. However, he had very little understanding of what it meant to be a spiritual leader, a true disciple, or to hunger and thirst after righteousness.

There is confusion in the camp! The cultural shock which rocked the sixties and the New Age philosophy of the seventies and eighties, and the narcissistic society of the nineties led us to confusion about the ministry of the Church in the twenty first century. Note Dr. Adams's comment:

> "Christians are being amalgamated into this system because of unbelief that leads to blindness. Because they have never been discipled as in 2 Peter 1:9, a new liberalism has entered the sphere of the conservative church. I call it neo-liberalism. The church preaches a conservative Biblical message but the lives of the people do not live the truth which shows the Church members are being deceived. They are still functioning with the old system of logic that they learned in their early years. They are unable to distinguish God's truth. Many Christians fall prey because they simply do not know how to distinguish truth from error. Slogans are bandied about such as 'All truth is God's truth.' Naturally, if it is the truth it is God's. No one in his right mind would deny that. But it is also a fact 'all error is the devil's error.'" Adams, *A Call for Discernment, p. 30.*

The Scriptures are very clear in what the truth is. In His prayer to the Father, Jesus said "Sanctify them by the truth, your Word is truth" (Jn. 17:17). The writer in Heb. 5:11-14 strongly indicates that maturity or the making of a disciple is partaking of solid food by knowing and applying the truth. Strict exercise of the truth produces in a person the continuing ability to discern between good and evil.

Therefore, being a true disciple is a disciplined process by which we can obtain the prize (1 Cor. 9:24-27). Paul says that the prize is Christ's reward for the believer at the *Bema* or the judgment seat of Christ (2 Cor. 5:10). The process is discipleship, to grow and learn as a newborn baby desires milk, so the new Christian has a desire to grow (2 Pet. 3:18). This desire is to be met by vigorously motivated disciplers in the Church to guide a disciple through the process. Note the following chart defining the BEMA seat.

> **BEMA is a Greek term describing a raised platform with steps leading up to a large rostrum, located in the marketplace of a city, where rewards were presented for victories at the Isthmian games. The term is also used as a tribunal setting in a law court. Biblically, it is used in 1 Cor. 3:12-15 and 2 Cor. 5:10 of the judgment of a believer's works in this lifetime, resulting in rewards (2 Cor. 5:10).**

The agonizing part is working through the process of sanctification. The idea in this process is to "put off" the "old man" thought patterns to be "renewed in the spirit of your mind" by allowing the mind to be filled with the Word and to "put on" the new man thought patterns as Paul explains in Eph. 4:20-24. This is the process we see as we pursue the Beatitude Model for Discipleship. There will be an Emptying

Process, the putting off of the old man thought patterns; the Discovery process of being renewed in the mind, and the Filling Process of putting on the new man. This demands a scrutiny of our personality development, uncovering any blind spots that would hinder our spiritual walk and being conformed to the righteousness of Christ; a constant putting off and putting on.

The Commission to Proceed

How do we do this? How are we sanctified? It is only by grace through faith plus obedience (Eph. 1:7-14; 1 Pet. 1:5-9). Jesus gives specific instructions regarding this process. The problem is massive from a natural point of view but from God's perspective it is a project. The project is given here as a command to the Church. We call it the great commission. Jesus said: "Go therefore and make disciples of all nations, baptizing them in the name of the Father and the Son and the Holy Spirit, teaching them to observe all things that I have commanded you; and lo, I am with you always, even to the end of the age" (Mat. 28:18-20). When we read this verse in the English translation, we tend to make the word "go" the main verb. The following diagram will help us understand the difference in reading it from the Greek. The word, *go,* is a participle that modifies the main verb "make disciples." Note the chart.

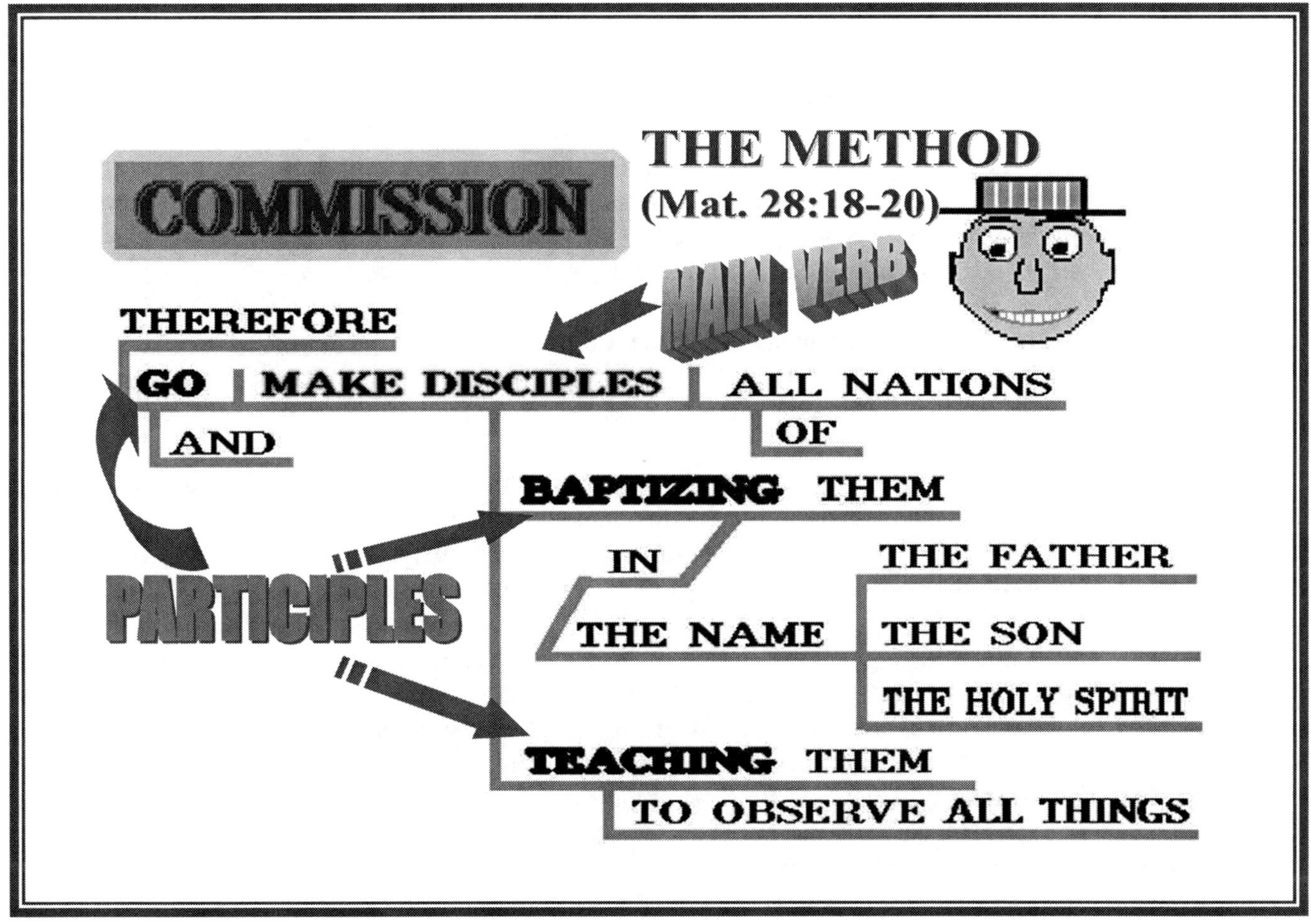

This book is designed to show that the Great Commission is to "make disciples." This commission is to the local church. In Mat. 28:19, Jesus establishes an education and training program for the Master's men. To state it another way, preparing future servant kings in and through the local church. It requires all the gifts and work of the corporate body to make a disciple. No individual possesses all the gifts. Therefore, the individual member is inadequate for the task. Jesus had all the gifts. Only He could meet all the needs of His disciples, but we are specially gifted in His process of making disciples.

The church, not the individual, is commissioned to make disciples. Each new disciple needs the nurturing of all the gifts, not just one or two. To the extent that a disciple does not receive this nurturing, there will be a weakness or unrighteousness in his spiritual growth. It's also true that if a member of the body is not functioning in their particular gift, they and others will become weak, sluggish and sickly (Heb. 5:11-6:12) because they do not receive the nurturing they need from the gifts. Note expanded definition.

> **"*Sluggish*… was used to describe the limbs of a sick lion. In the papyri, the corresponding verb is used of "sickness."** Rejecter, *Linguistic Key to Greek New Testament*, p. 333.

Unfortunately, this is happening too often, and as a result, few *true disciples* are being made. The King of Kings has given this commission to the Church, and the Church is the King's institution for preparing kings for their future reign with Him (2 Tim. 2:11-12; Mat. 16:24-27; Lk. 22:28-30; Rev. 2:26-27, 3:21). These future kings are called disciples throughout their training process. There are three participles that modify the main verb "make disciples" in this passage. The first is "to go;" the ending on the word indicates a participle and could be translated "as we are going, on our way, make disciples." In this context, it modifies the main verb which is an imperative and renders it a command. It is not that we are to go to Africa or South America; but wherever we go, whatever we are doing, we are to do something. The main verb tells us what to do.

The main verb is a descriptive term. It comes from the root word *math* in the Greek, which indicates a thought combined with action or a system of logic that demands action. Our English word *mathematics* is derived from this word. The ending on the word indicates a strong command, an active imperative. It is translated, "make disciples." The main idea is like the old Army command, "Do it now!" Therefore, an expanded translation could be: as we go, wherever we go, we should be changing the logic of those to whom we minister. Charles Ryrie defines the word disciple:

> "The word disciple itself means 'learner or pupil.' It always involved a teacher-student relationship. John the Baptist had his disciples (Mat. 9:14), the Pharisees had theirs (Mat. 22:16), and Paul had his" (Acts 9:25). Ryrie, *So Great Salvation*, p. 104.

Note again Paul's exhortation, "And everyone who competes for the prize is temperate in all things. Now they do it to obtain a perishable crown, but we for an imperishable crown. Therefore I run thus: not with uncertainty. Thus I fight: not as one who beats the air. But I discipline my body and bring it into subjection, lest, when I have preached to others, I myself should become disqualify" (1 Cor. 9:25-27).

This command is not to evangelize, although evangelization must precede it. It involves the whole process of spiritual development or discipleship. It is creating a desire in a person to learn, to know more about God. It can be an unbeliever who has never heard, or a believer who has never been discipled. Many who followed Him were not believers; they were seekers, desiring to learn. In the case of an unbeliever, they must be persuaded to follow Christ, and by faith alone receive him as Savior.

This is the regeneration experience, justification, or to be born again, declared righteous or one who has been persuaded in their heart that Jesus is the Christ their Savior. In those who continue to obey, God will create a desire—not just to know Him better but to follow Him. This is the process of sanctification, being set apart or made different, putting off the old man thought patterns, being renewed in the mind and putting on the new man.

When we lead someone to Christ as Savior for eternal life, we become obligated, as a new father or mother, to that infant Christian. With this parentage goes great responsibility as Jesus demonstrated with His disciples (Mat. 5:2). The first step in making a *true disciple* then, is justification (a person is made righteous by faith alone). But this is just the first part of salvation. The second step in making a *true disciple* involves the process of identification with Christ through the symbol of baptism. Here, Jesus uses a second participle meaning "to dip." It was a dyer's term in Christ's time. As a garment was dipped into the dye, it would become identified with the dye. This is a picture of a spiritual union, or Spirit baptism, which takes place when we believe and are baptized into the body of Christ. The ending on the word indicates three important things. It is an adverbial participle, indicating action and it takes on the mode of the main verb (make disciples), it modifies. Since this participle is modifying an imperative, it is not a take-it-or-leave-it proposition! It is a direct command.

Believers Identification with Christ

Dr. Radmacher sees baptism as identification with Christ. Jesus amplifies this imperative with the words "in the Name of the Father and of the Son and of the Holy Spirit." The indication here is that through baptism, we identify ourselves with the Father, Son, and Holy Spirit. The overall idea in this participle is that every time we make a disciple, or a person receives Christ as Savior, we must also guide them through a process of identification with His body or baptism. Note Dr. Radmacher's remarks:

> "Water baptism outwardly pictures the inner reality of our being identified with Christ in His death and His resurrection. Just as He died and was resurrected to new life, so individuals, at the moment of salvation, died to (were separated from) the tyranny of sin and were resurrected to new life (Rom. 6:4), and our bodies will be resurrected when He returns. (Rom. 5, 8-9)." Radmacher, *Salvation*, p.69.

I believe Jesus gave these participles in this order because it is the necessary process for spiritual growth and development of a *true disciple*. Christ's logic is that apart from justification, there can be no identification, and apart from identification there can be no sanctification.

The third step in making disciples involves sanctification. Because leading someone to receive Christ makes us a spiritual parent, we are given the responsibility to teach them all things He has commanded, that is, to train them up. The step of baptism is identification with Christ which produces in them a teachable attitude. If one rebels against—or resists—baptism, then the process of sanctification or learning will be hindered. The word Jesus uses here is *didactic* "to give instructions" or "to teach." The ending of this word is the same as above. It carries the same concept of an adverbial participle. It is a strong continuous command of responsibility. Jesus proceeds to tell us, as a part of this command, that we are to teach them—to observe (to keep, to guard, to be aware, to be alert to action) all—not just these things, but all—things that He commanded. The responsibility given here is not merely an intellectual ascent to some theological principles, but a physical and emotional awareness of what He did and taught.

He promises He will be with us to the end of the age, that is, He will never leave nor forsake us. His Spirit indwells us and gives us direct access to Him. The same Spirit that guided Jesus throughout His life on earth now lives in us (Rom. 8:9). The same Spirit made us alive, raised us up, and seated us with Him in the heavenly places in Christ Jesus (Eph. 2:5-6). He has now sealed us (eternal security) and will forever be with us, even to the end of this age (Mat. 28:20, Jn. 14:16). Joseph Dillow explains our dependence on Him:

> "If our eternal security depends on anything in us, it is certain it is not secure. However the Scriptures teach that our final entrance into heaven is guaranteed by the work of the Father, the Son, and Holy Spirit. Since it depends on an infinite person, who is faithful and true, it is inconceivable that the salvation of any child of God could ever be lost." Dillow, *Reign of the Servant Kings*, p. 513.

Next, He begins to select those who will follow Him as the king's men in the process of changing their minds, or those He will later call His disciples. He was making disciples that they may be with Him.

Matthew does not record the calling of all His disciples here, but He calls Peter, Andrew, James, and John, and they followed Him (Jn. 1:35-51). Remember, the word *disciple* means one who follows a master teacher as a learner. He has not yet called them disciples. While he was selecting His disciples throughout Galilee, He continued to preach the Gospel of the Kingdom, healing all kinds of diseases, pains, demoniacs, epileptics and paraplegics. People were coming from all over Israel and from beyond the Jordan (Mat. 4:18-22). Christ was giving spiritual answers to the complexities of the human heart and rescuing man from his depraved state. He is now ready to reveal the answer to man's basic difficulty in life which is fear resulting in anxiety and the need to become POOR IN SPIRIT or a humble servant.

PROJECT

1. Why are so many Christians spiritually malnourished? (Heb. 2-4)

2. How does the writer of Hebrews identify the Problem? (Heb. 5)

3. What does 2 Pet. 1:3 mean to you?

4. Why are all the gifts necessary in making a disciple?

5. List several things missing in discipleship today.

6. How is the Church like the Israelites?

7. Why test every spirit by the Word?

CHAPTER 4 - RIGHT THINKING ABOUT THE BEATITUDE MODEL

"And seeing the multitude, He went upon a mountain, and when He was seated His disciples came to Him. Then He opened His mouth and taught them saying: Blessed..." Mat. 5:1-2

The Making of a Disciple

There was a special meeting called at the north end of the Sea of Galilee on a hillside called the Mount of Beatitudes. The King had come and selected some of the King's chosen men, who would be His representatives (Apostles). Today they would be His cabinet officers. They are the ones He challenged to "come and see" and "come follow Me." These are the ones He had chosen to pour His life into for the rest of His life on earth.

After ministering to the multitudes, He went up the mountain and sat down. His disciples came to Him and He began teaching them. This is the first time the word "disciple" is used in the New Testament (Mat. 5:1). We established the meaning of the word disciple in Chapter 1 (Mat. 28:19). This is the same word Jesus uses to introduce the ministry of making disciples.

> **"LOVE FOR ONE ANOTHER DEMONSTRATES DISCIPLESHIP"**

He also established the message of the King: "Repent for the kingdom of heaven is at hand" (Mat. 4:17). Now He will demonstrate how to make disciples. In this context, it is difficult to discern if He is addressing the group he has called or the multitude. But one thing is sure—the multitude is listening and Jesus has some words for them: "Narrow is the gate and difficult is way which leads to life, and there are few who find it" (Mat. 7:14).

This is a unique ministry and certainly opposite of what the world teaches: "then He opened His mouth and taught them"---- (Mat. 5:2). This is the beginning of His teaching of the new logic for the citizens of the Kingdom.

The Subjective Cycle of Life

Larry, my client, was caught up in the Subjective Cycle of life. The old paradigms were dominating his thinking processes. Every time an old man thought pattern came up, he would respond according to the way he had been programmed in his previous formative years. These paradigms were buried deep in his memory banks; as a result he had become sluggish and needed a change of mind.

That is what Paul meant when he said, "Do not be conformed to this world" (Rom. 12:2). In other words, your old way of thinking about circumstances is distorted. We all have this difficulty since we all come into this world separated from God in darkness, under the influence of the world powers and controlled primarily by our emotions. In those early years we were exploding in our personality development and there were many broken relationships, conflicts, and deep hurts. In fact, psychologists tell us that by the time we are six years old, we have already developed 85 percent of our personality.

Because of all the pain and hurt in those formative years, we developed these layers of fear around ourselves, and as we grew into the adolescent years we became a very anxious personality. Anxiety drains us emotionally and we become depressed. No one likes a loser, so we proceed to build a defense system around us which causes us to manifest pride. This pride results in our becoming insensitive to those around us, and because of all this wrong thinking, impurity results and then we become extremely insecure.

This is the Adam and the Eve nature. This is a natural development under the influence of the world system. In those early years, we were influenced by the spirits of the world before we could rationally deal with God. We were exposed to fear, anxiety, depression, guilt, etc., causing chemical imbalance in our brain that causes bio-chemical changes in the organs of the body, and over a period of time affect the immune system. Note   Dr. McMillen's comments:

> "I am confident that the reader will be intrigued to discover that the Bible's directives can save him from certain infectious diseases, from many lethal cancers, and from a long gauntlet of psychosomatic diseases that are increasing in spite of all efforts of modern medicine. The highly important adrenal glands are frequently the target of emotional fire. Their secretions in abnormal amounts can cause high blood pressure, arthritis, kidney disease, and hardening of the arteries—the last killer alone is responsible for the annual slaughter of 800,000 in the United States. That is just one area of difficulty modern man has complicated his life with. God has a better way. He said to the Israelites three thousand years ago, 'If you diligently heed the voice of God and do what is right in His sight, give ear to His commandments and keep all His statues, I will put none of these diseases on you'" (Ex. 15: 26). McMillen, *None of These Diseases*, Preface.

Well, the Israelites did not keep his commandments and statues, and yes, they had all these diseases! Not only that, but we get new ones every year. Why? Because man continues to separate himself from God. The Bible is very clear about the misuse and abuse of our physical and psychological make-up. Our sins separate us from God and the wages of sin is death. For the unbeliever that is eternal death. For the believer it is physical death as James says, "But each one is tempted when he draws away by his own desires and enticed. Then, when desire has conceived, it gives birth to sin, and sin, when it is full grown, brings forth death" (Ja. 1:14-15). Whether we like it or not, this is the way we come into the world, separated from God.

Jesus shows us there is a better way, for you to be free from the bondage of this world. The old self-image we developed under the old world system must go. This starts the process of moving from the subjective cycle of life into the objective cycle of life. It demands a putting off of the old man and putting on the new (Col. 3:8-10). The old personality, or the old self-image, was developed under the influence of the world system and it must go (Mat. 5:1-16).

The subjective cycle is looking at life from our human perspective and the objective cycle is the greater sphere, looking at life from God's point of view. We see eight specific levels in the process. There are three levels in the Emptying Process and five in the Filling Process (Mat. 5:1-10).

The Emptying Process   OBJECTIVE CYCLE

Poor in Spirit: First Level in the Emptying Process

I will briefly explain the entire model and give an introduction to each level. Then we will go through a detailed study of each level. This is Christ's standard for the citizen of the Kingdom of Heaven. The first level of training in royalty or the making of a king is for one to become poor in spirit. The message from the King is, "Repent for the kingdom of heaven is at hand." That is, go on changing your mind, first about God, then about yourself, and then about His kingdom. Jesus is about to give the disciples a new logic that is in extreme contrast to the old.

He says "Blessed" (Mat. 5:3), which is the first promise to those who will follow Him. Each level in this process is introduced by this word *blessed*, which means to be happy or to have an inner contentment.

A better development of the word is "at peace inside are those who do certain things." It is a high and lofty position to be rich in the Spirit of God (Eph. 5:18, Gal. 5:22-25).

This promise of blessedness is based on becoming poor in spirit. The word *poor* is from a Greek word which means "lowly, beggarly." Other words expanded from this root indicate "to become poor or to be a beggar." It was used of Jesus by Paul, "For you know the grace of our Lord Jesus Christ, that though He was rich, yet for your sake He became poor, that you through His poverty might become rich" (2 Cor. 8:9). Here He is speaking of spiritual poverty—to be poor in the old spirit that was developed under the influence of the world system and rich in the new Spirit, the Holy Spirit of God.

The word *spirit* begins with a lower case, indicating it is man's spirit. A man's spirit that is poor in the human spirit but rich in the Holy Spirit. The human spirit was developed under the influence of the world system of fear, anxiety depression, defense, pride, insensitivity, impurity, and insecurity. The old personality is a product of the "old man" thought patterns from the Adamic nature (Eph. 4:22-24, Col.3:5-10). This was our condition before we became a believer in Christ.

Jesus said, "Blessed are the poor in spirit." Becoming poor in spirit is the first and most vital phase of the Emptying Process. It is a prerequisite for developing the other attitudes. This involves letting go of our old, pre-Christian identity—that old self-image—and adopting a new identity "created according to God" in Eph. 4:23-24. Being conformed to His image is the mandate for effective personality change: For "He is the image of the invisible God, the first born over all creation" (Col. 1:15).

To be conformed we must change our concept of God. This will help us get to know Him more intimately so we can build a proper God-image that will replace the old self-image. This knowledge will help us develop a better understanding of faith and how to apply it in every area of life. You see, the more we know Him, the more we can trust Him. It will increase our ability to communicate with Him in prayer, worship, praise and interact with Him in all areas of life.

Mourning: Second Level in the Emptying Process

The Greek word for *mourn* used by Christ means to grieve over past sin and change our old way of thinking. Such grief cannot be hidden. When we become poor in spirit, God's radiance will expose all the old man thought patterns and we just want to weep, cry and lament (Ja. 4:8-9). Mourning involves our conscience (Rom. 2:1-15); it involves repentance, confession, forgiveness, restitution and ultimately a new direction in life (Mat. 5:23-26). It demands a clear conscience (2 Tim 1:3-4). Like Paul before Felix, "In view of this, I also do my best to maintain always a blameless (clear) conscience both before God and before men" (Acts 24:16).

A disciple must reflect on all attitudes and actions in the past to detect any blind spots as a result of broken relationships, conflicts and deep hurts. The idea is to understand the conscience, how it functions and how to develop a good conscience that will free us from guilt and depression. Keeping a clear conscience is a valid life goal for any disciple (Ps. 32:1-5).

Meekness: Third Level in the Emptying Process

The word *meek* means, "gentle, or mild" and indicates a "softness." Meekness implies gentleness and humility, not a namby-pamby as the world sees it. Those who are meek are kindhearted; they search for ways to serve the Lord, no matter what the circumstances. A meek person is not spineless, but disciplined, unpretentious, and unassuming. Meekness is the absence of self-righteousness and malice. Christ and Moses were called meek men but not weak.

A meek horse is one that responds to the slightest movement or touch of tenderness; one whose strong will has been broken and is easily guided into a powerful task. This is God's desire for us—that our strong will would be broken and be guided by His Spirit into great accomplishments.

If you think meekness is weakness, then try being meek for a week! Dr. Radmacher

The disciple begins the process of learning the difference between self-righteousness and responsibility. It involves relinquishing personal prerogatives, assuming responsibility, and responding rightly in all circumstances (Phil. 2:3-4). The disciple must understand the source of conflicts and quarrels and be willing to surrender self-righteousness to God. He then appropriates God's grace to take on responsibility in his areas of weakness. Now we begin to tear down our defense or authority system that has been developed over the years and replace it with meekness. This causes us to hunger and thirst after righteousness so that we will not revert to former practices and possibly become even worse off than before (Lk. 11:24-26).

The Filling Process

Hungering and Thirsting: First Level in the Filling Process

Once we are empty, the natural response is to hunger and thirst after God. These are very strong words indicating necessity and urgency. It is a driving, compelling motivational force. In this case we are given the object of our hungering and thirsting after God's righteousness as demonstrated by Christ on earth. Not just any righteousness, but His righteousness manifested in Christ's life on earth. Hungering and thirsting is having a deep desire to do the things Jesus did when He was here. Christ functioned in all the gifts, all the time, so He was a perfect living illustration of God's righteousness in the flesh (Col. 2:9).

"Be all that you can be!" is a slogan of the U.S. Army and can apply to a physical accomplishment. Our desire should be "to be all that we can be" in the spiritual realm. This demonstrates His righteousness, by doing the things He did. First, each disciple must understand God's righteousness by the things He did and said. Secondly, we should understand what the Scripture says about spiritual gifts because that is our power to function. Thirdly, we should discover the specific gifting God has provided to each disciple (1 Pet. 4:10-11).

Merciful: Second Level in the Filling Process

The Filling Process includes "one who is merciful." The word *mercy* means to be "gracious, to console, to succor or to be sensitive." This is a characteristic of Christ. He demonstrates mercy all the time. It was by His mercy we are saved. It is by His mercies that we can dedicate our lives to Him as living sacrifices (Rom. 12:1). It is His mercy that enables us to discern human emotions; to identify with the problems of others. Jesus was "meek and lowly of heart" (Mat. 11:29). Jesus was sensitive to the needs of those around Him. He spoke with compassion to the multitudes, and fed them physically and spiritually. He showed kindness to a Samaritan woman and with His gifts met her needs. We now can realize how we fit into our local church and how to be able to discern the heartbreaks of others and develop sensitivity towards them.

We can become a vital functioning part of the body of Christ, joining with our brothers and sisters to accomplish the same types of things the Lord did 2000 years ago. We can become servants, as Jesus served; to acquire the ability to come alongside someone who is hurting and help them.

Pure in Heart: Third Level in the Filling Process

The concept of purity reveals the very nature of God. God is Holy. The heart (soul) is the source of impurity. It involves the mind, emotions, and the will, functioning with regard to moral issues. To purify the heart means to be sure you have a clear conscience (Acts 24:16). Robert Cook says regarding the heart:

"The central seat and organ of man's conscious life in it's moral and intellectual aspects; a term which comprehends all the elements of personality; in the New Testament, especially the epistles, with the addition of specific terms for will and mind it may sometimes be used in a more restrictive sense as representing the sensibility of man (the emotional qualities of personality)." Cook, *Systematic Theology, Vol II*, p.48.

Christ is the perfect example of a pure heart. Paul says, "Who may ascend into the hill of the Lord? Or who may stand in His holy place? He who has clean hands and a pure heart, who has not lifted up his soul to an idol" (Ps. 24:3-4).

In this area, each disciple learns how to stay above circumstances (1 Jn. 3:6-8). They develop the principles needed to enable them to deal with sin while it is still in the mind, before it becomes an action (1 Jn. 1:7-9, Rom. 12:2-6). It is not enough to simply be empty of excess behavioral, emotional, and spiritual baggage. We must also live above the circumstances.

Peacemaker: Fourth Level in the Filling Processing

A peacemaker is the logical outcome of concern. It demonstrates purity of heart. God would have each of us become a peacemaker. To fully understand God's idea of peacemaking, we must discard some of our preconceived ideas. From God's perspective, peacemaking has nothing to do with reconciling world powers or negotiating between nations. However, it does involve reconciliation of man to God (2 Cor. 5:17-21). Jesus was the ultimate peacemaker. Now He has commissioned us also to be peacemakers or reconcilers.

Each disciple needs to develop the skills needed to share the good news of Christ. We should be able to present the plan of salvation to those who do not know Him. We need to be able to tell and show them the security Christ promises to the believer in Mat. 28:19-20. The promise Jesus gives to those who become peacemakers is, "They shall be called sons of God" (Mat. 5:9, Jn. 1:12). In other words, they will see God in you and you shall be called a Son or Daughter of God. They will see you differently, and what an opportunity to explain what God has done in your life. However as you serve Him, you can be sure people will persecute you and say evil things against you (Mat. 5:10-12). This brings us to the next level.

Persecuted and Reviled: Fifth Level in the Filling Process

The word *persecuted* means to pursue or harass. The word's use here is a perfect passive participle that means there will always be a continuing persecution as a result of our godly conduct. We are constantly exposed to spiritual warfare and we are vulnerable to be attacked (1 Thes. 3:3-4; 1 Pet. 4:12-17). The idea of persecution is compounded by the words *revile* or *insult* in Mat. 5:11. This will be developed more in a later chapter.

KNOWING OUR ARMOR
FOR SPIRITUAL WARFARE

This is a spiritual battle we are in (Mat. 6:12, Eph. 6:10), and as we cut the psychological strings of the world through the Emptying and Filling Processes, we can recognize the seriousness and spiritual nature of the battle. Spiritual effectiveness signals that one has reached a level of maturity. Christians who regularly influence others for Christ often find themselves under attack from Satan's demonic forces.

Here the disciple understands suffering and spiritual warfare and learns how to put on the whole armor of God. We are able to activate our gifts and abilities in fighting these battles. We understand the dangers and realize that without the proper armor we might well be numbered among the wounded or sidelined in the fight (Eph. 6:10-20). Finally, Jesus gives the motivation force for our suffering and serving. There will be great rewards for those who participate in the Kingdom here and now. The concept of rewards will be developed in Chapter 13.

Conclusion to the Model

After going through the Beatitude Model of Discipleship, we discover we can handle any circumstance with which Satan and his demons confront us. We become the type of people Jesus calls, "the salt of the earth" (Mat. 5:13). We are the seasoning in a lost world! We cause those with whom we come in contact to thirst for what we have in Christ. Like salt, we are able to pierce or break down outer shells. We can help others where they are hurting.

Next Jesus said, "You are the light of the world" (Mat. 5:14). We become polished reflectors exposing this darkness with God's light. Some will respond; others won't. Some may even hurt us. Many will resist us. Some will flee, others will attack. No matter what the circumstances, God will give us His power and grace to stand firm for Him. We will experience inner peace even when persecuted. Finally, He says, "Let your light shine" (Mat. 5:16). These words contain one of the strongest imperatives in the New Testament. We really have no choice. We are commanded to let our light shine. As we will move through the process one level at a time and make sure there are no blind-spots left unresolved. Whether we like it or not we are reflectors of His light. This process will help you polish or brighten up your reflector.

PROJECT

1. Define the word disciple.

2. List the consequences of the subjective cycle.

3. What did Jesus do after calling His disciples?

4. List the elements of the subjective cycle.

   a. ______________________________   e. ______________________________

   b. ______________________________   f. ______________________________

   c. ______________________________   g. ______________________________

   d. ______________________________

5. List the elements of the objective cycle.

   a. ______________________________   e. ______________________________

   b. ______________________________   f. ______________________________

   c. ______________________________   g. ______________________________

   d. ______________________________   h. ______________________________

6. Describe what the model means to you now.

7. Draw the model and explain it to someone.

NOTE: I searched for years for a progressive process of discipleship that would take a disciple from ground zero (unbelief), to the grand meeting of our Lord and Savior at the judgment seat of Christ in heaven. It was not until I began counseling in 1972 after graduating from seminary as I was teaching a class on Mat. 5:1-16 that I realized, this is it. I was confronted with the Master Discipler Himself. After He called his disciples in chapter four He began teaching them a new logic of the Kingdom, A Kingdom that was not yet established in this world, the Kingdom of Heaven and He is the King. This Kingdom would one day in the future be established on Earth as it is in Heaven. The Beatitudes are an outline of the *Sermon on the Mount*. They present a solution to the behavior problems and growth processes that will guide them through this life time. All those who believe in this lifetime and persevere as a partaker to the end will reign with Him in that kingdom on earth. More on this as you study and do the things necessary to experience God's best in your life.

CHAPTER 5 - RIGHT THINKING ABOUT GOD

"Blessed are the poor in spirit, for theirs is the kingdom of heaven." Mat. 5:3

Emptying By Becoming Poor in Spirit

Here that process begins. I would like to remind you that this is not an exegetical development of the Beatitudes, but I am taking the principles of Christ, in the Beatitudes, as a frame work for the discipleship process. This process is also found throughout the Epistles (note 2 Pet. 1:1-11, Gal. 5:22-28, Ja. 4:1-12). The beatitudes make up an outline by which Jesus built a progressive process of discipleship. This is the introduction to the *Sermon on the Mount*, and the rest of the sermon is an amplification of these areas. In this area of poor in spirit, He emphasizes the authentication of the Word, the source of our knowledge of God, to know Him, to trust Him and to communicate with Him.

The idea of putting off and putting on starts with regeneration, or when we are born again (Eph. 4:20-24). This is also the first step in becoming Poor in Spirit. The self-righteous nature must be transformed. Jesus said, "For I say to you, that unless your righteousness exceeds the righteousness of the Scribes and Pharisees, you will by no means enter the kingdom of heaven" (Mat. 5:20). This statement leaves us with a question. Can we, in our own power, develop a righteousness that would exceed the scribes and Pharisees? No! Note Curtis H. Tucker's comments in his book:

"Practical righteousness that surpasses the scribes and Pharisees is seen as godly character. The first portion of the sermon (5:3-12) gives clear examples of the kind of character needed. Anyone who wishes to earn rewards and share in the Messianic kingdom on earth must be submissive and dependent upon God; he must be poor in spirit. He must be able to control his strength, strive to do God's will, be patient and forgiving (merciful), clean hearted, a peacemaker, and totally committed to Christ." Curtis H. Tucker, *Majestic Destiny*, p. 148-149.

The Scribes and Pharisees were the best at being righteous outwardly (Mat. 5:20); they really worked at keeping the law. The only way we can exceed the righteousness of the Scribes and the Pharisees is by believing in Him who is the righteousness of God, receiving His imputed righteousness—and it is by faith alone (Rom. 4:23-25). Jesus makes it clear when He says, "For God so loved the world that He gave His only begotten Son, that whosoever believes in Him should not perish but have eternal life" (Jn. 3:16). How can we know if we are born again or regenerated in His righteousness?

"In John's Gospel we see that the disciples of Jesus have already become believers before the public ministry begins (Jn. 1:35-51; 2:11). They are with him as He evangelizes (Sychar 4:27-42). There is no reason why they should have construed the Sermon on the Mount— when they heard it—as furnishing an ethical formula for reaching heaven. That would have been to forget the simple gospel which they already knew quiet well." Hodges, *Grace in Eclipse*, p. 20.

The following questions, designed by Dr. James Kennedy, in His book <u>Evangelism Explosion</u>, will help you discern your relationship with Jesus Christ. The first question is: *Have you come to the place spiritually in your life that you have the assurance, that if you died tonight, you would go to heaven to be with Christ?* If your answer was "no" or "I don't know," then see Resources page 154". If you answered yes, you need to know what you base that fact on.

The second question is designed to help you understand the basis of your salvation. *Suppose you were to die tonight, go to heaven, and God should say to you, why should I let you into my heaven?*

How would you answer Him? There is only one answer to that question and that is "Because I believe in Jesus for eternal life." If you weren't sure how to answer this question, then go to "Resources page 154."

When we believe in Christ for eternal life, we are born again and become His children (Jn. 1:12), so we are members of His Kingdom (Heb. 13:14). This is when acts of repentance (the changing of our mind) start. We will spend the rest of our lives changing our mind about God and His Kingdom. All those old principles of the old thought patterns stored in the brain must go. This process of changing the mind is what I mean by sanctification. You have been born into His family and that makes you royalty. We are born kings. We have begun the process of becoming *Poor in Spirit*.

> "But there is a progression from the curious to the convinced. These are those who gave themselves perhaps out of curiosity to the Word of God, who had an intellectual curiosity as to what Christ would say and teach, and as they listened to His words and beheld His works, they were convinced of the truth of His word and the truth of His person. They were convinced disciples." Pentecost, *Design for Discipleship*, p. 17.

The Need to Know God

Becoming Poor in Spirit is to "submit to God. Resist the devil and he will flee from you" (Ja. 4:7). It is not enough just to know Him as in justification; we must go on daily getting to know Him better in sanctification (Jn. 14:21-24). This is the attitude of one in the Kingdom of Heaven who desires to reign with Christ, the King of Kings. This attitude demands humility and a servant's heart; someone who desires to learn. Being "poor in spirit" is a learning attitude. The promise to those who desire to follow Him is that they shall inherit the kingdom of heaven. This promise is only for those who believe. Joseph Dillow comments:

> "If God's eternal plan revolves around demonstrating the moral superiority of humility and servant-hood, it is of the utmost importance that we learn this lesson now. All Christians are not servants, and only those who are will be great in the kingdom. Only those sons of God who are sons indeed will be co-heirs with their coming King in the final destiny of man. Many who have been saved by the King are not presently living for Him. Many who have begun lives of discipleship have not persevered. They risk forfeiture of this great future. But we are partakers (Gk. metochoi) of Christ, only if we hold our confidence firmly to the end (Heb. 3:14). However, those who are obedient and dependent servants now, and who persevere in discipleship to the final hour, will be among Christ's metochoi, the servant kings, in the thousand year kingdom of the Son of Man. All Christians will be in the Kingdom, but tragically, not all will be co-heirs there." Dillow, *Reign of the Servant Kings*, p. 6.

Becoming Poor in Spirit is being conformed to Christ's likeness—that is, becoming a partaker in His Kingdom in this lifetime. This is not only knowing Him from a justification point of view, but knowing Him intimately through sanctification, knowing we can trust Him in any circumstance. Unfortunately, Christians in general are lacking in their knowledge of God. A good help in this area would be to read *The Knowledge of the Holy*, by A.W. Tozer.

We need to experience Him and knowledge of Him is not enough. We need to experience His presence through obedience to his Word. Peter says this is the Christian's source of power: "Grace and peace be multiplied to you in the knowledge of God and of Jesus our Lord, as His divine power has given to us all things that pertain to life and godliness, through the knowledge of Him who called us by glory and virtue" (2 Pet. 1:2-4). Then again in verse five, Peter says, "Add to your virtue knowledge."

Solomon tells us the beginning of wisdom and knowledge is the result of the fear of the Lord (Prov. 1:7, Prov. 9:10). The fear of the Lord is a result of abiding in His word. As we get to know Him, we will become more sensitive to all that He has given us. We cannot trust a person we don't know. God is personality and the more we know Him the more we can trust Him. This demands a changing of our mind. Jeremiah states it this way:

> "Thus says the Lord: 'Let not the wise man glory in his wisdom, let not the mighty man glory in his might, nor let the rich man glory in his riches but let him who glories, glory in this, that he understands and knows me. That I am the Lord, exercising loving kindness, judgment and righteousness in the earth. For in these I delight,' says the Lord" (Jer. 9:23-24.

To know Him is to know His character or His perfections. Some are transferable and some are not. When we receive Christ as our Savior, He implants within us, by way of the Holy Spirit, the potential to exercise those attributes which are transferable. Some of these are righteousness, goodness, justice, graciousness, holiness, truthfulness, faithfulness, forgiveness, mercy, life, and love. However, there must be a reprogramming of our minds, which is getting our thinking straight about God. As Paul says, we must be temperate in all things (1 Cor. 9:25), especially in our knowledge of God. These are personality traits of a citizen of heaven, characteristics of royalty.

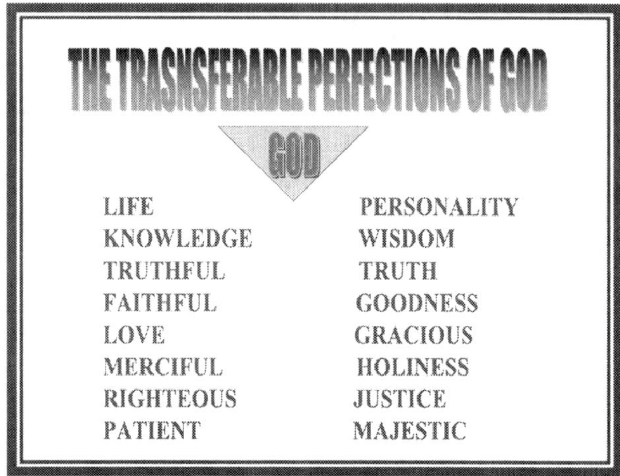

God also has non-transferable characteristics or perfections that we do not possess, but we do have access to them. God is omnipotent, omnipresent, omniscient, eternal, infinite, perfect, unchanging, self-existent, and sovereign. Jesus said, "And this is eternal life, that they may know You, the only true God, and Jesus Christ whom You have sent" (Jn. 17:3). This knowledge of Him is the source of the believer's power to function in this natural world. Peter says, "His divine power has given us everything we need for life and godliness, through our knowledge of Him" (2 Pet. 1:3). Seeing and knowing Him requires "abiding in Him, not just knowing about Him. Every answer we need has its source in our knowledge of Him. The question is how can we know Him? This knowledge comes through the Word. A. W. *Tozer* comments:

> "Left to ourselves we tend immediately to reduce God to manageable terms. We want to get Him where we can use Him, or at least know where He is when we need Him. We want a God we can, in some measure, control. We need the feeling of security that comes from knowing what God is like. What He is like of course, is a composite of all the religious pictures we have seen, all the best people we have known or heard about, and all the sublime ideas we have entertained. If all this sounds strange to modern ears, it is only because we have for a full half-century taken God for granted. The glory of God has not been revealed to this generation of men. The god of contemporary Christianity is only slightly superior to the gods of Greece and Rome, if indeed He is not actually inferior to them in that He is weak and helpless while they at least had power." Tozer, *The Knowledge of the Holy*, p. 13.

The Authority of His Word

How can we know Him? The Scriptures are God's revelation of Himself. That is, we get to know Him through His Word. Scripture says, "Faith comes by hearing and hearing by the Word of God" in Rom. 10:17. Paul clearly states this authority (2 Tim. 3:16-17).

We must be secure in the Word and respect it as His authority. Since the Bible is trustworthy and authored by God the Holy Spirit, it is the source of our knowledge of Him. To know Him is to know His Word and abide in Him (Jn. 8:31). Our ability to know Him and believe in Him is sourced in the Word. Therefore, we must be secure in the Word to respect it as His authority. How can we believe the Bible is God's Word? Note the diagrams below.

2 Tim. 3:16 Diagram

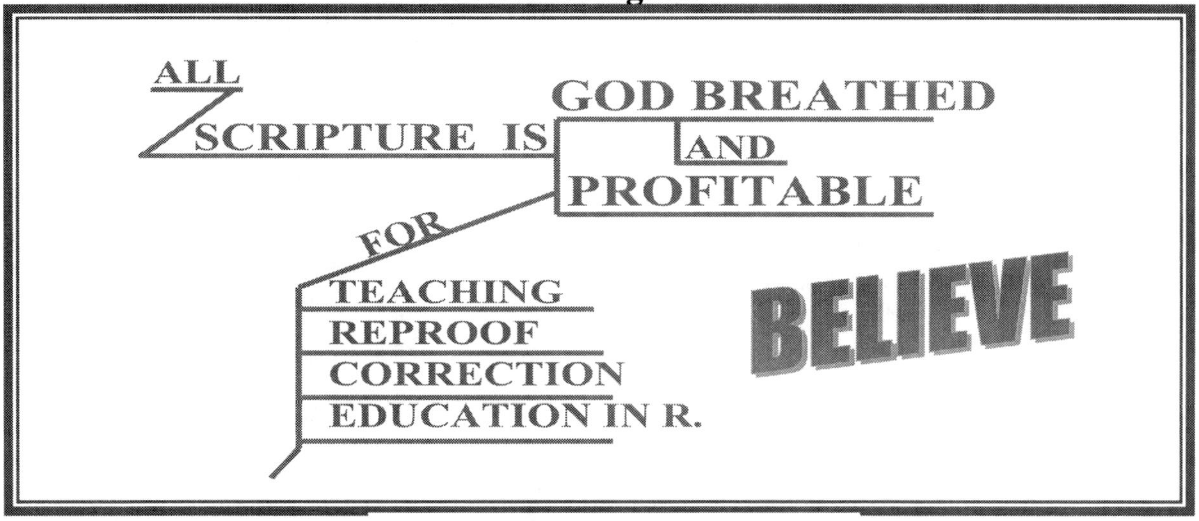

2 Tim. 3:17 Diagram

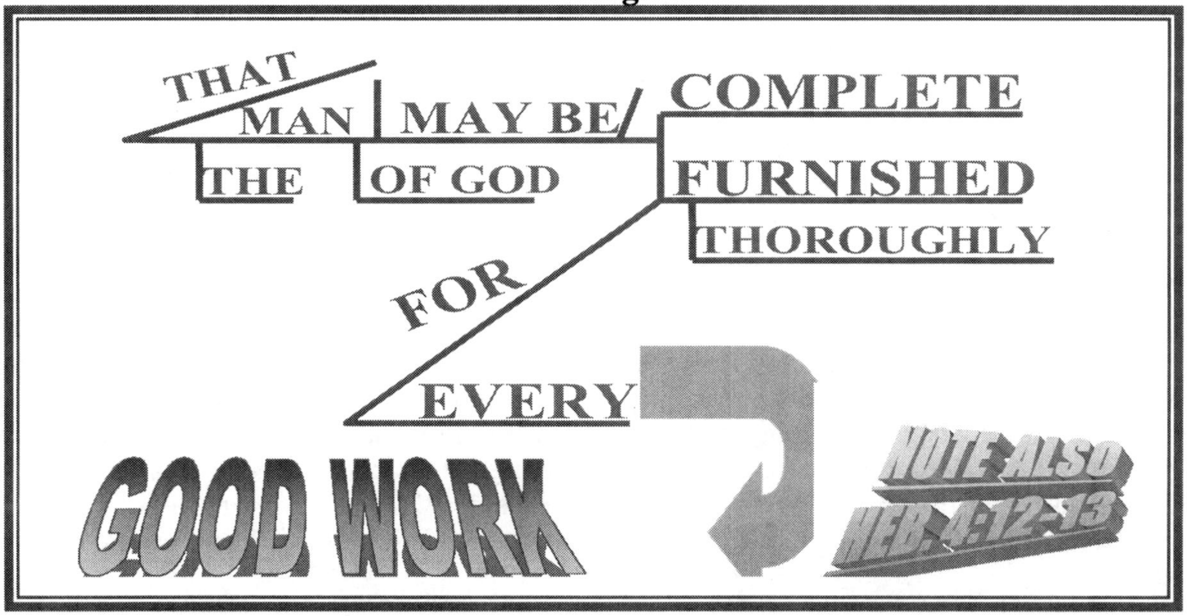

The Bible is a book of eternal truth that is not understood by the natural man. However, God created languages and reveals Himself in a way that those who have the Holy Spirit can understand. The Word is living; it is not natural, but has spiritual power even to the dividing of the soul and the spirit. We cannot even see the soul or the spirit, much less divide it. The Word has the potential to divide them, to separate them, take them apart, and know everything about them. The Word penetrates to the very core of man, even the discerning of the thoughts and intents of the heart. Thus, as the marrow gives life to the bones so the spirit gives life to the soul (Heb. 4:12).

From this text we have good evidence that the soul and spirit are not one and the same. Theologians and psychologists may not be able to discern them, but God's Word does. This is why the Bible is so significant in discipleship. It is God's way of giving us spiritual answers to psychological problems.

"Be diligent to present yourselves approved to God, a work-man who is not to be ashamed, rightly dividing the Word of truth" (2 Tim. 2:15). God is the designer of all things. He reveals them to those He chooses. Christ has delivered us from the powers of darkness. He has purchased us with His own blood. Therefore we really need to understand who He is.

Jesus Christ is God. He holds everything together (Eph. 4:15-16). Matthew says, "All things have been delivered to me by My Father, and no one knows the Son except the Father, nor does anyone know the Father except the Son, and He to whom the Son wills to reveal Him" (Mat. 11:17).

This is a special revelation that those who hold to a subjective view cannot understand. We are confronted with a society caught up in an ungodly humanistic worldview. Even Christians are being deceived by society's deceptive concepts. However, God reveals Himself to those who believe in Him (Mat. 24:21-22).

In other words we have everything we need for life and godliness because we have the Holy Spirit living in us. We have the scriptures to guide us. We have a body and soul to work out these powerful principles. Since we have all this, Paul admonishes us to take advantage of all we have:

"But as it is written: 'Eye has not seen, nor ear heard, nor have entered into the heart of man the things which God has prepared for those who love Him.' But God has revealed them to us through His Spirit. For the Spirit searches all things, yes, the deep things of God" (1 Cor. 2:9-10).

Paul gave us our mandate by admonishing us not to get caught up in controversies and quarrels of worldly philosophies (2 Tim. 2:20-23). This is a strong imperative. Paul exhorts us to be students of the Word and not be led astray by worldly philosophies and damaging others in the process (Col. 2:8-10). Our goal must be to please God, to be a diligent student of the Word of truth. The words "rightly divide" in the above passage are from a present active participle modifying the strong imperative. To be a good student, or diligent, is to cut a straight line through the Scriptures and to be straightforward in our understanding, contrary to the crooked and deceptive ways of the world. Jesus is the Living Word; we are created to live the Word. How?

Faith Plus Obedience = Sanctification

Now how do we do all this? We have the Holy Spirit and the Word. God has given us a special ability to believe what He says. This ability is called *faith and obedience*. It is an ability given by God. Faith with God as the object opens the channel through which grace flows, enabling us to function in our giftedness (Eph. 2:8).

When we are born again, God effectively and permanently connects us to Himself by grace. Our faith becomes the channel through which His grace flows. However, the object of faith must always be toward God (Jn. 10:28-29). It is like a hose connected to a faucet (God, the source). When the faucet is turned on, activating it as a carrier (believing), the water (grace) flows through, giving life to the soul that animates the body.

The concept of faith is to be convinced, to be persuaded, in our mind, whether in salvation or in sanctification. It is an innate human capacity in man to be persuaded to believe God or reject Him. It is that ability that when God draws us we have the ability to respond or not to respond. A good definition for faith can be found in Heb. 11:1: Faith gives substance (reality) to things hoped for and conviction about things not seen or faith substantiates things not seen.

> "Now faith is the substance of things hoped for, the evidence of things not seen." (Heb 11:1).

Faith sets us apart from sin. First, grace through faith delivers us from the penalty of sin. That is justification. But it is our faith plus obedience that frees us from the power of sin in our sanctification. We were saved, (past tense), from the penalty of sin by faith alone. We are being saved, present tense, from the power of sin by faith plus obedience. It is our faith that energizes obedience.

> "There are two things which differentiate saving faith from mere knowledge. The first may be summed up in the word 'trust.' It is one thing to intellectually accept certain propositions; it is another to be in a state of reliant trust. It is one thing to believe that Jesus is God and that He is the Savior, as the demons do; it is another to look to Him as one's personal Savior, from the penalty for sin." Dillow, *Reign of the Servant Kings*, p. 282.

When we believed, we were saved from the penalty of sin, regenerated, born again, and baptized by the Holy Spirit. We were taken out of darkness and placed in His light. But we brought all those old man thought patterns into our Christian life. This will often cause a crimp in our house of faith so the water or grace is slowed or stopped completely. Therefore, our natural tendency is to respond according to those old sinful thought patterns and quench the Spirit. To quench is to crimp, slow down, like pouring water on a fire. The danger is that the impulse of the flesh will hinder the energy or fire of the Spirit. Therefore, the object of our faith must always be God. We are vitally connected to God by faith. We have direct access to Him through the only mediator and that is Christ. He is at the right hand of the Father, making intercession for us. Any other object of your faith will quench the Spirit.

We are naturally conditioned to our old paradigms developed under the influence of the world system. The object of our faith is naturally ourselves. The process of sanctification in discipleship is translating the object of our faith from self to God. This faith enables us to believe in things we cannot see. We have always believed in things we could see, touch or feel. But as a believer we have the special ability to substantiate things by the Holy Spirit that are unseen.

When the object of our faith is God, faith gives substance or reality to unseen things. However, if the object of faith is in self then we can only believe natural things. A good illustration is that God is Spirit. We cannot see Him or touch Him, yet we believe He is. Note Sapaugh's comment:

> "Ephesians 2:7-9 is a magnificent statement concerning the eternal salvation which is graciously provided by God through the medium of faith in Jesus Christ. Faith is not a divine gift from God. Faith is a personal conviction which a person exercises when he or she encounters Jesus the Christ. The clear exhortation from Paul and the other NT writers is for people to believe. There is no biblical data to warrant the belief that faith itself is given by

God. Robertson correctly concludes, '*Grace* is God's part, *faith* ours.' God provides the free gift of salvation on the basis of His grace. People must receive the free gift of salvation by means of faith. Such is the clear and distinct message of Ephesians 2:8." Sapaugh, *Journal of the Grace Evangelical Society*, Vol. 7:12.

Prayer is Communicating With God

Another concept of Poor in Spirit is prayer. When we know the word and believe it, yet we still lack wisdom, what do we do? The Bible says, "… ask of God, who gives to all liberally and without reproach, and it will be given to him, but let him ask in faith" (Ja. 1:5-6). How does God speak to us? He answers us through His Word and by His Spirit interpreting the Word for us. When we have difficulties that we don't understand, we speak to Him about our situation, go to the Scriptures relating to our difficulty and allow the Holy Spirit to direct us.

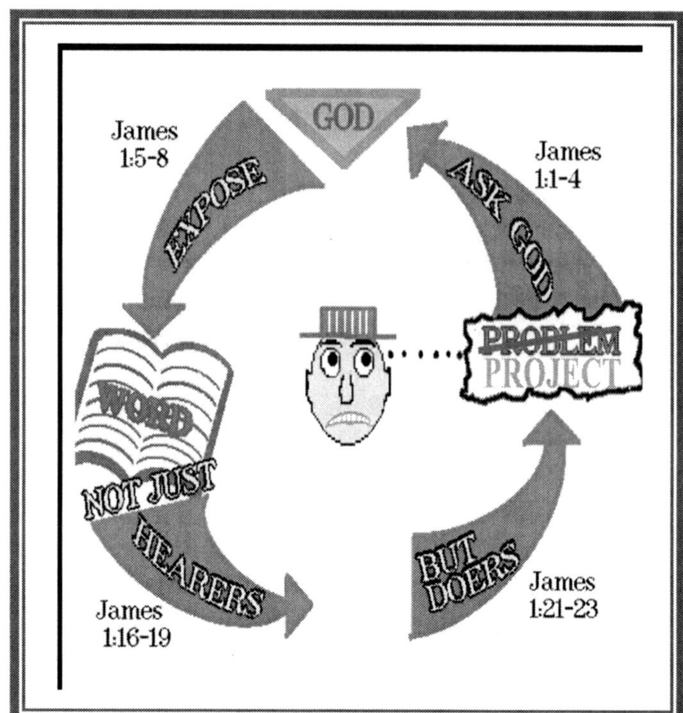

Many say that God does not hear their prayers. God always hears and answers all our prayers—not always the way we want but He answers. There are four ways He may answer. See diagram. There are many forms of prayer, such as thanksgiving, praise and worship, supplication, entreaty, etc. Prayer is a spiritual communion with God.

However, prayer is not a choice. We are commanded to pray without ceasing. That does not mean you must stay on your knees, close your eyes and go around audibly talking to God all the time. But it does mean to be in an attitude of prayer, experiencing "God's presence and always knowing He is there. His Spirit will guide you (Mat. 28:20, Gal. 5:16). Prayer then is an exercise of faith, an act of worship, a means of confessing our sins, an expression of love toward God and a way of giving Him thanks. James comment;

"If any of you lacks wisdom, let him ask of God, who gives to all liberally and without reproach, and it well be given to him. But let him ask in faith, with no doubting, for he who doubts is like a wave of the sea driven and tossed by the wind. For let not that man suppose that he will receive anything from the Lord; he is a double-minded man, unstable in his ways" (James 1:5-8).

James presents prayer in four elements. First, is to give your concern over to God. Since He is all-powerful, He can handle it. When you have difficult trials or temptations you don't know how to handle, stop! Do the opposite of what you would do naturally. Say something like this, "Lord, this difficulty is too big for me. I am going to entrust it into your hands and I thank you for the wisdom, grace and direction you are going to give me." Then we can consider it a joy. This difficulty is not a problem, but a project God has designed for my growth and development of character. My part is to surrender my will to His.

"My brethren count it all joy when you fall into various trials, knowing that the testing of your faith produces patience. But let patience have its perfect work, that you may be perfect, lacking nothing. If any of you lacks wisdom, let him ask of God, who gives to all liberally and without reproach, and it will be given to him" (Ja. 1:2-5).

Second, we must be sure we are asking in faith. When we are able to believe that God really is in control, we can trust Him in any difficulty. You see, prayer without faith is empty and ineffective because it is so important to have an intimate knowledge of God? If we don't know Him, we cannot trust Him. If you don't trust Him, it's because you don't know Him. He demands that we know Him well enough to believe what He says. The second part, then, is to exercise faith in what you know about Him.

Third, it is not enough just to read the Word. We must be diligent in our study and development of His principles from the Word, so that when trials and difficulties arise, the Spirit can bring to our remembrance the principles we should follow. If someone is praying about a marriage difficulty, the first project would be to talk to God. Then he or she should go to all the passages that deal with marriage and draw out principles. For instance, God gives a wife four basic principles: submission, purity, respect, and a gentle quiet spirit. Peter says, "even if he is disobedient, he may be won to obedience" (1 Pet. 3:1-6).

Fourth, we should "be doers of the Word" (Ja. 1:22-25). Start using all the principles you have learned. For a wife whose husband has left her, she can't submit when he is not around, but she can work on her conscience. Her "to do" list would start with working on her conscience, developing inner purity. Next, she could work on developing a gentle quiet spirit. She could do that at any time of the day. Also she would be understanding and work on restoring her respect for him. Finally, when she has the opportunity, she would practice submitting to him. Now she has the "to do" list that Peter indicates will have supernatural effects. Her problem becomes a project that God guarantees her the grace to work through. This is being a doer, not just a hearer.

In summary, then, to be a disciple one must become poor in spirit, to become poor in the old spirit or personality that was developed under the influence of the world system and to become rich in His Spirit. This involves getting our heads screwed on right about God by studying and developing the divine nature, by believing the Scriptures, by understanding faith, and becoming a prayer warrior.

This demands a renewing of the mind; all those old images and thought patterns must go (Rom. 12:2-6). Remember, we discovered earlier that there are disciples and there are true disciples (Jn. 8:31). To know

> "Then Jesus said to those Jews who believed him, 'If you abide in my word, you are my disciples _indeed (true)._ And you shall know the truth. And the truth shall make you free.'"
> Jn. 8:31-32
>
> "Sanctify them by your truth. _Your word is truth_"

Him is eternal life. This is what it means to enter into the sphere of royalty or partakers as kings in training under the King of Kings. We are promised that when we become Poor in Spirit, Jesus says, "Theirs is the kingdom" (Mat. 5:3). We become joint heirs with Him when we have humbled ourselves in His service by sanctifying Christ in our hearts. We must be sure we have a clear conscience.

Becoming Poor in Spirit is to become a follower of Christ as His disciple; we participate in His work now in this life time. In order to do this we must know Him in an intimate way through the Scriptures, believing what He says. When we have questions or doubts we must pray, asking Him for wisdom to become a participator with Him.

But that is not enough. As we get to know Him and trust Him, His radiance exposes all the darkness or wrong thinking and we just want to cry and mourn over our wrong attitudes and actions. That brings us to the process of mourning which we will deal with in the next chapter. Note what Jesus says about being a disciple (Jn. 8:31-32; 17:17).

PROJECT

Purchase a spiral note book, and then set up the first page as shown in the example below. Then skip four pages (space for future notes as you discover new principles about that attribute) and set up the next attribute with the same format. This is a lifetime study, so keep it in a safe place.

EXAMPLE FIRST PAGE IN YOUR SPIRAL NOTEBOOK:

LOVE

1. Define the word.

2. Look up and list references applicable to this attribute.

3. In your own words, write out what this attribute means to you.

Additional notes: In the future, when you are studying a passage and discover something new about an attribute, get out your note book and add the new information to your notes.

The Transferable Attributes are:

1. Love	9. Gracious
2. Truth	10. Holiness
3. Life	11. Goodness
4. Justice	12. Righteous
5. Person	13. Forgiving
6. Knowledge	14. Wrathful
7. Patience	15. Merciful
8. Faithfulness	

The non-transferable attributes:

1. Omnipotent	5. Unchanging
2. Omniscience	6. Self-existent
3. Omnipresent	7. Eternal
4. Perfect	8. Infinite

CHAPTER 6 - RIGHT THINKING ABOUT SELF

"Blessed are those who mourn, for they shall be comforted." Mat 5:4

Jerry was a trainer in the evangelism class. He was well trained in sharing his faith and was a Bible School student. One night he came into my office after a training session that had not gone well. He was really depressed. He said; "Bill, I'm going to give up; I'm just not effective in evangelism. I'm not doing well in Bible School or anything else. I'm going to quit school and get a secular job." My question to Jerry was, "How is your relationship with your father?"

He went on to explain how he had been very rebellious to his parents as a teenager, especially toward his father (an alcoholic). He had joined the Marines to get away from home. While in Vietnam he received Christ as Savior. He came home and attempted to share his faith with his father, but his father remembered his rebellion. He was still upset and told him to get out. The bitterness was rekindled, making Jerry a prisoner of his father.

We talked for over two hours as I tried to persuade him to clear up this conflict with his Father. His comment was; "I could never do that." He went home a bitter person. God did not give him any rest until he called his father and acknowledged his wrong attitudes and actions. What a release—Jerry was a different person! He completed Bible School and seminary. Now he is ministering for the Lord.

Unfortunately, no one had ever discipled him or held him accountable for his relationships with other people. Because of guilt, bitterness, and un-forgiveness, Jerry's life was in shambles. He had a great deal of knowledge about the Bible and knew how to study it, but his ability to apply it in his own life was lacking.

> "Therefore if you bring your gift to the altar, and there remember that your brother has something against you, leave your gift there before the altar, and go your way. First be reconciled to your brother, and then come and offer your gift. Agree with your adversary quickly, while you are on the way with him, lest your adversary deliver you to the judge, the judge hand you over to the officer and you be thrown into prison. Assuredly, I say unto you, you will by no means get out of there till you have paid the last penny" (Mat. 5:23-26).

Once we have escaped the darkness of the world and come into light, or we are born of the Spirit, the radiance of God's light begins exposing the dark areas and blind spots in our old man thought patterns. These old man thought patterns were developed under the influence of the world system in darkness. The people Christ called were proud fishermen, tax collectors, and other tradesmen. Their memory banks were filled with fears, guilt, rejection, and bitterness as a result of broken relationships, unresolved conflicts and deep hurts from their past.

Defining the Word

Jesus used the Greek word πενθεω, meaning "to mourn." Because of the tense that was used, it would translate, "go on continuously mourning over sin." James picks up on this power principle in Ja. 4:7-9. James, being the half brother of Jesus, was keenly aware of the dynamic principles Jesus had given in the *"Sermon on the Mount."* Here James reaffirms some of the principles from the beatitudes. Submitting and drawing near to God (Ja. 4:7-8a) is the idea of becoming poor in spirit. Zane Hodges amplifies this principle.

> "What follows at this point is an unmistakable call to repentance on the part of his readers. They should begin with submission to God, that is, with a determination to do what

is right and pleasing to Him. But as surely as they did this, Satan would test their resolve. Thus they should also resist the devil (just as Jesus did in His temptation), and they should expect victory over the enemy: he will flee from you. As great as are the powers of seduction employed by Satan, he is not invincible. A Christian firmly committed to God and the authority of His Word can rely on the help of the Spirit who dwells in him (4:5) and watches Satan flee when he meets this kind of resistance." Hodges, *The Epistle of James*, p. 95.

Then in the next phrase, James approaches the process of mourning. "Cleanse your hands you sinners" (Ja. 4:8b-9b) has reference to any outward manifestation of wrong doing. Then he says, "purify your hearts you double-minded," which has reference to the inward conditions of guilt, hostility, bitterness, un-forgiveness, etc. Again, Zane Hodges comments:

> "But it was not enough to reassert one's commitment to obedience and to resisting temptation. Resistance needs to have a personal dimension in which a Christian's fractured fellowship with God is renewed. Therefore; James enjoins his readership to draw near to God, knowing that such action will be reciprocated: and He will draw near to you. Of course, as the apostle John makes clear (1 Jn. 1:9) confession of sin is the first step in drawing near to God again. But renewed prayer and meditation on Scripture are also appropriate steps. God will respond to such steps, not only to forgiveness, but with other tokens of His nearness. He is always more eager to bridge the gap between ourselves and Him than we are. Restored closeness, therefore, between God and James' readers is precisely what James is aiming at here. God would meet them more than half way." Hodges, *The Epistle of James*, p. 96.

Paul also deals with this issue of repentance and conscience when he says, "… I myself always strive to have a conscience without offense toward God and men" (Acts 24:16). James and Paul see this idea of mourning as a vital issue. It is not a take it or leave it proposition. It is imperative! One needs to reflect on the past and detect the blind spots that offend God and man, as well as how others have offended Him. One needs to be able to detect anything that might hinder them from ministering to anyone at anytime.

We should examine our hearts daily as David did in the Psalms 32 & 52, Later he says, "Search me O God, and know my heart; Try me, and know my anxieties; And see if there be any wicked way in me and lead me in the way everlasting" (Ps. 139:23-24). The concept of mourning has been neglected, or in some cases forgotten, in the process of making disciples. How can we minister to those we have offended or those we fail to forgive? That is why Jesus says, "Therefore if you bring your gift to the altar, and there remember that your brother has something against you, leave your gift there before the altar, and go your way. First be reconciled to your brother, and then come and offer your gift" (Mat. 5:23-24).

This is the heart of the message of our King. Many times at funerals, you look back on a person's life and realize how much you are going to miss them and you begin to cry. This is the same idea in mourning. We come out of the darkness into the brilliance of God's light, and His radiance exposes our wrong attitudes and actions. You just want to cry. James says, "Lament and mourn and weep! Let your laughter be turned to mourning and your joy to gloom" (Ja. 4:9). Zane Hodges amplifies the idea of mourning:

> "If this were done with discernment and with a depth of commitment, it would be natural for them to lament and mourn and weep. Whatever exuberance they felt should be transformed into mourning, and whatever delight they were experiencing must be replaced with gloom. This does not mean, of course, that laughter and joy are wrong. On the contrary, both are beneficial to human experience (see, e.g., Ps. 126:2; Prov. 17:22). However, when an individual is dealing with personal sins in the presence of God, laughter

and joy are not merely inappropriate; such levity suggests a conspicuous lack of seriousness in the repentance. But when a person's heart is moved by the depths of his wickedness in the sight of God, the response enjoined here would seem not merely natural but also compellingly spontaneous." Hodges, *The Epistle of James*, p. 97.

Mourning then involves the psychological part of man; the heart, soul and emotions. We have been conditioned over the years through repentance, forgiveness, confession, and restitution, or the lack of it. If it is true that 85% of our personality is developed by the time we are six years old; it is not too difficult to figure out where it all originated.

Whether we like it or not, we are all products of the third and fourth generations. This is not just from genetic transference. We spent fifteen or twenty years rubbing elbows with our parents, them with their parents, and them with their parents. As a result, many of those personality traits passed down to us.

When our son David was a boy, he had a habit of rolling his eyes when I told him to do something he did not want to do. David is now married and has a son, Zach, who is five years old. One cold weekend when they were visiting our home, Zach wanted to go outside and play, but David thought it was too cold so he said "no" very firmly. Then it happened. Zach looked up at him and rolled his eyes back until all you could see were the white of his eyes. David cried out, "Oh no!" You know, I did the same thing when I was a child. Here, standing by the door, were three generations of rolling eyes!

That may sound funny but the Bible teaches in Exodus 20:5 and Deut. 5:9 that our sins, or negative personality traits, will visit the third and fourth generation. We can look at Abraham's family and see this principle amplified in his descendents (Isaac, Jacob, Judah and ultimately Joseph).

When Abraham went to Egypt, he instructed Sarah to tell the soldiers she was his sister. This was a half-truth—she was his half sister. God protected her from being touched by Abimelech. His son, Isaac, said the same thing, except Rebecca was not his half-sister she was his wife. This was an outright lie. Isaac's son, Jacob, was deceiving and deceptive in his relationship with Laban, not to mention his conniving with his mother to deceive Isaac. Finally, the whole nation of Israel was sold into slavery by Joseph's brothers. We can look back at our own forefathers and see the translation of their sins in the form of personality traits and temperaments in our lives. We are—whether we like it or not—products of the third and fourth generations. Only in Christ are we freed from the curse (Gal. 3:10-13).

Understanding the Conscience

The Bible has a lot to say about how important it is to have a good conscience. Paul is emphatic in his instructions regarding the conscience. Note the following references:

Acts 23:1	"I have lived in all good conscience."
Acts 24:16	"I always strive to keep a good conscience."
Rom: 2:15	"Their conscience always excusing or accusing."
Rom. 9:1	"My conscience also bearing me witness."
Rom. 13:5	"But also for conscience sake."
1 Cor. 8:7	"Their conscience, being weak, is defiled."
1 Cor. 10:25-29	"Why is my liberty judged by another man's conscience?"
2 Cor. 1:12	"The testimony of our conscience that we conduct ourselves in the world in simplicity and godly sincerity, not with fleshly wisdom but by the grace of God."'
2 Cor. 4:2	"But we have renounced the hidden things of shame, not walking in craftiness nor handling the Word of God deceitfully, but by

manifesting of the truth commending ourselves to every man's conscience in the sight of God."

1 Tim. 1:5	"Love from a pure heart, a good conscience, and from sincere faith."
1 Tim. 3:9	"Holding the mystery of the faith with a pure conscience."
1 Tim. 4:2	"Having their own conscience seared with a hot iron."
2 Tim. 1:3	"God, whom I serve with a pure conscience."
Tit. 1:15	"But even their mind and conscience are defiled."
Heb. 9:14	"Purge your conscience from dead works."
Heb. 10:22	"Having our hearts sprinkled from an evil conscience."
1 Pet. 3:15-16	"With meekness and fear, having a good conscience."
1 Pet. 3:21	"… Not the removal of the filth of the flesh, but the answer of a good conscience toward God."

Defining the Word

The word conscience, (συνειδεσισ), is a compound word meaning συν = with, ειδο = science or knowledge. The idea in the word, is acting with knowledge either from God or from the world. The conscience is the mind, emotions, and the will, all acting together with regard to moral issues. The conscience gives us the ability to discern right and wrong. The conscience is conditioned or trained by education. Psychiatrists tell us that by the time we are six years old; most of our personality was developed. This was the time our conscience was being conditioned to respond to our feelings. Almost without exception, the media and education system encourage us to live by our feelings. In other words, if it feels good, do it. We have been deceived. Note diagram.

The conscience is God's built-in warning system. Your conscience forms a grid, or a transition, between God's spiritual realm and our physical realm. It operates on information or knowledge stored in your brain. This knowledge has been stored as a result of attitudes and actions in our past. Paul says:

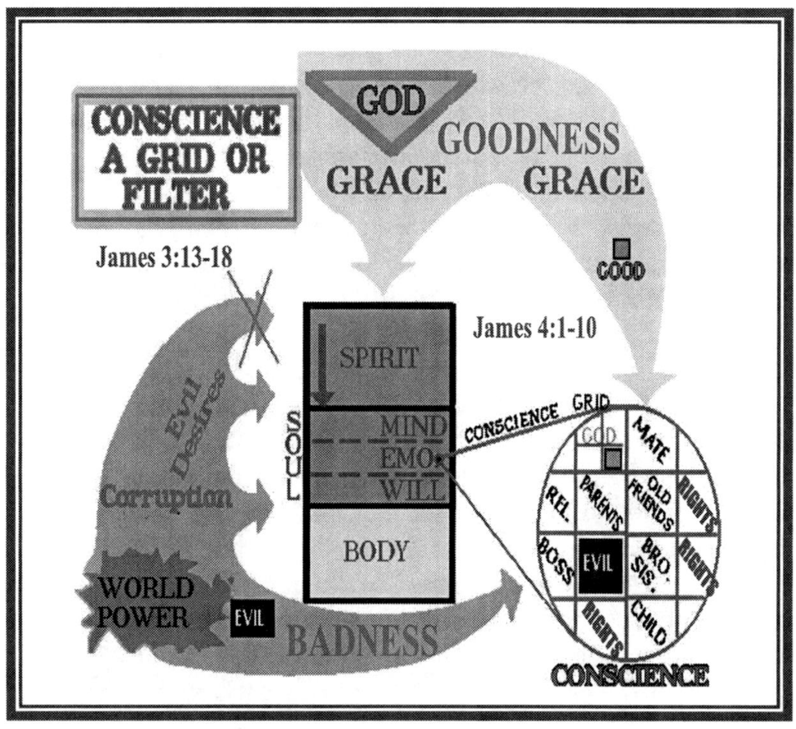

"But because of your stubbornness and unrepentant heart you are storing up wrath for yourself in the day of wrath and revelation of the righteous judgment of God" (Rom. 2:5).

Remember the conscience is a function of the soul. This is what makes you a person with a personality created in the image of God. Because of the sin of Adam, we all come into the world separated from God with a stubborn and unrepentant heart. Even though you have received Christ as Savior, you brought all those old memory banks, filled with the old man thought patterns into your Christian life. This is who you are. This is the way you respond to life's circumstances. In fact, this is your conscience. .

45

Our conscience has been developing over the years as a result of our attitudes and actions under the influence of the world system. The conscience is a grid through which we filter information. This grid originally consisted of large and small holes. The large holes allow wrong principles from an evil source to filter through and the small holes allow good principles from a godly source to filter through. The holes represent your conscience. In a practical sense it forms a grid through which information is processed from the world system or from God. This information activates the body. A good conscience is designed to eliminate wrong thinking that results in wrong actions (Rom. 2:1-15).

Now it is obvious that wrong principles can pass through the large holes. This activates the body with wrong attitudes and actions. The goal in discipleship is to reprogram the mind in order that only good data can pass through our thinking processes.

Paul gives us a process in Scripture for closing up those large holes in our conscience when he says that Scripture is given by the inspiration of God and is profitable for certain things in order that the man of God may be complete (2 Tim. 3:16). The idea is that you can be complete; all the large holes can close and only the good principles can filter through. You can function in a godly way under any circumstance. Your grid might be perfect to the point that no power in the world could manipulate you into an action contrary to His standard (2 Cor. 10:1-6).

How do we perfect our grid? You are fortunate because God has given you specific instructions. Paul says, "Do not be conformed to this world," and you must not be controlled by those old principles you learned from the world but "Be transformed by the renewing of your mind" (Rom. 12:2). This involves the biblical concept of repentance: changing your mind about old attitudes and actions and being persuaded to do the right thing. There are several commands that admonish us to keep a clear conscience in Mat. 5:23-24; Rom. 2:1-15; 2 Cor. 4:1-2; Heb. 9:14; 1 Pet. 3:16; 1 Jn. 1:9; and others.

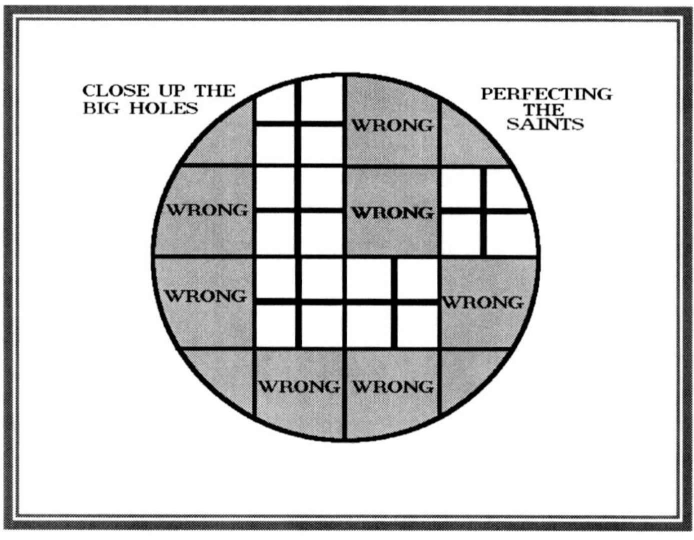

Paul says, "Faith comes by hearing and hearing by the Word of God" (Rom 8:17). It is through hearing the Word that we are established in our faith, not just hearing audibly, but hearing and believing. Repentance is changing the mind; faith is being persuaded concerning the change. The two always go hand in hand. Faith is not a synonym for obedience but has to do with the mind; to believe or be persuaded. Dr. Dillow speaks to this issue in his book:

"It is somewhat perplexing how this simple, universally understood, and commonly used term has been so freighted with additional meanings. Notions like obedience, yieldedness, repentance, and a myriad of other terms are continually read into this word in order to make it serve the purpose of some particular theological system. It is perplexing because the lexical authorities are virtually unanimous in their assertion that faith (pistis), means belief, confidence, or persuasion. The verbal forms all mean the same, to believe something, to give assent, to have confidence in, or to be persuaded of." Dillow, *Reign of the Servant Kings*, p. 271.

Repentance

Repentance is another area in the spiritual growth process. Remember, the word *repent* simply means changing your mind. The greatest contributor to this neglect is ignorance or disobedience. Ignorance is a result of not knowing. Unbelief, or disobedience, is a result of not being persuaded, which render one unable to believe. Both are a hindrance to discipleship. The concept is a process of renewing the mind by rethinking old attitudes, feelings and decisions. This process of reprogramming is what it takes to be transformed. Every conflict, hurt or broken relationship in the past caused a wrong principle to be recorded in our memory. Therefore, every time a stimulus comes, you will respond in that same way unless your mind is changed (Col. 3:8-10). Repentance results in a paradigm shift.

First, let's review how God designed you. You are a special creation of God with special parts, material and immaterial, which enable you to function supernaturally in a natural world Ps. 139:1-6). The Holy Spirit activates our spirit. Our spirit in turn activates the soul which involves the mind, emotions and will, which activates the body that involves the brain, limbic system, and nervous system. In contrast, the demonic forces appeal to the emotions which become dominant and negate the mind. The will is activated stimulating the old man thought patterns in the brain and we do what we feel like doing. The body will function according to what spirit is in control. When we are under the control of the Holy Spirit, we produce the fruit of the Spirit. When we are controlled by world powers we produce works of the flesh.

Our problem is not with our spirit, because it was made perfect when we were regenerated. It is also not with our body which is mature, even though it may need some adjusting here and there. The real problem is with our soul! Our psychological makeup still has the effects of the old man nature stored away in our brain. Every time a negative stimulus comes up, we react from our old man rather than acting rightly.

Most of our life principles were developed in our early formative years, as a result of the third and fourth generations. Therefore, there are many conflicts, broken relationships, and deep hurts remaining. Each problem or conflict in our memory bank has a principle that still controls us today. With each conflict the Holy Spirit brings to our attention, we should make a decision—to do or not to do. As we deal with it positively, we are cutting away those strings of the world's power that manipulate us.

The first step in mourning or cleansing the conscience involves the concept of repentance. The exhortation of John the Baptizer, who was the forerunner or announcer of the King is "Repent, for the Kingdom of Heaven is at hand" (Mat. 3:2). Then Jesus takes up the same message in Matt 4:17. The word "repent" used by John and Jesus is the method by which a paradigm shift takes place. Paul explains it as "renewing the mind" (Rom. 12:2). The idea is to change your mind. Dr. Dillow speaks to the danger of making the word mean otherwise.

> "Regarding repentance, a person could hold the view that repentance means 'turning from sin' and is a necessary ingredient of saving faith and still deny the Reformed doctrine of perseverance. However, it seems to me that those who believe that repentance is a condition of salvation and that it means turning from sin are sometimes guilty of Barr's illegitimate totality transfer. Most would agree that the basic meaning of *metanoeo* is simply to 'change the mind.' But often Reformed writers go beyond this meaning and read into it the notion of 'turn from sin.' In some cases they base their appeal on some standard theological dictionaries. Yet these lexical authorities have often been guilty of a 'theological idea' kind of lexicography. They have in mind a theological idea of repentance, that it involves turning from sin and conversion, and they read that theological idea into the various texts they quote." Dillow, *Reign of the Servant Kings*, p. 30.

In this context, the Word is commanding the Jews—who are deeply rooted in the idea of a physical kingdom in this world—to totally change their minds about the Kingdom. It is to be an earthly Kingdom with Jesus on the throne of David in His future millennial reign on earth. Jesus came and they rejected Him. The church age (or the times of the Gentiles) is between His triumphal entry into Jerusalem and the rapture. We are now in a period of being prepared as the bride of Christ. He directly addressed the preparation of this kingdom when He said, "Thy kingdom come, thy will be done on earth as it is in heaven" (Mat. 6:10). We are presently in a training process (sanctification) for reigning with Him in that future kingdom. Note Tucker's comments:

> "So why do we find ourselves so often back here struggling with guilt, shame and inadequacy? Why can't we accept that our performance doesn't impact or influence God's verdict about us? It is because we have blurred lines that need to be distinct-----.

> From Genesis to Revelation, the main theme of the Bible is the coming kingdom of Christ. It's not salvation. It's not heaven. It's not forgiveness or grace, or even eternity. It's the millennial reign of Christ, the total theocratic dominion we all long for." Curtis Tucker, *Majestic Destiny,* p. 36-37

The Kingdom is coming on earth as it becomes a part of the disciples' life as they prepare for the ultimate reign with Christ in the millennial Kingdom. The end product of our discipling is to be prepared for our position in the coming reign of Christ on earth. This is the process of sanctification. It is a constant changing of the mind. We will spend the rest of our lives in this process.

Repentance initiates a cleansing process. It is a "spiritual catharsis." My wife is a nurse and when our sons were growing up they would often get cuts on their fingers, arms, or legs. The first thing she would do is take them to the bathroom and wash the wound. Why? There were foreign bodies present in the wounds, which could cause an infection that would ultimately affect the whole body.

When you have a disease, the physician first diagnoses the cause. Then he begins a cleansing process to eliminate the cause. When you have surgery, the surgeon performs a cleansing procedure by removing infected or diseased tissue or a foreign body. Not only that, he performs a complete cleansing by sterilizing the area before he starts the operation. The reason behind all this is to remove the foreign material or the body could die. We must remove the wrong principles or the soul will die (Ja. 1:15). The surgeon who has a patient with acute appendicitis does not just give him an aspirin to control the temperature nor does a physician just put a band-aid on a skin cancer. You too cannot ignore past conflicts and broken relationships. Repentance demands confession.

Confession

The second step in mourning involves confession. Suppose I were a bank robber and had my gang trained the way I wanted. Then one day we went out and robbed a bank. Shortly after that someone presented the plan of salvation to me and I received Christ as Savior. As a result, I got all excited and went back to the hideout and tried to share Christ with the gang. They would think I was some kind of a nut and would probably respond with "You are nothing but a crook like we are." However, if I would go back to them and first share how wrong I had been in my influence on them and ask them to forgive me, then at a later time share Christ, they would be much more responsive.

God desires a clean vessel through which He can work to bring about responses in people. John speaks of a special way of cleansing; "but if we walk in the light as He Himself is in the light, we have fellowship with one another, and the blood of Jesus His Son cleanses us from all sin" (1 Jn. 1:7). But Jesus says in Matthew 5:23-24 that it is not enough to just confess to God. You must confess to those who have been offended and as you meditate on this passage you should sense a need for urgency.

There are four strong commands. The strongest is to leave your gift and be reconciled. I believe if Jesus were talking to you today, He would say that your body was never built to handle guilt. It will kill you (see Rom. 6:23). Go quickly to those who have something against you and confess. Then come and present your gift, for I want all of you free from any blind spots.

The word *remember* indicates things done in the past. It is not enough to deal with the present—there are past sins you must deal with. I might add that there is only one way to deal with sin. You cannot hide it, you cannot erase it, and you cannot ignore it or blame someone else. You can only confess it.

These are excuses I hear all the time from well-meaning people:

1. That happened before I was saved.

2. We must not live in the past but look to the future.

3. Oh, that was such a little thing.

4. They have forgotten about it.

5. You just don't know my parents.

You will be able to gain new insight if you will acknowledge John's next exhortation: "If we say that we have no sin, we deceive ourselves, and the truth is not in us" (1 Jn. 1:8).

This sin principle has reigned in your life through most of your developing years and you have been conditioned to respond to it naturally. Therefore, this verse demands an examination of past attitudes and actions to identify any offenses or un-confessed sins that would render you unclean. Make a list of broken relationships, and people you have—or had—conflicts with, or you have hurt. Start with those closest to you: parents, in-laws, mate, children, brothers, sisters, old friends, teachers, employers, and others. Once you have identified the broken relationships, conflicts or bitterness, you are now ready for the second principle regarding catharsis of past sins. John states emphatically, "If we confess our sins, He is faithful and just to forgive us our sins and to cleanse us from all unrighteousness" (1 Jn. 1:9).

Just like a surgeon or physician, we must not only treat the present symptoms but also deal with the root cause. There are some basic insights in this verse you need to understand. First, the word *confess* is a compound word meaning "same" and "to speak." Put them together and you have "to speak the same." In other words, in this context, as you look at the past from God's point of view, you can "speak the same" or "agree" with the ones you have offended.

But that is not enough. If you offend God, all you need to do is confess to Him. However, when you offend others you complicate the process. When sin gets out of the mind and becomes an action, you usually offend people. Then you must not only confess to God but also to all you have offended. In other words, the circle of confession must be as wide as the circle of the offense. James makes it clear that we not only confess to God but we must confess to one another as stated in (Ja. 5:13-16).

"Is anyone among you suffering? Let him pray. Is anyone cheerful? Let him sing Psalms. Is anyone among you sick? Let him call for the elders of the church, and let them pray over him, anointing him with oil in the name of the Lord. And the prayer of faith will save the sick, and the Lord will raise him up. And if he has committed sins, he will be forgiven. Confess your trespasses to one another, and pray for one another, that you may be healed. The effective, fervent prayer of a righteous man avails much" (Ja. 5:13-16).

Confession is part of God's healing process. This passage is often referred to as a basis for calling the elders to pray and anoint with oil. But James has much more to say about this process than praying. That is the first thing one should do. The word for *suffering* in verse thirteen is from a compound word meaning "evil" and "to have," thus it is translated evil treatment. In this context it would give the idea of one under heavy psychological or even physical, stress, either for one's own wrong doing or for the sake of the Lord. James is exhorting us to deal with it while it is in the mind before it becomes a flesh response. Hodges comments:

> "Calmness and appropriate behavior, even under stress, are what James is really seeking here. A rash oath is a poor response to any situation. But suppose someone was really suffering? In that case prayer was in order. The word rendered 'let him sing Psalms (φαλλετω) probably has the more general sense, 'let him sing praise,' although it is likely enough that in the early church such songs were often built on the Psalms of OT Scripture." Hodges, *The Epistle of James*, 115.

In the next phrase, James questions, "Is anyone cheerful? Let him sing Psalms." This is giving us a formula for fulfillment. If we will deal with our wrong thinking (trouble or stress) by means of prayer, then we will have a joy or praise in our hearts.

The word used here for *sick* in the context of Ja. 5:14 is the same word translated "weak or sluggish" (*astheneo*) in 1 Cor. 11:30. Paul is indicating to the Corinthians, they are doing the same thing the Israelites did, and like the Israelites, they are not going to make it. Indications such as this is not an acute illness, but a gradual weakness caused by psychological pressures causing you to be drained of strength that leads to ultimate physical illness (5:15). The word in 5:14 has the idea of *weariness of mind* or a psychological weariness. It is different from the word *sick (kamno) in verse 5:15*. The play on words here is significant. W. E. Vine gives some good insight on Paul's choice of words:

> "The choice of this verb instead of the repetition of *astheneo*, is suggestive of the common accompaniment of sickness, weariness of mind (which is the meaning of this verb), which not infrequently hinders physical recovery; hence this special cause is here intimated in the general idea of sickness." Vine, *Expanded Vine's Dictionary of New Testament Words*, p. 1040.

The idea then is a weariness of mind or wrong thinking. It is caused by constant pressure from work, home, or social activities which hinder you from getting proper psychological and physical rest. This is James' formula for a healthy lifestyle;

1. If you are suffering from difficulty, then talk to God about it.
2. If you are happy, then praise the Lord.
3. If you are without strength, like David (Ps. 32:3-4), call the elders who will help you recognize basic causes of your weakness through prayer and anointing with oil.
4. Confess any sins to those you have offended and to God.

This is a simple, but complex concept. It is not that God heals all sickness. Christ did not do that when He was here, but He can heal any disease according to His purpose. However, He has not chosen to heal everyone. Where weakness or being sickly is a result of past sins, conflicts and broken relationships (1 Cor. 11:28-31), as you remove the cause, the body is designed with a built-in healing system.

Most people I work with have no idea how to make a confession. The tendency is to say "I'm sorry" or "I apologize." Those words are abused and misused so much, it is best to just discard them. They do not convey the idea God intended. We must use the hard words, "I was wrong." These are the most difficult words in any language to say. However, this confession is what people need to hear and can understand.

The process of confession should be in a systematic order, beginning with those closest to you. Note the following order of confession:

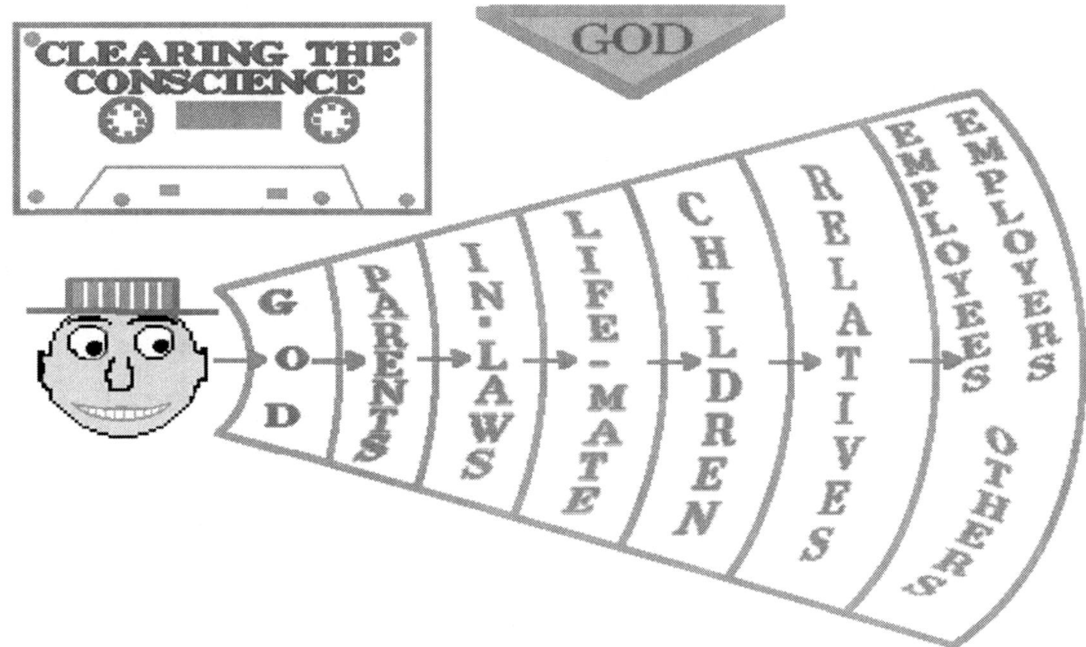

1. God: When you offend anyone, you offend God.

2. Parents: They are the root of your personality.

3. In-laws: When you marry, they become parents; you must honor them.

4. Mate: God has given you basic responsibilities to your mate.

5. Children: God gives you basic parental responsibilities.

6. Brothers, sisters, and friends: God expects us to live in harmony with them.

7. Employers: We are directed to obey them, even the harsh ones.

8. Enemies: God commands us to love them.

Make your list of those you have offended and then you can start the process of clearing your conscience of any guilt; there are certain principles that must be included:

1. Confess to God the basic Biblical offense.

2. Give the other person complete forgiveness before God.

3. Confess the basic Biblical offense to the person.

The next thing you need to do is start with the first one on your list and work out the wording you will use. There are three things that are very important in the wording of a confession:

1. Acknowledge you are wrong. Always say, "I was wrong," not "I am sorry."

2. Identify the specific (Biblical) offense.

3. Ask the person to forgive you.

Following are suggestions for the wording including the basic offenses.

Children to Parents (Eph. 6:1-3): Mom / Dad, I have been looking back at my younger years and I can see now how *wrong* I was in so many ways. I was often disobedient, and realize now that I have not really honored you as I know the Lord would have me to (illustrate one way you have dishonored them). Would you please forgive me?

BASIC RESPONSIBILITY
CHILD TO PARENTS
1. OBEY
2. HONOR

Mate's Parents (Eph. 6:1-3): [name], I have come to see how wrong I have been in our relationship. There have been so many times I have not shown you honor as I know I should have, (identify one area where you did not honor them). Would you please forgive me?

Old Friends (1 Pet. 3:8-12): [name], I have been reflecting back on our relationship, and I can see now how wrong I was in several ways: [list offense(s)]. Would you please forgive me?

Previous Mate (Eph. 5: 21-33): [name], I have been looking back at our past relationship in marriage and I can see now how wrong I was in so many ways, especially in the divorce and (identify some ways you failed 1 Pet. 3:1-7). Would you please forgive me?

Husband to Present Wife (1 Pet. 2:21-25 and 3:7 and Eph. 5:25-33): [name], I have come to realize how wrong I have been in my responsibilities as your husband. As a result of my relationship with my parents and our pre-marriage relationship, I have been unable to give myself totally to you in *love* as Christ loved the church. I have so often failed to *understand* your deep needs physically and emotionally, much less give fulfillment in those areas. I fail so often to *honor* you as the special person God has given me for completeness. I can also see where I have not *treated you as an equal* in our responsibilities before God. Would you please forgive me?

BASIC RESPONSIBILITY
HUSBAND TO WIFE
1. LOVE AS CHRIST LOVED
2. UNDERSTAND HER
3. HONOR HER AS A DELICATE INSTRUMENT
4. TREAT HER AS EQUAL IN RESPONSIBILITY

Wife to Present Husband (Eph. 5:18-24; 1 Pet. 2:21-3:7): [name], I have been looking back at our marriage, and I can see now how wrong I have been in several ways. As a result of my relationship with my parents and our pre-marriage relationship, I have been hindered (*impurity*) in being the *submissive* wife I know I should be. I can also see where I have failed to *respect* your ideas, plans, and decisions. Because of all this I have not been able to develop the *gentle, quiet spirit* that I know could make things different. Would you please forgive me?

BASIC RESPONSIBILITY
WIFE TO HUSBAND
1. SUBMISSION - POSITION
2. PURITY - CONSCIENCE
3. RESPECT - POSITION
4. GENTLE, QUIET SPIRIT

Parents to Children (Eph. 6:4): [name], I have been looking back at my responsibility as your parent and I can see so many areas where I have failed. I have been so inconsistent in my *discipline* in training you up in *the way of the Lord*. I have often *provoked you to anger* by my attitude and actions. I

BASIC RESPONSIBILITY
PARENTS TO CHILDREN
1. PROVOKE NOT TO ANGER
2. TRAIN UP
3. DISCIPLINE
4. ADMONISH IN THE LORD

have failed to *teach you* how to live by *Biblical principles* and how to relate to others. Would you please forgive me?

This is a general outline for working out the wording for all on your list. First, acknowledge you have been wrong. Don't use the abused phrase "I'm sorry" or "I apologize." Say the hard word. Just agree with the person you have offended, "I was wrong."

Forgiveness

The third step in mourning is forgiveness. This is another one of those theological concepts that is greatly misunderstood. There is wide-spread ignorance with regard to its depth of meaning. God pours love out to us and we transmit it to others so it is with forgiveness. God has forgiven us. Now we must forgive others! (2 Cor. 5:18-19, Col. 3:12-13).

> "Forgiveness has tremendous power. It is energized by the power of God. It has power over many situations. Forgiveness has the power to reconcile sinners to a holy God. It has the power to overcome the offenses of others and to repair relationships that have been damaged. It has the power to overcome bitterness, anger, and wrath." Miller, *Forgiveness: The Power and the Puzzles*, p. 5.

Let's consider the word *"forgive."* It is a compound word meaning "to remit or take away." When broken down, the word means "from" and "to send." The idea is "to send away from." God is forgiving, and has covered all our sins by the blood of Jesus. All our transgressions are paid for. David says, "As far as the East is from the West, so far has He removed our transgressions from us" (Ps. 103:12).

Dr. Wendell Miller developed six different categories of forgiveness that give us a better understanding of the significance and the broad sphere of forgiveness. The first two are based in our justification. The second two have to do with sanctification or our personal relationship with God. :

The following are definitions of his six categories:

1. Initial Judicial Forgiveness—Justified, conditional (dependent upon saving faith)
2. Initial Fellowship Forgiveness—Restored fellowship with God, conditional (depends on saving faith)
3. Repetitive Judicial Forgiveness—Unconditional (dependent only upon Jesus as our Advocate, interceding for each and every sin)
4. Repetitive Fellowship Forgiveness—Conditional on obedience (upon confession of sins)
5. Vertical Forgiveness—Unconditional release to God through prayer of the offender's supposed "right" to "get even;" release of the penalty that he might want to inflict onto the offender.
6. Horizontal Forgiveness—Conditional dependent upon release from estrangement (*alienation*) caused by the offenders offense.

This may seem complicated, but we need to understand forgiveness in its fullest sense. Remember Christ died in order to provide this spiritual freedom for us (Mat. 6:14-15, Eph. 1:7, 32). If we exercise three or four levels and fail to do the others, then the result will be incomplete forgiveness. Fellowship with God demands that we follow His precepts or we will place ourselves in bondage to the flesh. This is an impossible concept from a human perspective, but by His grace and all the spiritual abilities he has invested in us, we can do it.

Forgiveness is not forgetting. People will say, "I forgive but I will not forget." By this they mean that if I have really forgiven someone I should not remember it anymore. Well, that is generally not true to reality. For example, let's assume that you were sexually abused as a child. Do you think you would ever forget such a devastating event in your life? No, of course not! How unfortunate it would be if we tied our forgiveness to the concept of forgetting history or denying it ever happened. We might like to do that very thing but that does not work with God. He will keep on convicting us, and we will keep on denying it, and ultimately it will kill us (Ja. 1:14-15). Forgetting the event is not what God does with our sin. First, God is omniscient and cannot forget, and secondly, if that were all that was required, there would have been no need for Jesus Christ to die on the Cross.

The problem is we are trying to remove or forget the wrong thing. If we think that God is forgetting the event we are also wrong. God is not forgetting the historicity of the event. He paid your penalty therefore we must forgive the offenders penalty. You see, every wrong has a corresponding amount of damage. It is because of the damage that God declares a given act wrong. He does not just arbitrarily declare something wrong. He understands that a certain thought or behavior will cause certain consequences of hurt, damage or pain. Therefore, there is a corresponding payment due for such damage (Heb. 2:2-3).

Thus, when God removes our transgressions as far as the east is from the west, He is actually removing our personal liability to make payment for the wrong we did. So likewise for us, when we forgive we are not to attempt to forget the actual event. What we are to do is to release the person from their liability to make payment for the wrong they did to us. As God has canceled our debt, so too are we to cancel their debt. Note Paul's comment:

> "And you, being dead in your trespasses and the uncircumcision of your flesh, He has made alive together with Him, having forgiven you all trespasses, having wiped out the handwriting of requirements that was against us, which was contrary to us. And He has taken it out of the way, having nailed it to the cross" (Col. 2:13-14)

There are two things to be said in light of this verse. First, it mentions a debt that is canceled and nailed to the cross (Col. 2:14). In other passages of scripture, this is also described as a debt that was paid (Rom. 4:7-9). Without knowing how much the debt is, it is impossible to say that the debt has been paid. In regards to forgiveness, it is impossible to say someone is forgiven unless there has first been an accounting of the amount of wrong and corresponding damage done. God in his omniscience knew the amount of damage done. Therefore, He could also forgive us of our debt. When we forgive someone for the wrong they did to us, we must first calculate the amount of damage done before we can forgive them. But if we do not first calculate the damage, then our forgiveness will be incomplete and ineffective. If they are ninety percent wrong and we only forgive them thirty percent, then our forgiveness is ineffective.

The second thing is that God has paid the price for our wrong doing. In forgiveness, there is the release of the payment due but someone has to pay. What God has done is to make that payment by giving His only Son to pay the penalty Himself. Thus, when someone wrongs us, we must calculate the full amount of the debt. Take that total and give the debt owed to God. Next comes the dangerous part. Most people will take that debt back by putting it upon themselves, other people or things. God's intention is that we give that debt over to Him. Restitution is in God's hands. God's hands are perfect.

When we forgive another person what we are saying is, "Lord I am willing to take upon myself all the pain and hurt of this offense like Christ took my offenses. I'll give this person a clear record." The offense is off my record and in God's hands. Now God through your forgiving spirit, minister to that person. Loving confrontation often brings people to repentance. I know this is contrary to the world's philosophy but the Bible says, "bearing with one another, and forgiving each other whoever has a complaint against anyone; just as the Lord forgave you, so also should you" (Col. 3:13).

God not only forgives you, but He gives you the grace to forgive others. When another person offends you, you must immediately go to God and give them forgiveness (vertical forgiveness). However, they will not experience that forgiveness until they confess their wrong to you (horizontal forgiveness). If you fail to forgive immediately, you place yourself in bondage to that person. Remember, you are only releasing them to God for His discipline and He is able to keep their feet to the fire (2 Tim. 4:14-15).

Just recently I was driving down the freeway, minding my own business when a man turned in front of me, requiring me to slam on the brakes and move to the other lane. I immediately had a funny feeling in my abdomen, my heart rate spiked, my blood pressure shot up, and my face turned red. I was angry! Immediately I recognized the need to apply the principle of forgiveness. I confessed my wrong thinking and forgave that person to God (vertical forgiveness). If I had not, I would have been under the control of that person and could have had a wreck. Never tell a person you forgive them before they repent.

> "Therefore, loving an offender who has financially defrauded you may include requiring a plan for repayment (restitution) before granting horizontal forgiveness. To grant horizontal forgiveness to an offender who is not willing to make restitution may release the pressure that God wants to keep on him so that he will really repent. Don't fall into the "ditch" of easy forgiveness. Determine whether or not restitution is appropriate before you grant horizontal forgiveness." Miller, *Forgiveness: The Power and the Puzzles*, p. 213.

This compounds your responsibility to those you offend. Since conflicts are almost always two-sided, the person you have offended has probably offended you. So, before you confess to them, you need to have a spirit of forgiveness toward them. The only way you can accomplish this is to give them complete forgiveness for everything they have done or haven't done to you. *Remember, you never tell a person you forgive them, unless they ask.* This is between you and God. Also when you forgive a person, you are not saying they are right; you are only making the first step of reconciliation. The purpose here is that since God is faithful and just to forgive and cleanse you from all unrighteousness, you are now responsible to forgive those who offend you. Jesus makes this very clear, "For if you forgive men of their transgressions, your heavenly Father will also forgive you. But if you do not forgive men, then your Father will not forgive your transgressions" (Mat. 6:14-15).

Although God has forgiven you of all sin past, present and future you will not experience that forgiveness in this lifetime until you confess and forgive those who offend you. Remember, the basic principle is that God alone can forgive sin. Even when we forgive others, we are only acting as agents under His control and we must turn over the liability of other's sin to Him. What about forgiving myself? Dr. Miller speaks to this issue:

> "Forgive yourself? No." This idea is a stranger to biblical truth. Instead, confess your own sins, make Biblical changes in your life, and unconditionally forgive the penalties of everyone's offenses against you. Forgiving oneself is an un-Biblical exercise in futility. Instead, praying and unconditionally forgiving the penalty of each offense of others is God's will for all believers—it is a God-given power that relieves the offender from 'enemy control.' And sometimes forgiving the penalties of the offenses of others is the Biblical path for relief from guilt feelings, relief from feelings of guilt for sins that have been confessed." Miller, *Forgiveness: The Power and the Puzzles*, p. 213.

MY PART IN A CONFLICT IS TO CONFESS – GOD'S PART IS TO FORGIVE (1 John 1:9)

Restitution

The fourth element of mourning is restitution. The word is another compound word meaning "from," and "to put in order." The idea then is "to restore from disorder to order." Practically, if you have stolen money then the money must be repaid.

Recently I was discipling a young man, but after getting to a certain level, nothing was happening. He was not growing and he was unable to do some of the things he needed to do. I finally asked him, "Is there something you have not told me, something that is bothering you?" He began to weep and shared how he had taken a large sum of money from the bank where he had worked. He confessed to the bank president, worked out a plan of restoration and then we were able to continue discipleship.

However, restitution does not just mean material things. It involves relationships as well. When you are a part of a conflict, you have stolen a relationship. You have a responsibility not just to repent, confess and forgive, but to do everything within your power to restore that relationship. This is not always possible. Sometimes the other person will not cooperate in the restoration process. However, you must continue to exhort and pray for that person.

Having repented, confessed, forgiven and made restitution to all those on your list, you receive the comfort and peace Jesus promises to those who mourn. You are now on a new level of spiritual maturity. You have made a turnaround in your life's direction. You are now receptive to the leading of the Holy Spirit. Your old hindrances—guilt, bitterness and depression—are gone. You are now free to walk in the light. He is the light!

The discipleship process is designed to accelerate repentance. It closes all those large holes in your conscience (grid) which are a result of past attitudes and actions. These past attitudes and actions hinder us from looking at life from God's point of view. They must go!

When we are free from past sin, we will be able to see present trials as projects God has placed in our path to get our attention. For those who have become poor in spirit and mourned over past sin, a difficulty or trial is not a problem. We are now looking at a project God will use in perfecting us (Ja. 1:2-4).

Having mourned over past sin, Jesus says that they shall be comforted. The word used here means "to exhort, to comfort, to come along side." It is in the future tense and a passive verb. The idea is they shall (having mourned) be comforted passively by the Holy Spirit (Jn. 14:18). The result of godly mourning is always comfort. This idea of comfort is the freedom Jesus promised to those who abide in Him.

PROJECT

1. Define the Biblical concept of Mourning.

2. Have you confessed failures to your parents?

3. Have you confessed to your mate?

4. Have you confessed to your children?

5. Do you have plans to confess to others on your list?

6. Draw the GRID below.

CHAPTER 7 - RIGHT THINKING ABOUT RELATIONSHIPS

"Blessed are the meek, for they shall inherit the earth." Mat. 5:5

**"You have heard that it was said, 'An eye for an eye and a tooth for a tooth'
but I tell you not to resist an evil person. But whoever slaps you on the right cheek,
turn the other to him also." Mat. 5:38-39**

Leonard and his wife had spent years on the mission field and he is now a pastor in the southern United States. One day he received a phone call from the police in Washington State informing him that his daughter was a victim of a homicide. His first response was to find the guy and kill him. He was very angry! He was one of those people that if you violated his rights, he was ready to fight. He told me later that he had preached that God says 'vengeance is mine,' but when it happens to you or a member of your family, it's very different. He later found out this man had killed over 40 women. This angered him even more.

After working through this area of rights, he acknowledged to his wife that he had a terrible struggle to love this man's soul more than he wanted to kill him. He and his wife prayed together. He gave his right to have vengeance over this man to God. He is a meek man now, ready to continue his life ministry.

This attitude of meekness is a necessity for a disciple. Jesus lived and taught it. This is the last quality in the emptying part of the process. Poor in Spirit has to do with the mind or knowing God. Mourning has more to do with our emotions and clearing the conscience. Meekness has to do with our will as we deal with self-righteousness in relationships.

Defining Meekness

There have been endless discussions about the meaning of the word πραυσ, which translates "meek, mild or gentle," which indicates submissiveness to any offense, without malice. It has so many implications that one or two English words will not convey the full meaning. I will start out with a working definition—"power under control"—then expand that to a fuller meaning as you discover what "meek" is not.

Meekness demands an absence of malice. It means yielding my authority system to God. This necessitates a reprogramming of our personality developed under the influence of our old nature. It may be dead; but the memories of that old nature are still recorded in our old man thought patterns. All those old tapes recorded in our formative years to the present must be erased and reprogrammed with God's truth as Paul instructed in Rom. 12:2.

There are some beautiful promises in the Bible that bring out the significance of meekness:

1. The meek shall eat and be satisfied (Ps. 22:26).

2. The meek will He teach His way (Ps. 25:9).

3. The meek shall inherit the earth (Ps. 37:11).

4. The Lord lifts up the meek (Ps. 147: 6).

5. The meek also shall increase their joy (Isa. 29:19).

6. Satisfied are the meek (Mat. 5:5).

Meekness demands humility, which is the prerequisite to receiving grace (see Ja. 4:6). Grace is the source of power that flows through faith that enables us to function supernaturally in a natural world. Grace gives us the power to control our attitude toward circumstances. Meekness is power under control. Dr.

Radmacher stated in a recent conference that, "meekness is not weakness. If you think it is then try being meek for a week."

Meekness is the opposite of self-righteousness; the opposite of the Adamic nature. It is the character Christ claims, "I am meek and lowly of heart" (Mat. 11:29). Although He was offended every day of His life, He never took up an offense. And the Scripture says, "the man Moses was meek more than all men on the face of the earth" (Num. 12:2).

The attitude of a meek person is one of deference, or one who demonstrates deference in relationship with others (Phil. 2:3-4). Webster's Dictionary defines *deference* as "a yielding of opinion or judgment." It does not mean to become a weak person but it indicates strong character that is willing to defer one's own knowledge or rights to be able to understand the other person; to be able to help the other person understand or change their mind. This word is a synonym of honor. When we honor a person, we respect their position. It does not mean we compromise our position, but only defer in order to help the other person. Vine states it this way:

> "The common assumption is that when a man is meek it is because he cannot help himself, but the Lord was 'meek' because he had the infinite resources of God at His command. Described negatively, meekness is the opposite of self-assertiveness and self-interest; it is equanimity of spirit that is neither elated nor cast down, simply because it is not occupied with self at all." Vine, *Expanded Vine's Dictionary of New Testament Words*, p. 56

Meekness Expanded

This is such a broad subject that the whole Bible addresses this issue. It all started when Adam and Eve responded wrongly to Satan's influence. It will all end with the fulfillment in Revelation. Some classic passages that would be beneficial for you for a personal study are: Rom. 6-8, 14; 1 Cor. 8:11; Phil. 2:1-10; Ja. 3:13-4:10.

The basic principle is that Christ has been given all rights or authority in heaven and on earth. That does not leave any rights for those who believe. Christ has all rights; we have responsibility as disciples or His servants (Mat. 28:18, 11:25).

It was a hot summer afternoon in Texas. Jill and Bob were getting hotter and hotter, not from the heat outside, but from a marital conflict that had been raging all day. Jill just wanted to share her unexpressed desire with Bob that their daughter needed to do her homework immediately when she comes home from school (Eve nature). Bob just wanted to share his unexpressed desire with her that they should be gentler with their daughter and let her do it later (Adamic nature).

Now that seems like a simple matter to resolve, but it wasn't. This simple disagreement grew rapidly into a full conflict. Jill brought up all the old charges she had against Bob and his list was as long as hers. This episode ended like all the others—with no winner, no resolve, no softening. The wedge just went a little deeper and the division more obvious.

The problem was not the daughter, although subconsciously, they tried to blame her. The problem was with Bob, primarily, and secondarily, with Jill. Bob had failed to take his responsibility as the spiritual leader so Jill had assumed his responsibility. They are both out of control spiritually. They were not receiving the grace from God to manage this crisis. Just like Adam and Eve in the Garden of Eden, they did what was right in their own eyes. They stood in their own self-righteousness, which resulted in a no-win situation with an abundance of hostility being directed at each other.

As our personality develops, each of us builds a system of personal government that seeks to establish and maintain an emotionally controlled life style. What this means is that out of the desire to be in a state of harmony, we set up a system of rules, guidelines, ordinances, laws, or statutes that guarantee—or at least to the best of our ability—we get what we want.

For example, Bob grew up as an only child. Everything he wanted he got. Now he wanted peace in his house, and in order to maintain that, he had set up the personal law that gentleness is required with one another. The logic of this idea is that if a person is gentle, then there will be peace and a pleasing environment. So far, so good. But there was Jill. She grew up as the oldest of five children, and had to fight for everything she got. Now because of her system, she was ready to fight, and this really complicates things. A person can set up a personal government that can be kept by one, but when another person is involved, then the prospect of two personal governments merging together becomes much more arduous. Inevitably, Jill's law will violate Bob's personal law and Bob's will violate Jill's—sometimes knowingly and sometimes not. Everyone has a personal government with certain established laws to maintain peace and pleasure.

> **GOD'S DESIRE IS THAT HE IS THE ONLY ONE CONTROLLING YOU.**

Problems develop when a personal law has been violated. To put it more bluntly, people fight when someone has done them wrong! People get upset when someone does what they don't like. People get angry when they get something they did not want, or did not get something they wanted. They are controlling you.

I desire that which will please me. So I set up a personal system of government that will more consistently produce what pleases me. This personal government is made up of hundreds of rights that I believe will insure my happiness. Then it happens! Someone violates one of my rights! They commit a sin against me. They transgress my commandment. This brings down my wrath upon them. My wrath is against the perpetrator of the offense. My wrath is designed to do several things:

1. Teach them a lesson.
2. Change their behavior.
3. Make them pay for the damage they caused in my pleasure.

You may be thinking: I see myself as having a right to punish all violations of my laws. What would my world look like if I let violators get away with such lawlessness? I feel I have a right to punish those who break the law. In fact I think it is righteous to do so.

The above is the process that describes the hostility and the harm people do to each other. It is just as Ja. 4:1-2 says—that you lust for your personal law to be fulfilled, but it is not because someone has violated it. So you exercise your personal authority to punish the violator and reestablish your law so that you will be pleased. Likewise, James continues with another example by saying that we desire to have but cannot obtain so we fight and quarrel.

> "Where do wars and fights come from among you? Do they not come from your desires for pleasure that war in your members? You lust and do not have. You murder and covet and cannot obtain. You fight and war. Yet you do not have because you do not ask" (Ja. 4:1-2).

Jill and Bob were standing in their own authority in their own little kingdoms. They were each standing on their own self-righteousness. Jill was deeply hurt, angry, and insecure. The only tool she knew was to take control. So she took control of the children. She became the spiritual leader in the home. Bob was also hurt, but he responded differently. He withdrew further from his leadership responsibilities. He began to spend more time at work and with his friends. Therefore the conflicts continued. They had lost sight of the kingdom of God where unconditional love rules, not personal law and self-righteousness.

Jesus said, "Blessed are the meek." Meekness is the attitude Jesus demonstrated all His life. He is the perfect example of meekness. Meekness is the opposite of self-righteousness or personal law. Jesus never once stood in His own self-righteousness, but went to the cross in obedience to the Father. Jesus never once defended Himself, but always trusted His Father to protect Him (1 Pet. 2:21-23).

Meekness is the attitude Jesus is referring to when he talks about denying self, bearing the cross, hating his family, his own life and counting the cost. To do this demands reprogramming of our old man thought patterns. Note the remarks of Jesus regarding this:

"Then Jesus said to His disciples, 'If anyone desires to come after Me, let him deny himself, and take up his cross, and follow Me. For whoever desires to save his life will lose it, but whoever loses his life for My sake will find it" (Mat. 16:24-25).

In this passage He says if we do not do these things we cannot be His disciple. This is an awesome responsibility. What we are talking about here is loyalty. We cannot be loyal to our old life and to God's new life. We cannot serve two masters (Mat. 6:24). The old self-righteousness patterns must be reprogrammed.

The Source of Rights

The word that best describes our self-righteousness or rights is the Greek word *exousia*. It is often translated liberty, freedom or authority. However, the best translation in this context is "rights." The prefix means "out of" or "from." The root word means "ownership or possession." In 1 Cor. 8:9, we are told to "beware, lest somehow this liberty (rights) of yours become a stumbling block to those who are weak."

When we are standing in our own rights or self-righteousness, we are actually looking at God and saying, "I am God of my life; you are not." We think of one of the curse words as blatantly taking His name in vain. However this self-righteousness is idolatry and God does not take this lightly.

Exousia is used when Jesus says in Mat. 28:18, "All authority (*exousia*—authority or rights) has been given to me in heaven and on earth." We only have responsibility (not rights) within His will which gives us His special power when we are walking in the Spirit. John confirms this as a part of our being born again: "But as many as received Him, to them He gave the right to become children of God" (Jn. 1:12). However, Paul warns us not to abuse our rights in 1 Cor. 8-9. Demonic forces desire that we abuse or misuse our power. Paul says, "For the weapons of our warfare are not of the flesh, but divinely powerful for the destruction of fortresses. We are destroying speculations and every lofty thing raised up against the knowledge of God, and we are taking every thought captive to the obedience of Christ, and we are ready to punish all disobedience, whenever your obedience is complete" (2 Cor. 10:4-6).

You can readily see the overwhelming implications and widespread effect of embracing this concept. This concept is so powerful that you need to understand its origins in order to recognize and identify self-righteousness that keeps pulling you down. Your rights cause you to feel insecure, trapped, inflexible and powerless. These are strongholds in your memory banks that were developed under the influence of the world during your developmental years. They cause you to have vain imaginations that affect your present thinking. This results in your mind having lofty ideas, pretensions and self-deceit.

"For we do not wrestle against flesh and blood, but against principalities, against powers (εξουσια), against the rulers of the darkness of this age, against spiritual host of wickedness in the heavenly places." (Eph. 6:12)

Our weapons are spiritual. We are God's instruments for warfare, "The battle is the Lords" (1 Sam. 17:47b). We are His soldiers. Our goal must be to please Him by obeying His commands. When we are standing in our own rights, we are literally shaking our fist at God and setting ourselves up as a god. It is very subtle! We would never consciously acknowledge this attitude but it is always there in our old thought patterns. In most cases we don't realize what is happening because it is a conditioned response of our authority system.

Where did this concept originate? It was not in this world. Jesus indicated in Jn. 8:44 that Satan (Lucifer) is the father of lies, a fallen being (with reference to the spirit world). The only fallen spirits we know about are in Isa. 14 and Ezek. 28. A beautiful angel with power and dignity was created by God to have charge over other angels. He was the most beautiful angel; he was a ruling angel named Lucifer. He became puffed up and proud. He actually wanted to be like God! Satan did not want to be conformed to God's image, he wanted equality with God. Satan wanted to be another I AM with God. We know from Scripture that God cast him out of glory into the sphere of this world or into our time and space capsule. He is known in this sphere from Scripture, as Satan, that old serpent, the tempter, the prince of the power of the air, the accuser, the god of this world, and many other titles (Eph. 6:12, 1 Pet. 5:8-9).

It was in this sphere that God created Adam and gave him dominion over the world. Then God said, "It is not good that man should be alone, I will make him a helper suitable" (Gen. 2:18). He formed the woman from the bone and flesh of man and brought her to the man. They became one flesh in a permanent relationship. This was the institution of marriage. Indications in Scripture are that God designed man to be strong, decisive, protective and directive. He designed the woman to be gentle and quiet in spirit as the emotional focus in relationship. As a result, she was quite deceived (1 Tim. 2:14). In fact, the Scripture specifically states that because Adam was formed first, God gave him the responsibility of being the servant leader, or protector of Eve (to serve and to lead) (Gen. 1:28). Satan deceived Eve; she ate of the forbidden fruit and brought it to Adam. He ate and this was the outward manifestation of his failure to provide leadership in preparing and protecting Eve.

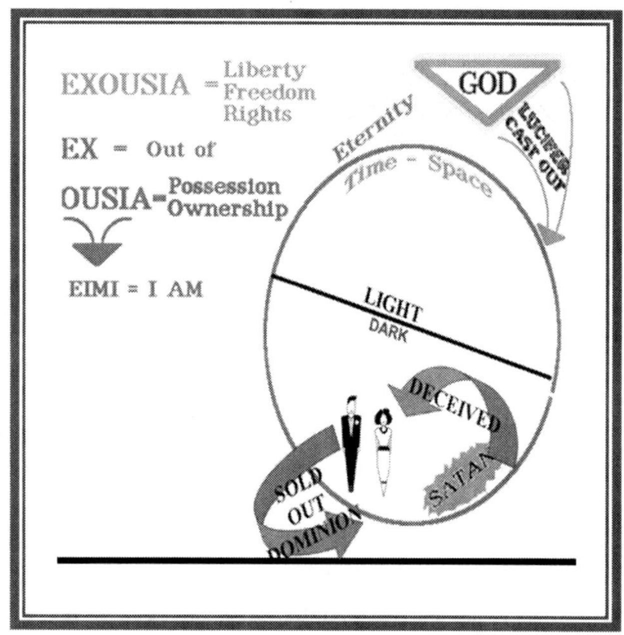

At this point, Adam yielded his dominion over the world to Satan. That is why we read in the Bible that Satan is the ruler of this world (Mat. 12:24, Eph. 6:12). Immediately, Adam and Eve died spiritually and were separated from God. God removed them from the light of the Garden and placed them into the darkness of this world. They were spiritually dead; therefore, they had spiritually dead offspring. Look what happened to their children. The scripture says they began to do what was right in their own eyes.

After 1600 years, God destroyed the world by a flood. Only the family of Noah escaped. After the flood, God gave the law to protect man from destroying himself again. He sent the prophets and they killed them. He sent the Scriptures and they rejected them. Finally, God sent His only Son, Jesus, into the world for three reasons. First, Jesus offered Himself as an example, a servant, and was obedient even to death. Then after three days God raised Him from the dead. Now He offers eternal life to all who believe. Second,

He modeled the way we should live in this world and directed believers to follow Him. Third, He gave us the truth about how to have victory over this sphere of darkness is to walk in His steps (1 Pet. 2:21).

However, we are naturally descendants of Adam and Eve. We come into this world spiritually dead; separated from God. When we believed, we received Christ as Savior. He actually gave us His righteousness and made us one with Him. He made us to sit with Him in the heavenly places (Eph. 2:5-6). He placed us within His body as a body part, in order that we, as a body, would keep on doing what He did when He was here.

In a spiritual sense, you were amalgamated into His Body. Now you are identified with Him in His life, His death, and His resurrection. Paul says, "Or do you not know that all of us who have been baptized into Christ Jesus have been baptized into His death? Therefore we have been buried with Him through baptism into death, in order that as Christ was raised from the dead through the glory of the Father, so we too might walk in newness of life… Likewise you also reckon yourselves to be dead indeed to sin, but alive to God in Christ Jesus our Lord" (Rom. 6:3-4 and 11).

You have been raised from the dead spiritually, although physically you are still in this world. Being raised spiritually is an eternal concept revealed in time and space by the Scriptures. Paul sheds more light on this truth. "Therefore if anyone is in Christ, he is a new creation; the old things passed away" (2 Cor. 5:17). Paul confirms our being raised from the dead, "And do not present your members as instruments of unrighteousness to sin, but present yourselves to God as being alive from the dead, and your members as instruments of righteousness to God" (Rom. 6:13). You are raised into newness of life, even though physically, you are still in this world.

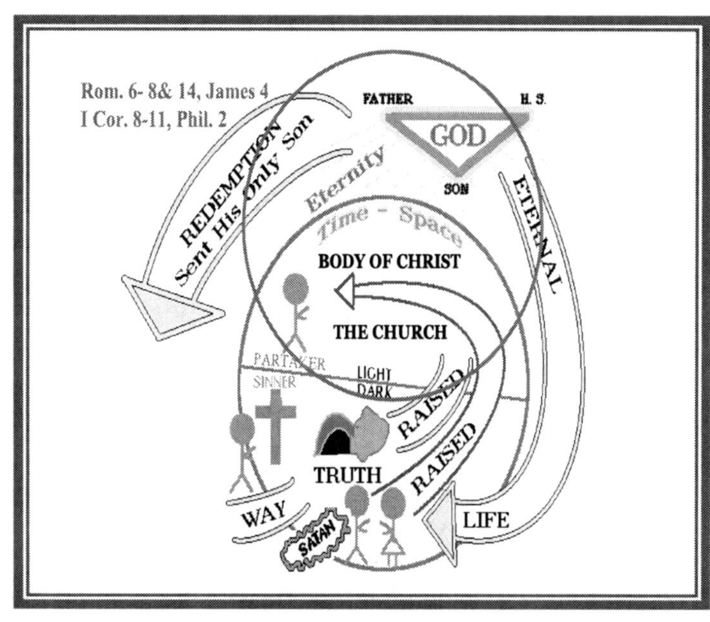

That is why many have such a hard time believing it. You have been made perfect spiritually, the old man spirit is dead but the old man's thought patterns are still in this new life. If someone is a Christian, why then do they go on sinning? We sin because we bring all those old man thought patterns into our new life. Every time one of those old principles comes up, we think wrongly. Because the old sin nature was not eliminated, death in the Biblical sense means separation from God. Although the old man is dead (separated) the old man thought patterns are buried in our memory banks. Therefore, we will spend the rest of our lives renewing our minds, eliminating the old way of thinking or repenting.

However, we now have the Holy Spirit living in us and that Spirit is greater than the spirits in the world (Jn. 14:16,-17, Acts 1:5-8, 1 Jn. 4:4). But every time we think wrongly or are not exercising our faith, we perceive ourselves as sinners. We are no longer sinners, we are saints who sin. The old sinner was crucified with Christ. We have been made saints.

The Solution to Self–Righteousness

When we see ourselves as sinners, we tend to act like sinners and keep on sinning. We must stop and look unto Jesus (2 Cor. 3:18; Heb. 12:2). We must change our minds by repenting in that area. David, in the Psalms, had this same difficulty.

> "How can a young man keep his way pure? By keeping it according to thy word. With all my heart I have sought thee; do not let me wander from thy commandments. Thy word I have treasured in my heart that I may not sin against Thee" (Ps. 119:9-11).

Here we have the answer to the deceitfulness of the world system in which we mature. Our work in the process is obedience to His Word, which will result in renewing our mind or changing our mind according to what He has said in Rom. 12:2. We must not only know or believe, but also do what it says. Even though we cannot see how it could possibly work; we know that He will not allow us to wander from those commands unnoticed. David goes on to say we do this in order that we might not sin against Him.

The sinner has died. We have been made a saint (1 Cor. 1:1-2) who sins, but whose sins have been forgiven. His blood has covered all our sin. (1 Jn. 1:9). You are now a part of His body! You have been set free! Stop acting like a sinner and think like a saint. You only sin when you yield your mind to do what comes naturally. Stop it.

Jill and Bob's conflicts continued to get worse. They just could not understand who they were in Christ and still sinning. Yes, they knew a lot about the Bible, but they could not get past those natural responses that come from the old thought patterns. The Bible says, "The heart is deceitful above all things and desperately wicked; who can know it" (Jer. 17:9). They were not recognizing their old man thought patterns of wrong thinking. Jill was assuming more and more control over the family and now was withholding herself physically from Bob. Her rationalization was that she felt used. Needless to say, Bob was drifting further and further away. He was still at home, but his heart was not.

They were still unaware of the damaging effect and subtle control their "old man" thoughts patterns had over them. They were living out the traits passed down from the third and fourth generation. Like Jill and Bob, our personalities are also a result of exposure to the philosophies of this world and or the result of being under the influence of the world system in our formative years. This is not the type of personality God designed for us.

The process of sanctification began when we believed and is continuing through our growth in our knowledge of God by being poor in spirit (continuing action). Keeping a clear conscience in mourning, we are now proceeding through the process of gaining freedom from self-righteousness in meekness.

Translating Rights into Responsibility

The first thing we need to do in translating rights into responsibility is to confess to God all self-centeredness or conceit. It is a natural tendency to stand in our self-righteous attitudes, but when we do, we sin against God. So it is important to identify our natural tendencies, to acknowledge them and to agree with God that our attitude is wrong and accept His forgiveness (Jn. 1:9).

Second, make a list of all your self-righteous attitudes. This is the most difficult part of the process for most people. Spiritual forces will hinder us in every way possible. They do not want us to identify inner conflicts. These are the strongholds evil has on us. One of the reasons evil is so hard to identify is because of our own sin nature. We must purpose before God to discipline ourselves to make this list. One of the ways to go about this task is to make lists of tangible and intangible self-righteousness.

Things on the tangible list are usually very easy to identify, but difficult to give up. Those things on the intangible list are very difficult to identify and even more difficult to give up. We must remember this is not a natural task. It can only be accomplished by God's grace through the Holy Spirit. So gird up your mind and purpose in your heart to discipline yourself to make the list (Ps. 32:3-5; Ps. 139:23-24; 1 Cor. 11:31-32).

TANGIBLE	INTANGIBLE
Parents	To be accepted
Mate	My privacy
Children	To be loved
Home	My right-of-way
Clothing	To be first

Third, yield all your self-righteousness to God. This is a project between you and God. You don't give your rights over to people, you give them to God. He is the only one that can handle self-righteousness (Mat. 28:18; 11:27). In the past, we've tried and just ended up making a mess of things. Now wouldn't it be logical to just place them in the hands of God, who can really handle them? We are not giving up anything; we are just placing them in the hands of the one who can handle it. If He really is all-powerful, all-knowing, everywhere present, eternal, infinite, etc., and He lives in you, then certainly He is trustworthy. You can believe Him (Mat. 11:25-27; Jn. 3:35-36; 1 Pet. 5:7-11). However, it is not enough to just give up your rights; you must continue to "grow in the grace and knowledge of our Lord and Savior Jesus Christ" (2 Pet. 3:18).

Fourth, give Him—along with your rights—all expectations in each of these areas. Our self-righteousness produces an expectation or hope in people and relationships. You must always place your expectations or hope in the Lord and show deference in all circumstances (Ps. (62:5-6; 1 Tim. 4:10). People will disappoint us, but the Lord never will. We can trust Him (1 Cor. 10:13; Phil. 4:13).

How often have you had an expectation of a person and he didn't measure up? What happened? We become frustrated and probably develop some bitterness toward them. Now wouldn't it better to place your expectations in the hands of God? Let me assure you that if our expectations are within God's will, and we sincerely give them over to Him, He will do whatever is best for us. Don't stop now. Steps one through four are not enough! We must continue.

Fifth, discern what your responsibility is in these areas and take that responsibility by His grace and under God's authority. God has given us principles in Scripture for situations we will face. He will give us the ability to respond rightly. However, it is up to us to discern our personal responsibility and do it. "Therefore do not be unwise, but understand what the will of the Lord is" (Eph. 5:17).

For instance, if a wife leaves her husband for another man, what is the husband's responsibility? It does not change. He is to go on loving his wife as Christ loved the church. This is an unconditional responsibility (Eph. 5:25-33, Hosea 1-3). Not only that, he is to understand why she has done this. He must still honor her as that special person God has given him for fulfillment. He also must treat her as an equal in the graces of life. You see, God's principles are unchanging and unconditional responsibilities (1 Jn. 2:5, 1 Cor. 4:6, Rom. 11:29). If she should remarry he must still forgive her and treat her as a sister for there is a blood relationship between them as parents of their children.

Sixth, be prepared for a test in each area we give over to God. When we give our self-righteousness and expectations over to the Lord, He will test us in those areas (Ja. 1:2-3; Heb. 12:3-11). Why does He test us? It is not for Him to see if we pass the test. God tests us so that we may prove to ourselves that we have victory in that particular area. God knows when we have given up our self-righteousness to Him. We also need to know.

Seventh, be ready and willing to give thanks for whatever happens. Our willingness to give thanks demonstrates our having given up a right (Ja. 1:2-3; Heb. 12:3-11). Whether the results appear good or bad, we have yielded our rights. We are to give thanks in all things when we believe that all things work together for good to those who love the Lord and are called according to His purpose (Rom. 8:29).

Now, this does not mean I am thanking Him for the fact that my wife has left? I am thanking Him for the lessons that I can learn by working through this difficult project God has provided just for me. God then gives me the grace to work, to do it His way. All this is not just for our benefit, but also for all who are involved in the circumstances. Paul says, "Giving thanks always for all things to God the Father in the name of our Lord Jesus Christ" (Eph. 5:20). You must realize that this is not something you do only once. You will spend the rest of your life identifying and giving your self-righteousness over to the Lord. The reason we emphasize dealing with the past is that all our rights are rooted in the past.

Therefore, reflect on your past. Then, simply identify your rights that have caused problems. We can avoid much difficulty in the future by dealing with self-righteousness that is rooted in our past. God has a special plan for your life. He loves you very much. He will not let you do your own thing and get away with it because whom God loves He disciplines. If you are one of His, you can be sure He is going to discipline you. When you are caught in something that is detrimental to your growth and development, God will have already been working to provide what you will need. For further study in this area meditate on the following passages: Heb. 12; Ja. 1; Rom. 6:8.

You have come a long way. Now you should experience that inner peace Jesus promised to those who become *Poor in Spirit*, to those who *Mourn*, and to those who become *Meek*. But there is more. The greatest experience a person can have is salvation. The second is dedication. You are now ready to present yourself to Him as a living sacrifice. If Paul were here talking to us today, he would plead by saying, "I urge you therefore brethren, by the mercies of God, to present your bodies a living and holy sacrifice, acceptable to God, which is your spiritual service of worship" (Rom. 12:1).

Rights! They cannot be taken lightly. Presenting ourselves as a sacrifice is not something that is done in your own power. Paul says that it is done by the mercies of God. What are the mercies of God? Paul has just enunciated them in the first eleven chapters of Romans. He has made it clear that we are saved because God is rich in mercy. He saved us, not on the basis of our righteous deeds, but according to His mercy, by the washing of regeneration (a cleansing) and renewing (changing our mind) by the Holy Spirit (Tit. 3:5). We are not only born again by His mercy, we are kept by the sanctifying process by His mercy (1 Pet. 1:3-5).

Since He died, was buried and ascended into glory in His spiritual, resurrected body, no one can see Him in the flesh any longer. He now uses us to make His invisibility, visible. Reflecting His image is our special service of love to Him. Therefore, He has chosen our physical bodies offered up as a living sacrifice so people can see Jesus in us now.

For others to see Christ in us, our life must agree with what we say. What we speak must agree with what we are doing or it will be worthless. Paul tells us that sacrifice should be holy. To be holy means to be set apart. You are a special person, set apart by God, for God. A spiritual sacrifice is well pleasing to God.

Finally, in that last phrase in Rom. 12: 1, Paul says that "this is your spiritual service of worship." The idea here is that as we function in this capacity, we are doing the most logical or reasonable spiritual service. This is the most intelligent and logical thing we can do. The challenge is to dedicate our body to God. This prayer is designed to help you work out the wording for a total commitment to Him. However, this is just a guide. Put it into your own words, from your heart.

Thank you, Lord, for your forgiveness and cleansing from my sins and blind spots, and for taking all my rights and setting me free from conceit and selfishness. Now, by your grace and mercy, I purpose to dedicate myself to you as a living sacrifice, set apart totally for your service. I wish to be an instrument through which your spirit can translate spiritual principles through my psychological make-up into physical actions that people can see. I realize this is the most logical spiritual thing I can do. I commit myself into your hands. Amen.

The promise to those who have become meek is that they shall inherit the earth. Those who have yielded their strong, self-righteousness over to Him, will take up their cross, and follow Him, will reign with Him as servant kings. I will describe ruler-ship, rewards and inheritance more fully in the last chapter of this book. Jesus is the King of Kings and we will serve with Him. Our position will be kings over the earth during His future millennial reign in this world on the throne of David (Mat. 5:5, 10:38-39; Mk. 9:34-38 Rom. 8:17; 2 Tim. 2:11-12; Rev. 1:6).

"In conclusion, 'to inherit the kingdom' is a virtual synonym for rulership in the kingdom and not entrance into it." George N. H. Peters is correct when he says, 'To inherit a Kingdom, if it has any propriety of meaning, undoubtedly denotes the reception of kingly authority of rulership in the Kingdom.' All saints who endure, who overcome, and who perform works of righteousness (e.g. ministering to Christ's brethren), will inherit it, i.e. rule there." Dillow, *Reign of the Servant Kings*, p. 82.

In the meantime, we are still in training for reigning in the future. Our Master Teacher has given basic instructions regarding the Emptying Process which is changing the mind, reprogramming our emotions, and yielding our strong will over to Him. Now our job is to continue growing and learning.

We have been exposed to the Emptying Process and as we work through this simple but profound process (Poor in Spirit, Mourn and Meek) we will be ready to pursue the most important part of the process. Rom. 12:1-2 prepares us for Rom. 12:3-8, or the Filling Process.

Having completed the Emptying Process and all the projects, you are now ready to start filling. Remember, it is not enough to empty the old thought patterns. We must fill the void with those characteristics Jesus demonstrated when He was here. Next, we will look at what happens when are we empty of self-righteousness. There will be a void in our life if we do not seek something more. That is to "hunger and thirst" after righteousness.

PROJECT

1. Define meekness.

2. Explain the Greek word "exousia."

3. Give a broad definition of the word "deference."

4. How would you explain it to someone and what Scriptures would you use?

5. Draw the diagram explaining the source of rights or the absence of meekness.

6. List the seven steps for transforming rights to responsibility.

    1)

    2)

    3)

    4)

    5)

    6)

    7)

CHAPTER 8 - RIGHT THINKING ABOUT HIS RIGHTEOUSNESS

"Blessed are those who hunger and thirst for righteousness, for they shall be filled."
Mat. 5:6

Daniel had worked through the Emptying Process. His marriage had been restored and things were going well, he thought. He did not make time for discipling, consequently, he began to fall back into his old ways. He tried to become involved in his church, trying one program and then another. Each time he felt a little more rejected and finally became weary in well doing. Daniel was suffering the Galatians 6:9 syndrome, "And let us not lose heart in doing good, for in due time we shall reap if we do not grow weary" (Gal. 6:9). He was not being satisfied because he was doing it in the flesh, rather than in the Spirit's power. He did not have a teachable spirit and was not willing to go on to discover what God had in store. Watchman Nee speaks to this in his book:

"Never for a moment think that because the grace you have received is so insignificant you therefore have no place in the church. As long as you are a member, you have a definite function. There is no one having the life of God who is not a member of the body of Christ, and no member is so small as to have no function of his own. The less than the least of the members still has his function in the body, and that particular function cannot be replaced by any other member. No matter how tiny is that function, no one else can substitute it. Not even the greatest function in the body can stand in for the smallest one: none can take the place of the other: you cannot be a substitute for me, nor can I be a substitute for you. Oh, if we could see this we would leap for joy." Nee, *The Body of Christ*, p. 44-45.

God had given him a capacity to function and all the tools he needed. Peter says, "He has given us everything we need for life and godliness" (2 Pet. 1:3). But Daniel was not functioning in his gifted abilities; in fact he did not even know what his gift was. He was ignorant in regard to his potential and the results were devastating. He had lost his wife, could not provide for her and was totally miserable. There was the sin of omission in his life not to mention the sins he was committing every day; he was dysfunctional. Paul says, "Do not neglect the gift that is in you" (1 Tim. 4:14). Again the writer in Hebrews says, "How shall we escape if we neglect so great a salvation" (Heb. 2:3). The construction of this passage demands a negative answer, thus, the idea is you will not escape, you will suffer the consequences (Result, a loss of joy in his life, and other disciplines by God). Daniel was neglecting that great salvation and the people who had ministered to him were neglecting their responsibility to strongly encourage him. That is a serious charge and they will not escape the discipline of the Lord. Note Hebrews 2, 6, 10 and 12.

Jesus sets an example of humility and deference toward His disciples. There was an occasion where the disciples gathered in the upper room, to eat the Passover meal in Jerusalem. The disciples were already neglecting their responsibility. Instead of washing each other's feet, they were arguing over who would be the greatest in the kingdom and the devil had already placed in Judas's heart to betray Christ (Lk. 22:3). Christ and the disciples had walked from Bethany to Jerusalem. They were tired and their feet were dirty. The custom was that the servant of the house would wash their feet. Christ then sets an example for His disciples. He exercised His ability to show mercy. He washed their feet (John 13:1-7).

You see, it is not enough to just empty, or as Paul would say "Put off concerning your former conduct" (Eph. 4:22). There is a process of discovery and filling that begins with hungering and thirsting after His righteousness. These are very strong words. To hunger is a driving force that will cause a person to go to extremes to receive food (work hard, steal, lie, cheat, etc.). There is even a greater urgency in thirst because a person can only live a few days without water. Jesus chooses these words because there is urgency in our need for His righteousness. When we believed, He imputed (gave) to us His righteousness. Therefore, we are obligated to surrender our righteousness and work at discovering His righteousness.

Now we have two kinds of righteousness: (1) our natural self-righteousness we developed as a result of Adam's sin, and (2) His righteousness which was imputed to us when we believed. By faith He declared us righteous (Rom. 4:5-8). This is what the Bible calls justification, and this righteousness comes by faith alone. However; this begins a process of putting off our self-righteousness and putting on His righteousness (Eph. 4:20-24). The Bible calls this sanctification which is the process of being conformed to His righteousness. This righteousness comes by works of obedience. Note Dillow's comments:

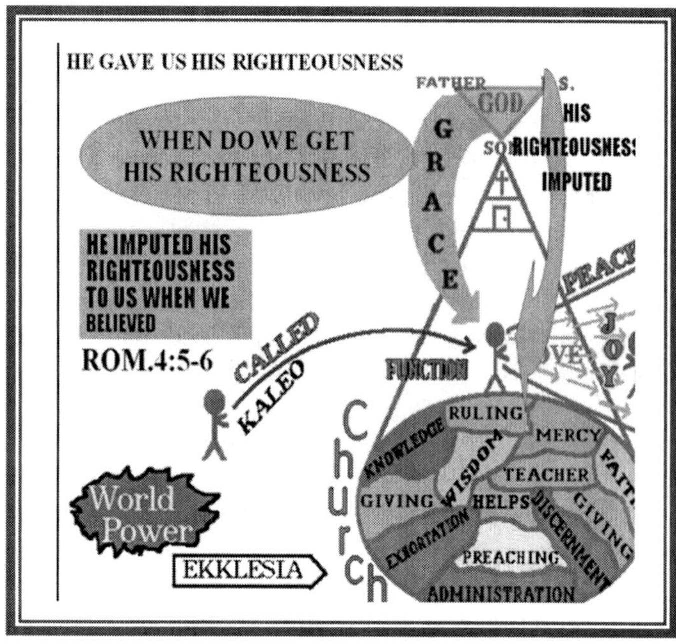

> "Slavery to sin leads to death, and obedience leads to moral righteousness. Death for the non-Christian is, of course, eternal and final. For the Christian, death is temporal judgment and spiritual impoverishment as in Rom. 8:13. The righteousness here comes as a result of obedience, and therefore we may conclude that moral, and not forensic, righteousness is in view. Paul has said earlier that, 'if Abraham was justified by works, he has something to boast about' and 'to the one who does not work, but believes in him who justifies the ungodly, his faith is reckoned as righteousness' (Rom. 4:2, 5). Forensic righteousness comes by faith alone; this righteousness comes by works of obedience." Dillow, *Reign of the Servant Kings*, p. 184.

The Need for Hungering and Thirsting

Christ is giving us a solution to the emptiness of the world system: to be filled with His righteousness. He said, "I am the bread of life, he who comes to Me shall never hunger, and he who believes in Me shall never thirst" (Jn. 6:35). It is not enough to empty out all the old concepts developed under the kingdoms of the world. When we empty, there must be something to replace it, to fill the void. We must fill up. This is a new kingdom and we are new creatures. The old logic must go and we must be filled with new logic. We do not put new wine in old wineskins (Mat. 9:17).

The word hunger is emphatic and demands fulfillment. A desire to eat or find satisfaction, which in a metaphorical use means to desire earnestly or to long for, indicates emptiness. The word thirst also has a metaphorical use meaning to long for ardently or to thirst after. Jesus is speaking metaphorically, which would translate, blessed are those who earnestly desire and ardently long for His righteousness. Both hunger and thirst mean a continuous action for one's own benefit. This is not a one-time act. It means to go on hungering and thirsting after His righteousness. He has imputed His righteousness to us, we now have His righteousness. When we are controlled by the Spirit, we will manifest it.

The Object of Hungering and Thirsting

After we have emptied of all the fear, guilt and bitterness, the Holy Spirit creates a hunger and thirst for His righteousness. Righteousness comes from a word meaning the quality of being right or righteous. In fact, this is an attribute of God. Jesus came into the world to demonstrate His righteousness so that man could see and understand. How did Jesus manifest His righteousness? It was through what He said and did, or the way He spoke and served. The key to righteousness is observing the things He taught and the way He served.

His Righteousness Demonstrated

In the gospels He demonstrated the righteousness of God through the speaking gifts: *preaching, teaching, exhorting* and <u>*word of wisdom*</u>, and *word of knowledge*. The serving gifts demonstrated was *mercy, helping, faith, giving* of Himself, and *ruling*. He was an excellent manager or *administrator* and was a *discerner of spirits*. Those are the five speaking gifts and seven serving gifts listed in Rom. 12 and 1 Cor. 12. He also demonstrated two sign gifts, *miracles* and *healing* to authenticate His Messiahship (Heb. 2:4). The only sign gifts not demonstrated by Christ were tongues and interpretation of tongues. It is interesting to note that Jesus had all the speaking and serving gifts. Here Christ is giving us a solution to the emptiness of the world system. His desire is that we be filled with His righteousness, doing and speaking in the power of His Spirit (1 Pet. 4:10-11). He said, "I am the bread of life. He who comes to me shall never hunger and he who believes in me shall never thirst" (Jn. 6:35). The bottom line is we will find our fulfillment or completeness in doing His righteousness or using the grace gifts He has given us.

Therefore, to hunger and thirst earnestly after His righteousness is to study the things He did and said. Then proceed to be conformed to His image of righteousness and to demonstrate it in the same way He did, through the gift he gave you. We can experience His righteousness as we are obedient, because if we have received Christ, we have been made righteous. This righteousness was demonstrated every day of Jesus' life on earth. In fact Paul says, "For in Him dwells all the fullness of the Godhead bodily" (Col. 2:9). Note chart on the things Jesus did and said while on earth and has given us ability to continue His work.

Note also Peter's comments:

"As each one has received a gift, minister it to one another, as good stewards of the manifold grace of God. If anyone speaks, *let him speak* as the oracles of God. If anyone ministers, *let him do it* as with the ability which God supplies, that in all things God may be glorified through Jesus Christ, to whom belong the glory and the dominion forever and ever. Amen." 1 Pet 4:10-11

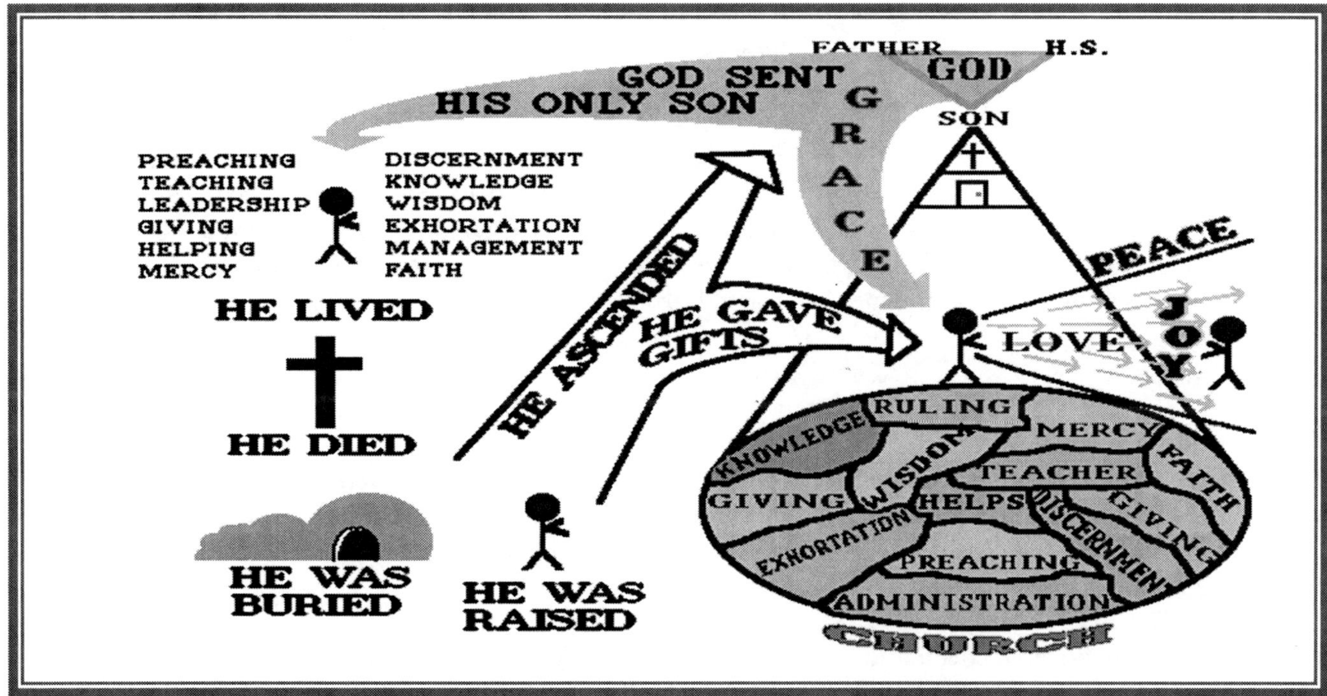

His Righteousness in Justification

Our first glimpse of the righteousness of Christ was in the Gospels, the good news shared by someone or discovered in the mirror of the Word. It was through the coming together of the Word and the Spirit within us that a conception resulted and ultimately a spiritual birth took place and we became children of God. We were born into the Kingdom of God; we were justified, born again, saved from the penalty of sin. This birth was a genuine and permanent implantation of God's Spirit in us, the penalty of original sin was removed. This began the process of salvation that has three parts that are specifically discussed by Paul in Col. 3:1-4. The following diagram will give us a visual view of the three parts of salvation and how we relate to God's design of the body, soul and spirit.

His Righteousness in Sanctification

We were justified when we believed. He saved us—declared us righteous (Rom. 3:24, 4:1-6). We were sinners separated from God, spiritually dead, and unable to help ourselves. "But God, who is rich in mercy, because of His great love with which He loved us, even when we were dead in trespasses, made us alive together with Christ---" (Eph. 2:4-5); this is justification. When we became believers, we began a process of what the Bible calls sanctification, or being set apart, made different, to be conformed to His image and likeness. The power of sin is being removed and the power of God is being enhanced. Working through the Emptying Process is not enough. We must go on and develop our spiritual skills and gifts to full capacity.

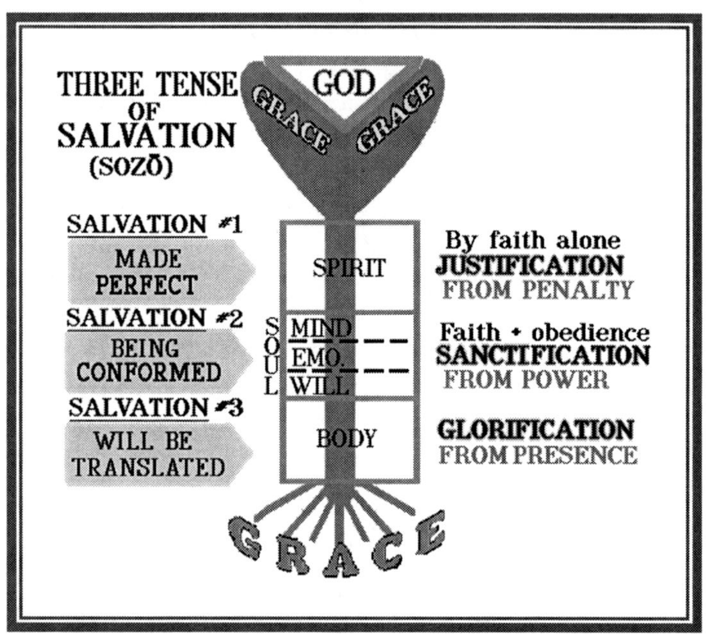

In our development up to this point, our focus has been to help get the image of God straight in our mind and to remove any blind spots or self-righteousness that would hinder us from manifesting His image. Now we are ready to concentrate on His likeness, which is sanctification. Ultimately, when He comes, we will be taken up to be with Him; we will be glorified.

In the meantime we are to be in a process of being conformed to His likeness. To hunger and thirst after righteousness is the basic stimuli for us to be conformed to His likeness. Paul admonishes us to present our bodies as a living sacrifice. Since God has chosen us and gifted us with a special ability, our responsibility is not to be conformed to the old man thought patterns, but to be transformed by renewing the mind which includes the changing of our mind about our abilities to serve Him by faith plus obedience (Rom. 12:1-6).

Paul exhorts us regarding how to do this. First we are not to think more highly of ourselves than we ought. We are not to have an inflated view of ourselves nor we should not think too lowly; but to think soberly or to think rightly about ourselves (Rom. 12:3). We have been supernaturally amalgamated into His body as functional body parts, vitally connected to all the other parts. He has not only given us a specific function - our gift; but He has also given us the capacity by faith to function in the specific task He has called us to perform (1 Cor. 12:3-7).

Our gifts differ according to the grace He has given us. We have been given certain tasks to perform in this lifetime. He gives us the power to channel the exact amount of grace to function in the way He desires. Then He commands us to exercise that gift accordingly (1 Pet. 4:10-11). He encourages us in another passage to earnestly desire the best gifts. <u>The best gift is the one He has given you</u>. The special ability to do the things He did and said when He was here. Therefore we are directed to hunger and thirst (Mat. 5:6), or earnestly desire the things that will demonstrate our partaking in His divine nature.

> "Having then gifts differing according to the grace that is given to us, *let us use them:* if prophecy, *let us prophesy* in proportion to our faith; or ministry, *let us use it* in *our* ministering; he who teaches, in teaching; he who exhorts, in exhortation; he who gives, with liberality; he who leads, with diligence; he who shows mercy, with cheerfulness." Rom. 12:6-8

The idea of hungering and thirsting is a stimulus for us to eat and drink and is related to the consuming of food and water, which are filtered or digested through an intricate digestive system. All the nutrients are then filtered into the blood, ultimately to each individual cell where they actually become a physical part of us. So it is when we feed on the Word and drink of the living water, we become partakers of Christ. Eating and drinking are often synonyms for believing. We can transfer that same concept to our spiritual hungering and thirsting after His righteousness. As we consume His righteousness, saturating our mind with Scripture, it is digested through meditating on it day and night. It penetrates every part of our life, becoming an integral part of our being (Ps. 119: 9-11).

In other words, it is not enough to just take food into our mouth and chew it. We must carefully chew it well and consciously choose to get it into our digestive system so that it can assimilate and become a part of us. Otherwise we will become malnourished and ultimately deteriorate. The same is true with your hungering and thirsting after His righteousness. We must choose to get the Word into our head so that we can translate it into righteous thinking that will stimulate the will (volitional). This will allow His righteousness to become a physical part of our life. Otherwise we will become malnourished and finally deteriorate. Note Dr. Ironside's comments:

> "Righteousness. We had none of our own. 'There is none righteous, no, not one.' All that we thought to be such we have learned is but as polluted rags in the sight of an infinitely holy God. But He has set forth Christ, the risen Christ, who once bore our sins in His *own* body on the tree, as the expression of the righteousness of God. We are made the righteousness of God in Him. 'This is His name whereby he shall be called, Jehovah and so we stand before God in a perfect, unchallenged righteousness, complete in Christ." Ironside, *1 Corinthians*, 76.

It is not enough just to know about His righteousness, but we must be so filled with it that we actually demonstrate it with our physical lives. Others will be able to see His likeness in us. It is necessary then for us to discover from the life of Christ the things that He did and said. What did Jesus do when He was here in the flesh? How did He go about doing it? Did He have opposition? Did He suffer while doing these things? What are the things I should be doing? Am I prepared to suffer? These are questions that demand answers if we expect to demonstrate His likeness in our life. Note Paul's comments;

> "… and that he was seen by Cephas, then by the twelve. After that He was seen by over five hundred brethren at once, of whom the greater part remain to the present but some have fallen asleep. After that He was seen by James, then by all the apostles. Then last of all He was seen by me also, as by one born out of due time." (1 Cor. 15:5-8).

Jesus Christ actually came out of glory, took on the form of man and lived His life in the flesh (just as we do). He performed His responsibilities using all His gifts as an example to us. He died on the cross for our sin; He was buried in a tomb; on the third day God raised Him from the dead. He appeared in His resurrected body and the Scripture says again in Eph. 4:7-8, "But to each one of us grace was given according to the measure of Christ's gift. Therefore He says: When He ascended on high, He led captivity captive and gave gifts to men." The key phrase is "according to the measure of Christ's gifts." The things He did and said by His gifts when He was here in the flesh, He has now given these same gifts to men that they might continue His ministry through the Church (Eph. 4:13-16).

His Righteousness in His Death and Resurrection

He has been glorified and just as he was glorified we shall also be changed into our spiritual body (1 Cor. 15:41-44). Christ's death was the final dead sacrifice for the sin of man. It was the termination of the Old Covenant and His resurrection was the initiation of the New Covenant. The law had been fulfilled in Him and the period of grace had its origin in the resurrection. But that was not the end of His earthly ministry.

After His appearance to the five hundred, He ascended into glory (Acts 1:9-14, 1 Cor. 15:5-8). This completed the transition from the old covenant to the new covenant. What had been—under the old covenant—only a copy or a shadow of what was to come, had now been fulfilled. God ministered to Israel through prophets, high priests, and kings under the Old Covenant. In the New Covenant, Christ is The Prophet, High Priest, and King of Kings. He has now taken His position at the right hand of His majesty as High Priest and is appointed to offer both gifts and sacrifices (Heb. 1:3).

Since Christ exercised all these gifts in making His disciples, it would seem logical that the church (His Body) should utilize the same supernatural abilities He used when He was here and has given to man. He has appointed certain men in the church to oversee this task as stated in Eph. 4:11.

"And He Himself gave some to be apostles, some prophets, some evangelists, and some pastors and teachers, for the equipping of the saints for the work of ministry, for the edifying of the body of Christ" (Eph. 4:11-12).

"You also, as living stones, are being built up a spiritual house, a holy priesthood, to offer up spiritual sacrifices acceptable to God through Jesus Christ" (1 Pet. 2:5)

"But you are a chosen generation, a royal priesthood, a holy nation, His own special people that you may proclaim the praises of Him who called you out of darkness into His marvelous light" (1 Pet. 2:9).

"Do you not know that you are the temple of God and that the Spirit of God dwells in you?" (1 Cor. 3:16).

"Or do you not know that your body is the temple of the Holy Spirit who is in you, whom you have from God, and you are not your own?" (1 Cor. 6:19).

The writer of Hebrews clearly differentiates between the old covenant and the new (Heb. 8:7-13). After Christ took His position as High Priest, it was necessary that He have something to offer. All the gifts and sacrifices of the Old Covenant were material and dead (blood). He has made all that obsolete (note Heb. 8:13). When He said, 'A new covenant,' He has made the first obsolete. But whatever is becoming obsolete and growing old is ready to disappear. Jesus was the last of the dead sacrifices. He made the supreme sacrifice and passed through death into life eternal in order to offer a better way. He now ministers through spiritual gifts and living sacrifices (that is through our physical bodies) Rom.12:1-6. It is necessary for us to understand that the old covenant is finished, we are now under a new covenant, and we are now body part in this living organism called the Body of Christ. (1 Cor. 12:12-27) Note also:

"In that He says, 'A new covenant,' He has made the first obsolete. Now what is becoming obsolete and growing old is ready to vanish away" (Heb. 8:13).

His High Priestly Position

The shadow of the Old Covenant is now fulfilled since the high priest always ministered the gifts and sacrifices through the priest of the temple. The New Covenant has a new priesthood and a new temple. That is where we enter the picture.

His Priest and His Temple

We are now His Temple. All believers are living stones in this new building, not made with hands but built upon the foundation of the apostles and prophets, Jesus Christ Himself being the chief cornerstone (Eph. 2:20). We have been selected and fit into a special niche in his body (1 Cor. 12:27), forming a vital part of the temple. In fact, we are physical parts that people can see. We are also His priests serving in the temple (1 Pet: 2:5,9). Just as He offered Himself as a sacrifice (dead), fulfilling the old covenant, He now desires that we offer ourselves as a living sacrifice, His agents in the world (Rom. 12:1). To be a living sacrifice is to proclaim His Excellency (righteousness) with our words (lips) and our action (spiritual gift). Note Heb. 10:23-25:

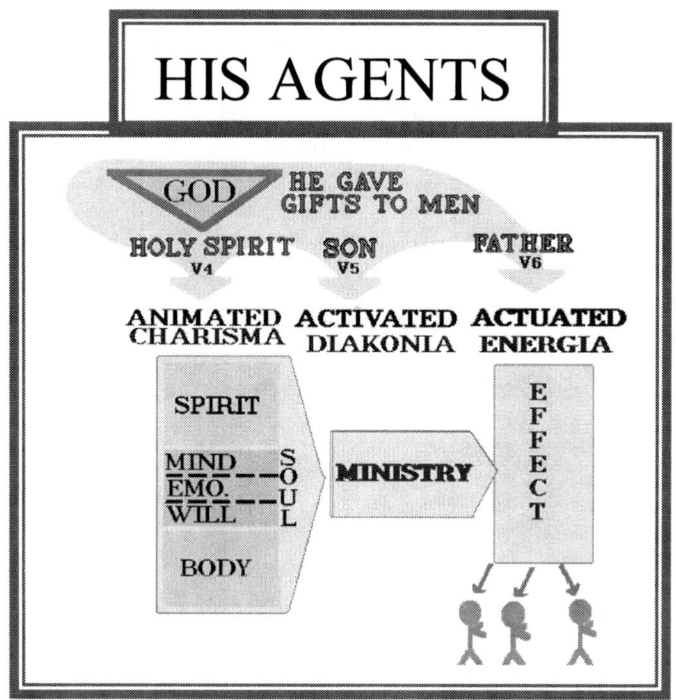

"Let us hold fast the confession of our hope without wavering, for He who promised is faithful. And let us consider one another in order to *stir up* love and good works, not forsaking the assembling of ourselves together, as is the manner of some, but exhorting *one another* and so much the more as you see the day approaching" (Heb.10:23-25).

Having boldness, holding fast without wavering, considering one another, stirring up, and doing good works—all these echo Paul's exhortation, "do not neglect the gift that is in you" (1 Tim. 4:14). Also, "stir up the gift of God which is in you" (2 Tim. 1:6). These are strong imperatives. It has been shown that all who believe have a spiritual gift. However, I often hear Christians say, "I don't think I have a gift." I think it is a must to know what the Scripture says about our spiritual abilities. The problem in most churches is that they do not amplify this unique power God has provided for the Church. They are caught up in a Hebrews 5 syndrome—they are satisfied with milk (being fed), rather than desiring meat (feeding themselves) and are in danger of discipline. They are not skilled in the Word therefore are not participating to the fullest in their giftedness (Heb. 5:12-14). There are several verses that confirm that each person has at least one gift and strongly encourages us to function in it (Rom. 12:3-8).

The Believer's Priestly Position

I have already noted that when He ascended on high, He gave gifts to men (generically speaking), and He commissioned us as priests (1 Pet. 2:1-10). We have one of those special gifts that were given "according to the measure of Christ's gift" (Eph. 4:7). Paul makes it very clear in this context that each one of us has received one grace gift to carry out our priestly functions. The distribution of spiritual gifts is a work of the Father, Son and Holy Spirit. The Trinity is a vital part of our ministry. The Holy Spirit indwells our being, animating (charisma) us in a special ability to perform a ministry (diakonia) that Jesus, the Son, did when He was here. God, the Father, then actuates (energizes) our giftedness in the lives of the ones to whom we minister. The chart above illustrates how the Holy Spirit animates us to function in a special gift (1 Cor. 12:4-6).

Jesus Christ ministered in all the gifts when He was here, and has now commissioned us to build a ministry around our gift and activate it by ministering to those around us. God the Father then effects or actuates it in the lives of those being ministered to, in order to accomplish His will in the world.

These changes will bring about eternal rewards for the servant and for the one being served. This passage indicates that each one of us has received a gift from God to enable us to represent Him in this natural world in a supernatural way. It is not something we work up or call down. It is a gift given at the time of our new birth. Another thing we notice in these verses is that since we have been given a gift (past tense) then we are obligated to get out there and use it:

> "Now concerning spiritual gifts, brethren, I do not want you to be ignorant: you know that you were Gentiles, carried away to these dumb idols, however you were led. Therefore I make known to you that no one speaking by the Spirit of God calls Jesus accursed, and no one can say that Jesus is Lord except by the Holy Spirit. There are diversities of gifts, but the same Spirit. There are differences of ministries, but the same Lord." (1 Cor. 12:1-5)

Priestly Functions

Remember the temple priest concerns were gifts and sacrifice. We are now a priest in the royal priesthood and must be presenting our bodies as a living sacrifice and serving in our giftedness (Rom.12:1). Since it is true that we all have a gift, then it would seem reasonable that we should know what the Scripture teaches on the subject. Paul directs Timothy to stir up (keep fanning into flame) the gift he has been given. He is even stronger in his first letter to Timothy exhorting him, "Do not neglect the gift that is in you" (1 Tim. 4:14). Paul again states in Rom. 12:1 "Do not be ignorant (unaware) concerning spirituals." We will understand the word *unaware* better if we know the root of the word. It is the same root word from which we get agnostic. It literally means "without knowledge of spiritual things." The situation has not changed that much through all these years. Most Christians do not understand what the Scripture says about gifts, much less discovering and using them.

We are fortunate because most Christians never experience the freedom we have. There are two words in this context that translate *spiritual gift*, each having a sphere of meaning within the ministry of the church. The first word, *spirituals (pneumatikos)*, involves the whole sphere of spiritual functions. It is a broad and descriptive term. It involves the concept of power and things not seen. It involves a work of the Spirit. It includes salvation, sanctification, spiritual gifts, reconciliation and anything that is spiritually motivated.

The second word charisma which translates spiritual gift and it is one of the spirituals because it is a work of the Spirit. When we believed God's Spirit was given to us as a seal as a guarantee of our inheritance (Eph. 1:13-14), and later Paul adds that when Jesus ascended to the father he gave gifts to men (Eph. 4:7-11). This enables us to function in a supernatural way, according to His specific motivation. Galen Currah comments on the relationship between gifts and grace:

> "The connection of Gifts with grace is two-fold in verse 10. First, the very word *charisma* implies that it comes from grace, *charis*. Second, the person who has received a charisma is a steward of God's manifold grace. That there is great variation in gifts is evident from the word 'manifold.' That is to say, 'the grace of God manifests itself in different ways.' Now regardless of the nature of a person's particular spiritual gift, he is

responsible to God to use that gift. 'It is required of stewards that one be found trustworthy'" (1 Cor. 4:2). Currah, *Spiritual Gifts, Designed and Described*, p. 10.

A spiritual gift produces supernatural results in the person being ministered to. It does not mean we can go around moving mountains or raising the dead. These gifts are given for the purpose of accomplishing His purpose or His ministry in the life of the receiver. As we function in our gift, we become God's instrument of grace to that person.

The word for spiritual gift is very descriptive. The first part is *char* and would translate to "joy." In the second part, we add two letters and get *charis*, which translates to "grace." The third part is the suffix, or ending, and that is by adding two letters on the end of the word, *ma* that indicates a function. Put it all together and you get *charisma*, which translates "a gracious spiritual function." The manifestation of spiritual gifts also has three elements that describe the function. Paul describes it in 1 Cor. 12: 4-6 in verse 4, *animation*; verse 5, *activated*; and verse 6, *actuated*.

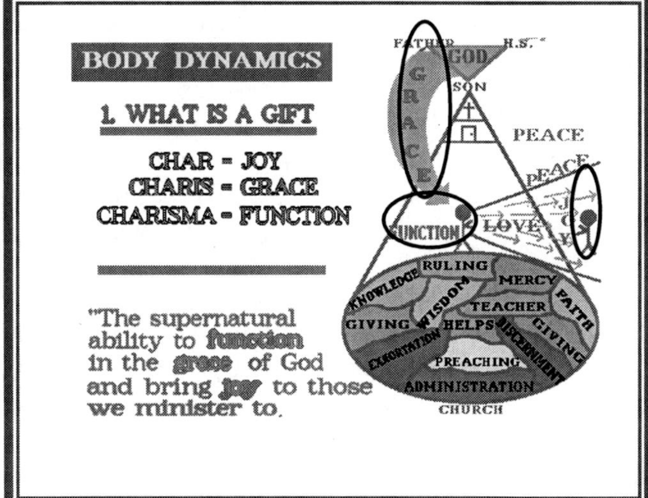

Discerning the Warnings

Gifts are our motivation to function. However, you are probably still wondering if you are functioning in the power of the Spirit or if you are functioning in the power of the flesh or some other spirit? Well, Paul does not leave us in the dark here. From 1 Cor. 12:3, he gives us a quality control checklist. It is obvious from this text that the Corinthians were attempting to bring into the church the same worldly attitudes and actions they had practiced when they were unbelievers. They were actually worshipping these pagan idols, indicating they were communicating (in a state of ecstasy) verbally, and were being led astray. They were evidently receiving spiritual guidance from these speechless idols.

The first test is a warning against binding up the message of Christ through our wrong thinking and selfish attitudes that allow the demonic forces to manipulate us. The word *accursed* is from a compound word meaning "up or back" and "to lay aside, bind, or curse." Together it means to bind up the message of Christ, either with our lips or with our life.

The second test is pride; that is, by saying Jesus is Lord of our life when we are totally self-controlled or being manipulated or controlled by demonic forces. We know that anyone can say the words "Jesus is Lord" or "Praise the Lord" with their lips, but no one can say it with their lips and live it with their life except by the control of the Holy Spirit. The lips and the life must be in agreement.

Tragically, many of the Corinthian Christians had fallen back into some of their old idolatrous beliefs and practices. They could no longer distinguish the work of God's Spirit from that of demonic spirits or God's true spiritual gifts from Satan's counterfeits, or true worship of God from the perverted worship of idols. They forfeited God's blessing and received none from their false gods. They were quenching the Holy Spirit.

We too, will have this tendency since our memory banks are filled with principles we developed before we believed in Him. These principles were all developed from the influence of the world powers, the same spirit that controlled the Corinthians through the speechless idols. This is the primary reason many churches are so ineffective today. Everyone tends to bring some worldly ideas (that often sound good and have an appearance of good) into the church and the message and ministry of Christ is bound up in our attitudes or actions.

That is why Paul writes from Corinth to the church in Rome, exhorting them, not to be conformed to this world, to get the old way of life out of their system and to be transformed through (metamorphous), an Emptying and Filling Process. Then He tells them how to do it: "By the renewing of your mind" (reprogramming), that you may prove what is that good and acceptable and perfect will of God" (Rom. 12:2).

If we are functioning under the control of the Holy Spirit, our life will represent and identify with the name of Christ and our lips will proclaim His Excellencies. Neither our lips nor our life will hinder the message and ministry of Christ! However, if the Spirit is not controlling, we will bind up the message and ministry of Christ with our own self-righteousness. Our gift then will no longer be spiritual and will only demonstrate carnal or counterfeit actions known as the works of the flesh.

The Tri-Unity of God in Gifts Animated by the Holy Spirit

Now that we have an understanding of the words and the warning, we need to understand how the Body functions. There are three basic elements in the function of spirituals. First we are animated by the Holy Spirit (1 Cor. 12:4; Eph. 4:4). In verse 4 you will notice the function of the Holy Spirit; varieties of gifts, but the same Spirit. This is the basic spiritual motivation. After we have discovered and developed our gifts and we allow the Holy Spirit to control our mind, emotions and will, our physical body will manifest a special spiritual manifestation of the things Christ would do if He were here. The word used for spiritual gift means a joyous, gracious function. That is not a natural function and will accomplish the things Jesus began to do and teach on earth. This brings us to the next basic element. John MacArthur comments:

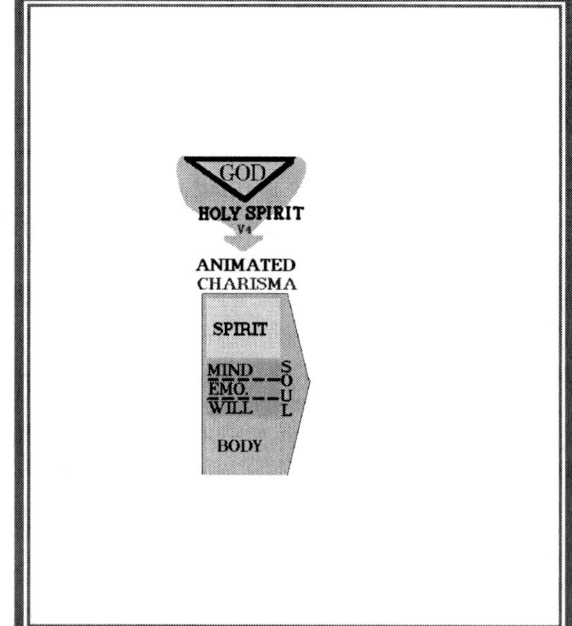

> "Spiritual gifts, however, are not natural, but rather are supernaturally given by the Holy Spirit only and always to believers in Jesus Christ, without exception (v. 7). Spiritual gifts are special capacities bestowed on believers to equip them to minister supernaturally to others, especially to each other. Consequently, if those gifts are not being used, or not being used rightly, the body of Christ cannot be the corporate manifestation of its Head, the Lord Jesus Christ, and the work of God is hindered."

MacArthur, *First Corinthians: New Testament Commentary*.

Activated by the Son (Messiah)

The second element is *Activated*. You will notice in 1 Cor. 12:5, the function of the Lord Jesus, "there are varieties of ministries and the same Lord." The word used here—and elsewhere in the New Testament—for *Lord* always refers to Christ the Son or the Messiah. It is His ministry and His righteousness being demonstrated in our spiritual gift. You see, Jesus is now in a glorified state at the right hand of the Father, and no one can see Him as they did when he was here in the flesh. Note the chart.

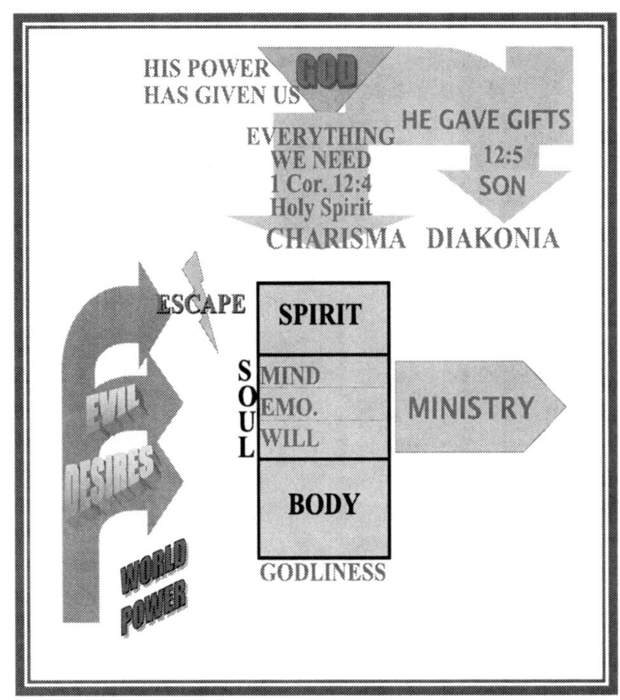

He has chosen us to demonstrate His gifts through our physical body in order that people might see *Him*. But that's not all. Even though two people may have the same gift, they may use it in a different way. One may be gifted to teach young people, another may be more adapted to teach adults. All gifts are different and produce different ministries. Our ministry is built around our spiritual gift. This passage indicates there are many different kinds of gifts and one Spirit (1 Cor. 12:4). Now in verse 5, He indicates each gift has a unique ministry of performing as a part of His Body, doing the things He did when He was here. The following diagram will amplify how God, the Father, the Son, and the Holy Spirit function through us.

The result of our ministry is the energy of God effecting change in the heart of the person to whom we are ministering. This no doubt has reference to God the Father who is the energizer of all things. He is the one that affects all things in the universe. Spiritual gifts are so unique because of the power involved and the unity they display. They involve the Godhead totally; that is the Father, the Son and the Holy Spirit each manifesting Himself in a special way through the believer. You are also unique; in fact, so unique that each of the persons of the Godhead has a special part in the function of your gift. The Holy Spirit supernaturally enables you to function in the same ministry Jesus performed when He was here, totally energized and effected by the Father. You are fully energized with all the power of God and as you humble yourself in obedience to Him, the Tri-Unity of God begins to work through you affecting His will in a supernatural and eternal way.

Actuated by the Father

You will notice in 1 Cor. 12:6, the function of the Father. There are varieties of effects, but the same God. The word *effect* is from the Greek word from which we get the English word "energy." In this context, there is clearly indicated an active functioning energy or manifestation of that energy. Therefore, it is the energy of the Father (note

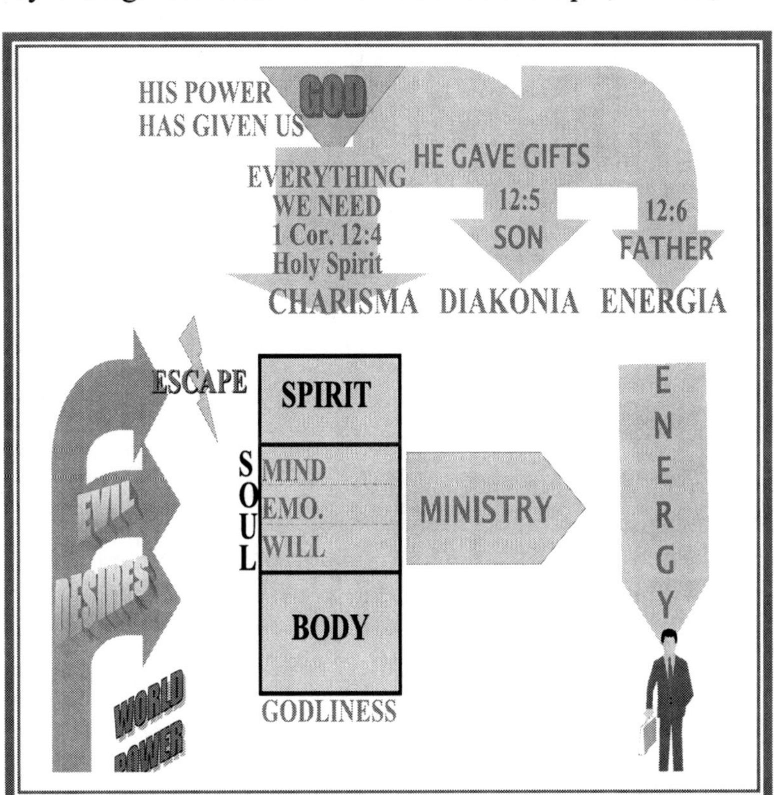

also Eph. 4:6) effecting the ministry (the same things Christ did), motivated by the Holy Spirit. This is a clear manifestation of the power of God.

The Holy Spirit dwelling in us has given to each believer a spiritual gift which provides a channel through which God can affect a ministry in the same way Jesus ministered when He was here. This is our motivation to function supernaturally in a natural world. It is God's means of effecting a supernatural change in another person. This is the result of the body being one, united in its function. Note Paul's comment.

"There is one body and one Spirit, just as you were called to one hope of your calling" Eph. 4:4.

That one Body is the Church. Paul makes reference here to the universal church; however, our local church should be a replica of the universal body. A personal application would be the church (local) to which you have submitted. This is where we were called, when we were united in the one Spirit who dwells in the one body the church. This is our hope (1 Cor. 12:4; Eph. 4:4). This is our means of "keeping the unity of the Spirit in the bond of peace" (Eph. 4:3).

The Purpose of Gifts

The results of your ministry will change lives just as Christ did when He was here. The difference is that He had all the gifts and totally submitted to the Father. We normally have only one gift and our tendency is to fail to discover or submit to the use of it. Hopefully, that will become less and less of a problem as you grow in the grace and knowledge of Him. Remember, "His divine power has given to us all things that pertain to life and godliness" (2 Pet. 1:3); to live this life and demonstrate godliness with this life in the energy of the Triune God.

Designed to Bring the Body Together

Discern the specific purpose from Paul's exhortation in the following verse: "But the manifestation of the Spirit is given to each one for the *profit of all*" (1 Cor. 12:7). Paul does not want you to be unaware of the purpose for spiritual gifts. The word translated here is a compound word (*suv* and *phero* or *sunpheron*) translated to bring together or *common good*, is a picturesque word that leaves no question about the purpose. The body is drawn or cemented together by the functioning of the gifts of the body. Note chart:

Paul clarifies the purpose of His word, and then dramatically illustrates the purpose of your gift. Your gifts are given for the building, uniting, drawing together and developing oneness in your local body (church). It is for qualitative development; that is, each member being built up, growing into the mature state demonstrated by Christ when He was here. Each member is being perfected as they rub elbows with each other. Note chart:

One of your friends has a deep difficulty, allowed by God in order to stimulate growth. You come alongside and minister to the basic need with your gift and a supernatural change takes place. Not only is your friend's life built up, but the whole body is built up, including you (1 Cor. 12:25-26). You see, God not only meets needs, He also allows those needs in order to stimulate growth through a disciplined life. Study (Phil. 2:1-4).

In the perfecting process, you have been called (as all other believers) to be a living stone to fill a special niche that no one else can fill. We are all being fitted for a special function—God's will. As we become mature—understanding our place and functioning in it—every encounter we have will be a divine appointment for a special purpose. The real beauty of this is that as we function in the power of the Spirit, those we encounter will see Christ in us and they will respond. Notice how the philosophers responded to Paul's gift of preaching in Athens:

> "And when they heard of the resurrection of the dead, some mocked, while others said, 'We will hear you again on this matter...' However some men joined him and believed" Acts (17:32, 34a).

Designed for Meeting the Needs of Others

The purpose of your gift is never for your own benefit or for the building up of one's self. Our Lord practiced this principle every day of His life. He lived a life of humility and obedience to the Father, and His only purpose was to glorify the Father. He continually reminded His followers that He came to do "the will of my Father." He never once used his spiritual ability for His own edification, but always considered others more important than Himself. In fact, Paul exhorts us as members of Christ's body:

> "For as the body is one and has many members, but all the members of that one body, being many, are one body, so also is Christ. For by one Spirit we were all baptized into one body—whether Jews or Greeks, whether slaves or free—and have all been made to drink into one Spirit. For in fact the body is not one member but many. If the foot should say, 'because I am not a hand, I am not of the body, is it therefore not of the body? And if the ear should say, 'because I am not an eye, I am not of the body,' is it therefore not of the body?" (1 Cor. 12:12-16)

We are to put away the old attitudes of self-righteousness and conceit in order to hunger and thirst after His righteousness. Spiritual gifts function as a unit, all fitting together to form the Body of which Christ is the Head. We are the functional parts of His body (Eph. 4:16). All of the gifts have a specific function and they all are different. If you have the gift of giving and I have the gift of giving, each will function differently according to our faith. Some gifts are more prominent than others, although they are all very special to God. "He gives more honor to the less honorable gifts" (1 Cor. 12:23a).

I will summarize the purpose of your gift by emphatically stating that the gifts are given for building up and bringing together the body as a unit. No one gift is ever isolated for self service and most of all, no one has all the gifts, nor does everyone have the same gift. They are given by the Tri-Unity of the Father, Son and Holy Spirit for one purpose, to glorify Him.

Differentiating Between Gifts and Talents

Gifts and talents are often confused. After a beautiful solo is sung, you might hear someone say that the singer really has a gift for singing. Singing is not a gift; it is a talent. There are clear distinctions between gifts and talents.

However, I do not want to minimize talents. God has predetermined our talents as well as our spiritual gifts. Your talents were given to compliment your gift. Being a schoolteacher in a public school does not mean you have the gift of teaching but it will compliment your gift of mercy, administration, or whatever gift you have. Gifts also work the other way. Your spiritual gift will amplify your talent. It will give you the ability to stay with a project others have given up on.

Discovering My Spiritual Gift

Can you really know what your gift is? Certainly you can know! Some would say there is no need to put an emphasis on knowing your gift. I would agree that we should not put more emphasis on this than we find in Scripture. I might add, however, that the Bible has a good deal to say about knowledge of spiritual gifts. In fact, Paul says, "Brethren, I do not want you to be ignorant" (1 Cor. 12:1b) (without knowledge). Once a person said to me, "I got along without them for 25 years, why should I get involved now?" I believe that borders on ignorance and is exactly what Paul was referring to. It is also a violation of Paul's exhortation, "Don't you dare neglect the gift that is in you" (1 Tim. 4:14, paraphrased).

Paul gives us some guidelines in several places: First in 1 Cor. Chapters 12, 13 & 14; in Rom. Chapter 12; and very succinct statement in 1 Pet. 4 and in Eph. 4. All this is to enable you to discover your gift. I will give you several insights I have drawn from the Scripture to aid you in the discovery process, but ultimately, only the Holy Spirit can reveal your gift and confirm it in you.

Study Scriptures Relating to Gifts

You must study the Scriptures with an emphasis on spiritual gifts. I have given you many principles regarding spiritual gifts, but that does not eliminate the necessity for personal study and practice. James exhorts us; "Be doers of the word" (James 1:22). Practice, practice, practice. Your mind must be saturated with the passages. Make them a part of your life. You need to discern, and then write out, all the principles you can find in these passages regarding spiritual gifts. You may be encouraged by all the insights the Holy Spirit will give to you.

Submissive to Christ

You must be empty of self. There is no room in a servant's life for pride. Anything that would give the world powers access to your mind, such as guilt, broken relationships, deep hurt, bitterness, or any moral impurity will hinder you from being able to freely function as a member of His Body. Note 2 Pet. 1:3-11:

> "His divine power has given to us all things that pertain to life and godliness, through the knowledge of Him who called us by glory and virtue, by which have been given to us exceedingly great and precious promises, that through these you may be partakers of the divine nature, having escaped the corruption that is in the world through lust. But also for this very reason, give all diligence, add to your faith virtue, to your virtue knowledge, to knowledge self-control, to self-control perseverance, to perseverance godliness, to godliness brotherly kindness, to brotherly kindness love. For if these things are yours and abound, you will be neither barren nor unfruitful in the knowledge of our Lord Jesus Christ. For he who lacks these things is shortsighted, even to blindness, and has forgotten that he was cleansed from his old sins. Therefore, brethren, be even more diligent to make your call and election sure, for if you do these things you will never stumble, for so an entrance will be supplied to you abundantly into the everlasting kingdom of our Lord and savior Jesus Christ" (2 Pet. 1:3-11).

Note Dillow's comments:

> "Peter's meaning is that we must make our Christian lives impregnable against falling into sin by adding the virtues in the preceding context to our foundation of faith. We must strengthen our lives. This will make us unshakable and firm in the midst of suffering. To say it differently, to make our calling and election sure is to purpose that they will achieve their intended aim, a holy life, perseverance in suffering, and inherit a blessing." Dillow, *Reign of the Servant Kings*, p. 298.

If you have unresolved conflicts, conceit or self-centeredness, you will not be ready to give an answer for the hope that is in you with meekness and humility. And therefore, you will not be able to persevere as a partaker following Biblical principles.

Making Sure of Your Calling and Election

These verses are not related to your justification or new birth. Peter has already discussed this when He said "To those who have obtained (note this is past tense) like precious faith with us, by the righteousness of our God and Savior Jesus Christ" (2 Pet. 1:2). It is obvious here that he is addressing those who are already elected and called out of darkness into the Body of Christ. So there must be another calling and election. The first order in our salvation is that we are first elected (selected), and then we are called (see Rom. 8:28-30)—that is our justification. Here in 2 Pet. 1:3-11, we are dealing with sanctification, a life time process of being transformed into Christ's likeness (Rom. 8:28-29; Phil. 3:10, 20). Here Peter gives the solution to "make our call and election sure." He starts verse 3 "His power has given us everything we need." We have all the resources to be a participator in the divine nature. Then he gives us a list of the things we must do to make sure 2 Pet. 1:5-7. That is our calling, and as we persevere as partakers to the end, we will be elected (selected) as kings to reign with Him in the future millennial kingdom. We will discuss this area more later. Your calling is your ministry here on earth (your giftedness), and your election will be in the future BEMA where you will be elected to reign with Him in the future kingdom.

How then can we make sure of our calling? Just as Peter said, "by being diligent in exercising your faith; by adding virtue, knowledge, self-control, patience, godliness, brotherly love and *agape* love." Developing these characteristics will qualify you as a partaker and give you the assurance of your calling, election, and guarantees your inheritance (2 Pet. 1:5-8).

Dedication of Yourself

You must acknowledge you are empty of self and by the mercy of God, dedicate yourself to Him (Rom. 12:1). You are ready to take up your cross (life ministry) and follow Him (Mat. 10:38). Peter again exhorts us in this area, "you also, as living stones, are being built up a spiritual house, a holy priesthood, to offer up spiritual sacrifices acceptable to God through Jesus Christ" (1 Pet. 2:5a). This is a once and for all act of considering yourself dead to sin and alive to God, not giving yourself to acts of unrighteousness, but instruments of righteousness to God (Rom. 6:11-16). The following is a prayer of dedication; rewrite it in your own words:

"Lord, I thank you for your grace and love that has enabled me rethink all those old attitudes and actions that were contrary to your Word, to be able to confess those areas of failure and receive your forgiveness. I praise you now for the new freedom I am experiencing as I obey you, according to your Word. Now Lord, in this new freedom I wish, by your mercies, to dedicate my body, soul and spirit to you as a living sacrifice, holy and acceptable to you. I realize now this is the most reasonable spiritual service I can perform. I purpose now to be a partaker in your divine nature (Rom. 12:1).

Determine Spirituality

Determine if you are controlled by the Holy Spirit and not out of selfishness or some other spirit. We discussed this before but now it is time to make sure you are controlled by the Holy Spirit. Note Paul's exhortation in this area:

> "You know that you were Gentiles, carried away to these dumb idols, however you were led. Therefore, I make known to you that no one speaking by the Spirit of God calls Jesus accursed; and no one can say that Jesus is Lord except by the Holy Spirit" (1 Cor. 12:2-3).

The word *accursed* here is from the root word "to bind" with the prefix meaning "up" or "back," and together they mean to "bind up" or "accursed." The idea here is no one speaking by the Holy Spirit can bind up the message of Christ. The second part of this test is "no one can say that Jesus is Lord except by the Holy Spirit." These verses pose the following questions:

1. Is there anything in my life or by my lips that would bind up the message of Christ through me?

2. Can I, by the Holy Spirit, demonstrate with my life and with my lips that Jesus Christ is truly Lord of my life?

Can you answer these questions without any doubt? 1) I am not binding up the message of Jesus Christ with my life or my lips." And, 2) "Yes, Jesus Christ is Lord of my life." (Note also Eph. 5:18-21).

The Discovery of your Giftedness

Paul and Peter give us some guidelines in several passages of Scripture. We have already discussed several passages directly related to discovery; 1 Cor. 12-14, Rom. 12, Eph. 4:1-16, 1 Pet. 4:7-11, 1 Tim.4:14, 2 Tim. 1:6. These verses should stir up a burning desire in our hearts to leave no "stones unturned" until we discover this special ability God has given us. Remember the Holy Spirit is the only one that can confirm in you the gift God has given you. Note the following guidelines.

<u>Ask</u>

James says "But if any of you lack wisdom, let him ask of God" (Ja. 1:5). Jesus also said, "Ask and it will be given to you; seek, and you will find; knock, and it will be opened to you" (Mat. 7:7). "But seek first the kingdom of God and His righteousness and all these things shall be added to you" (Mat. 6:3).

First, ask your pastor. God has given certain men to the Church for the perfecting of the Saints for the work of the ministry. These men are the evangelist, pastor, and teacher (Eph.4:11). They would likely compose your pastoral staff, depending on the organization of your local church. Their equipping you includes the discovery and development of your gift.

Second, ask your mate. Generally, no one knows you as well as your mate. God has given you this intimate relationship, and it should be used for Spiritual growth. God gave the wife the responsibility of being a suitable helpmate. This is also in the spiritual realm. The husband is to give spiritual protection and direction, including the discovery and development of her spiritual gift.

Third, ask your friends and acquaintances. God is not hiding your gift. When you are functioning under the control of the Holy Spirit, people will see this special ability in you. Therefore, ask your friends, teachers, deacons or anyone that knows you well.

<u>**Affirm**</u>

Affirm or confirm the gift God has given you and make them real in your life. You have been through the process of discovery, and now you have a good understanding of all the gifts and many of the principles governing them.

God is not hiding your gift from you, in fact He exhorts you to not be ignorant concerning spiritual gifts (1 Cor. 12:1-3), in another place it says, "Don't neglect the gift that is in you" (1 Tim. 4:14), and again, "Fan into flame the gift that is in you" (2 Tim. 1:6). It is very obvious in all the passages relating to gifts that it is the believer's responsibility to discover and develop their gift, and He will give you the grace to accomplish the task. This demands that you understand the tendencies and trends of each gift listed in Romans 12 and First Corinthians 12.

<u>**Accept**</u>

You can narrow the gift list down to two or three, then begin to work out projects to use those gifts in an experiential way. Keep a record of how you used it and what the results were. No one test or inventory is going to tell you what your gift is; only the Holy Spirit can reveal the fact that you have a certain gift, and then only as you function in it. There are several ways you will become aware of your gift. People will begin to see unusual responses to your ministry. People will receive the fruit of the Spirit (love, joy, peace etc.) as you minister to them. Others will be drawn to desire more and more of your ministry. You will experience an inner sense of fulfillment as you minister. Continue to narrow down to one major area. The following is a list of speaking and serving gifts:

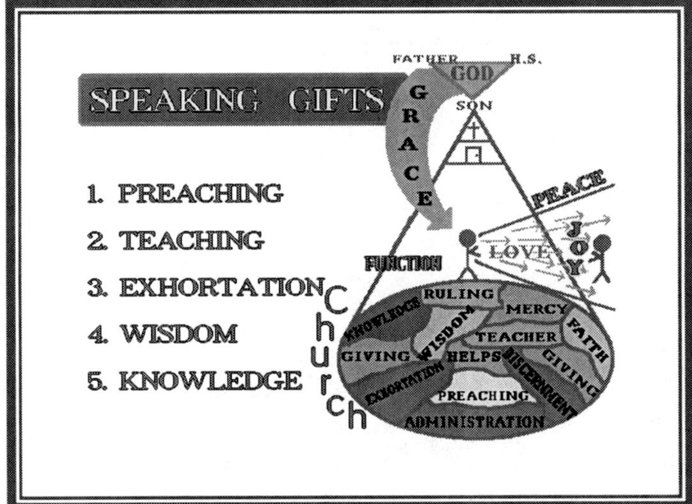

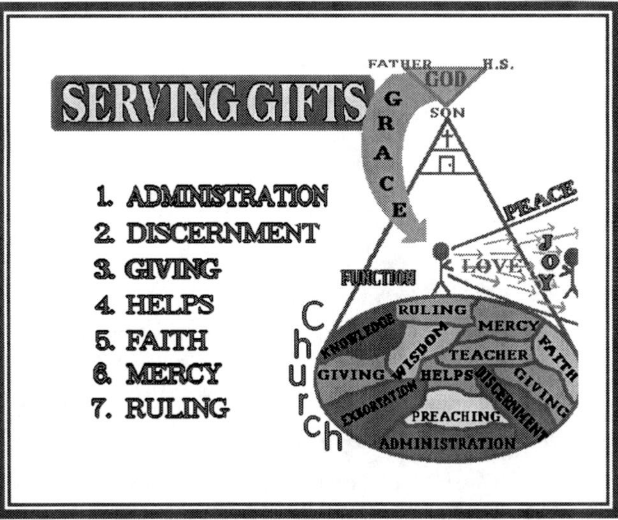

You might want to consult your pastor, teacher, or other leaders and let them know you are interested in developing some projects that would enable you to function in these areas. Read all the material you can find on the gifts God has given you. Give all your energy to developing your life ministry and life message around the strong areas you have discovered in your studies. Note Paul's exhortation:

"But earnestly desire the best gifts. And yet I show you a more excellent way"
(1 Cor. 12:31).

Paul's concern is that when you are walking in the Spirit, you will not desire a gift that is not a Body gift that does not build up the body—such as tongues, healing, or miracles. What is the greater gift? It is the one God has given you. Just accept and activate the gift God has given you.

You are now ready to be fitted into your special niche in the building. You should be able to exercise your gift with full knowledge. Exercise is the key! Practice! Practice! Practice! You need a means of quality control. God is not interested in quantity so much as quality that comes when you function at full capacity. Note Peter's exhortation:

"As each one has received a gift, minister it to one another, as good stewards of the manifold grace of God. If anyone speaks, let him speak as the oracles (Word) of God. If anyone ministers (serving), let him do it as with the ability (power) which God supplies. That in all things God may be glorified through Jesus Christ, to whom belong the glory and dominion for ever and ever. Amen" (1 Pet. 4:10-11).

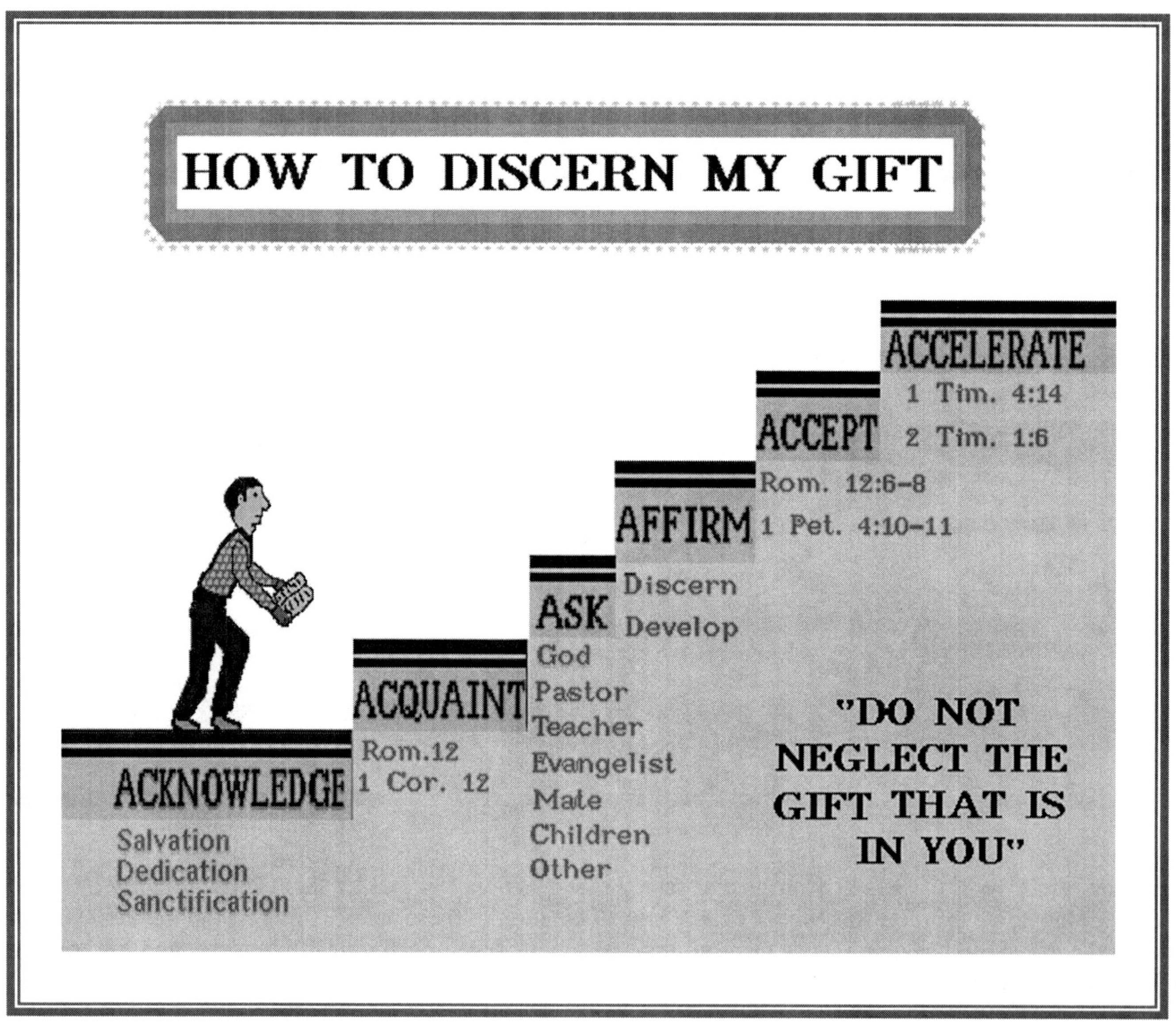

PROJECT

1. What is the ministry of each member of the Trinity regarding spiritual gifts?

2. Describe the three parts of the word CHARISMA.

3. What is the purpose of spiritual gifts (1 Cor. 12:7)?

4. To whom has God given spiritual gifts (1 Pet. 4:10)?

5. What are the vehicles for spiritual gifts (1 Pet. 4:8-9)?

6. Describe a spiritual sacrifice (Heb. 13:15-17).

7. List the major passages dealing with spiritual gifts.

8. How do spiritual gifts and talents relate?

CHAPTER 9 - RIGHT THINKING ABOUT SENSITIVITY

"Blessed are the merciful, for they shall obtain mercy." Mat. 5:7

Rick was anxious to serve the Lord after he had worked through the "emptying" process. After an extramarital affair, his wife had come back home and he felt so good about the way the Lord was working that he discontinued his counseling. He completed a Spiritual Gifts seminar and discovered his spiritual gift, but he failed to understand how he uniquely fitted into the total program of the church. As a result, he never got involved in the church, and his abilities were not used.

You need to understand that God has given us the ability to function by faith in our life ministry (Rom 12:3). Not only has He given us this ability, He has prepared beforehand the exact work He wants us to do, as well as the means to do it (Eph. 2:10). Therefore, to the extent that we function to the capacity God has given us, we will experience the fulfillment God has for us.

Rick was able to function for a while, but guilt was compounding daily and hindering his ability to handle it. First, he began to reproach himself because he could not make the right decisions. Then he began neglecting his wife, which resulted in her leaving him again. Finally, he came in for help. His condition was worse now than before. Not only that, but his wife was adamant about getting a divorce. Rick's life was in a pitiful state. With tears he asked, "Bill, what went wrong? What can I do?" I told him that we would start over. Rick had offended many people in the previous eight months and needless to say, he was ready to do whatever was necessary to receive the best that God had for him.

Defining the Word *Merciful*

You see, it is not enough to just go through the Emptying Process or just through the Discovery Process. A disciple never quite finishes the learning process in this lifetime. In the previous Beatitude, we learned that those who hunger and thirst after His righteousness shall be filled, so we must not stop but go on hungering and thirsting. Note Peter's exhortation:

"For if these things are yours and abound, you will be neither barren nor unfruitful in the knowledge of our Lord Jesus Christ. For he who lacks these things is shortsighted, even to blindness, and has forgotten that he was cleansed from his old sins" (2 Pet. 1:8-9).

The first characteristic we are to be filled with is mercy. Jesus says, "Blessed are those who are merciful for they shall receive mercy" (Mat. 5:7). David's prayer was "God be merciful to us and bless us" (Ps 67:1). In fact, it was by His great mercies we were saved (Eph. 2:4-55), and it is by His great mercies that we dedicate ourselves to His service (Rom. 12:1). God has not only been merciful to you and blessed you but now He gives you that inner satisfaction as you show mercy to those who come to you. You are now becoming a means of His blessing to others. You are now His agent of mercy in this dark, dismal world.

What is mercy? The root word, ελεοσ, signifies a deep empathy for one who is suffering physical pain or hurting psychologically. It indicates an outward demonstration or sensitivity to those who are in need. It is empathy not sympathy. Vine states:

"Wherever the words mercy and peace are found together they occur in that order, except in Gal. 6:16. Mercy is the act of God; peace is the resulting experience in the heart of man. Grace describes God's attitude toward the law-breaker and the rebel; mercy is His attitude toward those who are in distress. In the order of the manifestation of God's purposes of salvation, grace must go before mercy only the forgiven may be blessed. From this it follows that in each of the apostolic salutations where these words occur, grace precedes mercy, 1 Tim. 1:2; 2 Tim. 1:2; Tit. 1:4 (in some mss.); 2 Jn. 3 (Trench, Syn. & xlvii)." Vine, *Expanded Vine's Dictionary of New Testament Words*, p. 733.

Mercy is more than an attitude; it is an action toward a person who is in misery. Specifically, it is the attitude Jesus demonstrated in His walk on earth. We are becoming His instruments of mercy. But even more personally, it was because of His great mercy toward you that He came into the world (Eph. 2:4). His greatest mercy was that He died on the cross for your sins. He was made sin for us; now we have been commissioned to show mercy.

Rick failed to develop this characteristic. When we become merciful, we get out of ourselves and into the lives of others. We reach out and touch someone with a new sensitivity. Everyone tends to put up a front, the idea "I'm okay, you're okay," when deep inside they are dying. Having developed our spiritual abilities with this new sensitivity, we can reach through the front people put up and meet their needs. There are some basic principles we need to understand in order to function at capacity.

Like all the other Beatitudes, merciful is the opposite of the world's logic. The kingdoms of the world have always demonstrated pride, arrogance, egotism and self-righteousness. The Jews, especially in that day, did not understand what the word meant, and the Romans saw mercy as a weakness. They looked down on the merciful. Look at America! We are riddled with self-centeredness and have become a society animated by narcissism. We have fallen in love with self and are unconcerned about the other person. We even have a Bill of Rights that will ultimately be our downfall just like Rome. Someone has said we need to change the Bill of Rights to a Bill of Responsibility and Mercifulness.

The Forgotten Concept—Deference

We need to understand the depth of the concept of deference ($\alpha\nu\alpha\beta\alpha\lambda\lambda\omega$), a merciful act of setting aside my desires to meet the needs of another. This attitude demands that we see the other person as more important than ourselves (Phil. 2:3-4). This attitude of mercy is the ability to love the unlovable, to be able to see through an offense to see the offender's need. These last four Beatitudes are the characteristics Jesus demonstrated all of His life here on earth. At this level, the disciple—having emptied and discovered his gift—can begin to develop a new sensitivity toward his contemporaries; the same sensitivity Jesus demonstrated when He was on earth. Grace and mercy always go together. Grace is the power we receive from God to show mercy. To be merciful is not the natural thing to do. By grace, it becomes a supernatural function. Lenski amplifies this attitude:

> "The 'merciful' are, of course, the same persons as those referred to in the previous beatitudes. Luther well says that in all the Beatitudes faith is presupposed as the tree on which all the fruit of blessedness grows. This, then, is not mere natural mercy as it is occasionally found among men generally but the mercy growing out of our personal experience of the mercy of God. God's mercy toward us always makes us likewise merciful, 18:21, etc. The noun $\epsilon\lambda\epsilon o\varsigma$ and its derivatives always deal with what we see of pain, misery and distress, these results of sin; and $\chi\alpha\rho\iota\varsigma$, 'grace,' always deals with the sin and guilt itself. The one extends relief, the other pardon; the one cures, heals, helps, the other cleanses and rein-states. With God $\chi\alpha\rho\iota\varsigma$ is always first and $\epsilon\lambda\epsilon o\varsigma$ second." Lenski, *Interpretation of St. Matthew's Gospel*, p. 191.

Jesus was always above circumstances, never taking up an offense, but utilizing His gifts to reach out to people. Take, for instance, the woman at the well. They were talking about water; he sensed a need in her life. He began talking about living water and met needs in her life and she was never the same again.

Nicodemus came to Jesus asking questions and Jesus sensed a need, reached out and met that need. Nicodemus was never the same again. Now we have that same power, the same Spirit dwelling in us to reach out and meet needs (Jn. 3:1-21).

Illustrated Through Doing the Work of Ministry

The first level in the process of becoming merciful is to help the disciple thoroughly understand the function of the church; the leadership, the ministry of all the gifts, the organization and all the members.

The second level is to help them get involved with others who have already established a ministry around their spiritual gift. The most merciful thing we can do for a person—and the most merciful thing that person can do—is to develop the skills for service. That will place them in a position of overwhelming blessing from the Lord (Mat. 5:7). They, in turn, will guide and assist others in building a life message and ministry around their gift. This is a team effort, with all the parts working together. The key verse, 1 Cor. 12:7, indicates the clear purpose of spiritual gifts is bringing the Body together.

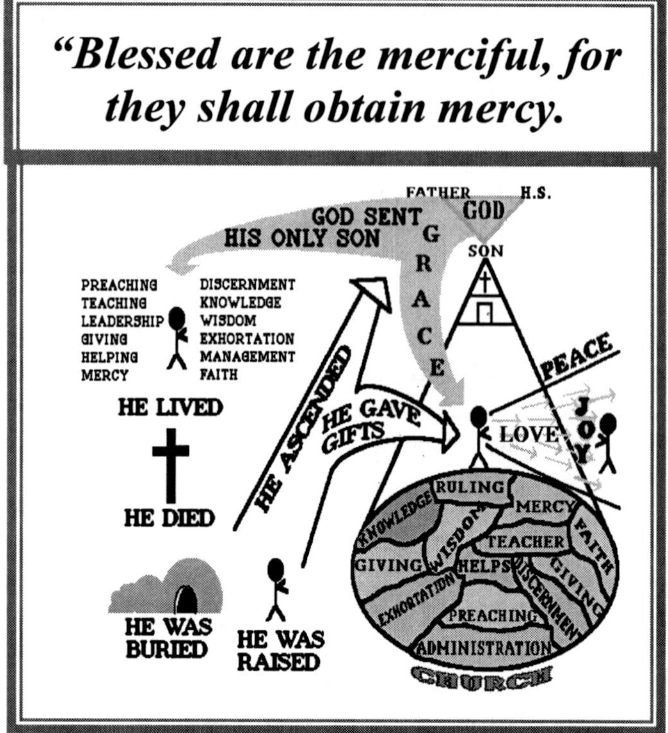

The third level is to develop a Biblical understanding of the sensitivity Jesus demonstrated in His ministry. Examples of this mercy were demonstrated to us through our salvation (Eph. 2:4-5), to the disciples through His washing of their feet (Jn. 13:1-17), in the high priestly prayer (Jn. 17:1-5), and to the soldiers who took Him into custody (Jn. 18:1-11).

The fourth level is to guide them in ministering to those rejecting God's best. These could be the poor, the hungry, the sick, the needy, the depressed, the anxious, the widows and orphans, the divorced, those with family conflict, those with addictions, the harassed and those in prison.

The promise that results from being merciful in the life of a disciple is that they shall obtain mercy. The verb is passive and in the future tense, indicating it is God that returns mercy for mercy. This is a promise to those who show mercy. Remember, now we are serving the King of Kings as student kings, and we are aliens in a foreign kingdom, so we desperately need His mercy. It is also important to remember that out of mercy flow forgiveness, justice, and all the fruit of the Spirit.

Christ's Mercy in the Metaphors of the Church

The Church is God's agent of mercy in world. It is not a building, it is a place where Christians gather to be educated in how to go out and show mercy to the ungodly world system. Radmacher defines the Church as God's agent in the world doing His business, in His place, through His people, at His pace:

> "The Bible gives us several metaphors that are designed to give us a better understanding of the sensitivity Christ demonstrated when He was here. We as members of His body now have the responsibility to develop that same sensitivity through the use of our spiritual gifts. Each metaphor gives a deeper understanding of the spiritual depth of this special temple not made with hands. In other words we become His instruments of mercy. The most profound truths concerning the nature of the church are pictured by Paul through the literary vehicle of the figure of speech. From these figures one can learn more of Paul's

conception of the church than from any other source. Not only do they communicate profound doctrinal concepts, but they add color, life, and emphasis to the truth." Radmacher, *The Nature of the Church*, p. 221.

The Church is a supernatural sphere. It is not a building made with hands. Even though it is in the world, it transcends the world. It is Christ's spiritual body indwelling a multitude of physical bodies for the purpose of teaching and accomplishing those things He did when He was here. You see, God has not only allowed needs within the Body, He has provided a means of fulfilling those needs through the gifts and abilities of the members.

In his book, *The Nature of the Church*, Radmacher lists six metaphors that amplify the dynamics of the Church. These six bring out the solid foundation on which we stand, the protection it offers, the source of direction, the sacrificial nature of its servants, the sensitivity of the bride and bridegroom, and the solidarity of its parts. Note Radmacher's comments:

"In the present study the criterion for the inclusion of a particular figure was its specific contribution to and elucidation of the New Testament doctrine of the corporate universal church. Therefore, those listed by Chafer are the ones herein investigated with the exception of 'the Last Adam and the New Creation' which this writer feels has more individual and cosmic significance than contribution to the explanation of the corporate church." Radmacher, *The Nature of the Church*, p. 222.

Christ's Mercy is seen in the Building Metaphor

Paul and Peter both refer to the Church in metaphor as a building—not a building in the physical sense, but with the characteristics of a building. It is a safe place, a lighthouse in a dark world. All buildings naturally have a foundation and Paul clearly indicates the Foundation has already been laid (Eph. 2:20-22).

It is a spiritual building not made with hands. It rests on the foundation of which Jesus Christ is the Chief Cornerstone. Jesus said to Peter, "On this rock I will build My church and the gates of Hades shall not prevail against it" (Mat. 16:18). That Rock is Christ Jesus and it is the same spiritual Rock that followed the Israelites in the wilderness (1 Cor. 10:4). It is the same stone spoken of in Ephesians: "Jesus Christ Himself being the chief cornerstone" (Eph. 2:20).

The Foundation

This architectural term, the cornerstone, refers to the first stone laid in a new building. It was usually a specially designed stone made sometimes of gold or silver. Not only was it ceremonially valuable, it was placed strategically for establishing lines and direction for the foundation as well as the rest of the building. Another very important factor is that it gives support to the building. So the building of which you are a part has a beautiful and sound basis in the Chief Cornerstone.

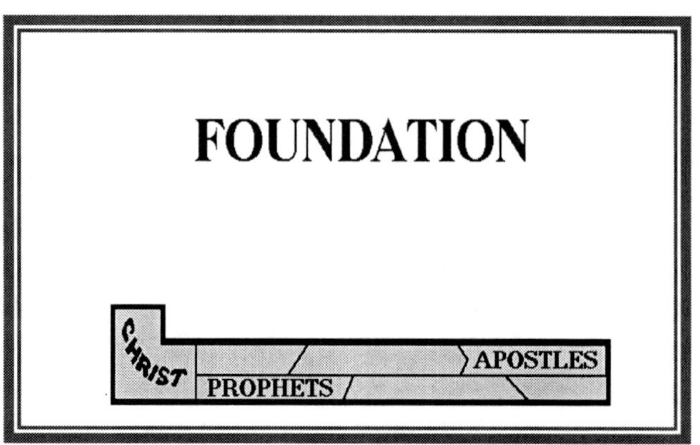

How did He build the foundation? Paul identifies Christ as the Chief Cornerstone. Now He begins the process of selecting the stones for the foundation. All these stones came from the Israeli stone quarry. He spent three years personally preparing these living stones to fit into a special place. He did not entrust this work to anyone. It was not until this work was finished that the world powers were able to touch Him, and He said his time was at hand. Then finally on the cross, He said that the work was finished. Then in Acts 2, He laid the foundation, consisting of Christ as the Chief Cornerstone and then the apostles and prophets (Eph. 2:20). He has torn down the dividing wall (Eph. 2:14). Radmacher comments on the foundation:

"The foundation of the building, the universal church, consists of persons, namely the apostles and prophets of the present dispensation in its initial stages. It is significant to note that the foundation is not Peter; he is only a part with the others of the foundation. Thus, this verse as well as Peter's own discussion in 1 Peter 2:4-7 should be helpful commentaries on Matthew 16:18." Radmacher, *The Nature of the Church*, p. 260.

The formation began on the day of Pentecost. After His resurrection, Jesus gathered the apostles and prophets in the upper room where the Holy Spirit descended and filled the room. They were all submerged in the Holy Spirit and the foundation was complete. They were now ready, trained and thoroughly equipped for the building of the superstructure (Acts 2:3).

The Superstructure

All those stones on which the whole building is being built and everyone who has believed since that day of Pentecost, has been fitted into a special niche in the superstructure. We who believe today are being joined—as living stones—to take our place as a physical part of His building, amalgamating His divine qualities to our contemporary qualities.

This is a spiritual building and if you are not properly functioning, then you allow the walls to be penetrated by forces of darkness or spiritual forces of wickedness (Eph. 6:12). We have each been given a task, commissioned as His ambassadors in the world. Paul refers to our position in the world as ambassadors with a message and ministry of reconciliation:

"... you also, as living stones, are being built up as a spiritual house for a holy priesthood, to offer up spiritual sacrifices acceptable to God through Jesus Christ" (1 Pet. 2:5).

Finally, this building has a future. This building is the dwelling place of the Holy Spirit and you are a part of that building.

> "In Him, you also trusted, after you heard the word of truth, the gospel of your salvation; in whom also, having believed, you were sealed with the Holy Spirit of promise, who is the guarantee of our inheritance until the redemption of the purchased possession, to the praise of His glory" (Eph. 1:13-14).

You have been chosen for a strategic place in this building and this special place guarantees you an inheritance in his Kingdom. Your protection and security—even now as you read this—has been guaranteed until the final redemption of all those who are His. Your future has been sealed by the Holy Spirit until He, Christ, comes for you—His Bride.

Christ's Mercy is seen in the Bride Metaphor

This illustrative metaphor brings out the deep sensitivity of the bridegroom for His Bride. The subject is unconditional love. His love is the vehicle through which He demonstrates His mercy. In Ephesians, Paul captures this sensitivity and protection (Eph. 5:23-24).

The Ephesians passage covers the betrothal period or the preparation of the Bride and the fact that Christ laid down His life for her. He lived as a servant for 33 years, ultimately dying on the cross for her in order that He might set her apart; that she would be cleansed and that He might present her as the perfect bride at the wedding alluded to in the Revelation passage. Radmacher comments on the Bride metaphor:

> "Having rejected the theory that the church as the bride is entirely future and the theory that the church as the bride is the past Jewish church, there is a third alternative which this writer believes to be the correct one. The church, the bride of Christ, includes all those who have put their faith in Christ in this age of grace which had its beginning at Pentecost and will continue until the Bridegroom comes to receive His bride unto himself to consummate the marriage. Although the bride of Christ is the same group as the body of Christ, this figure brings out certain distinctive ideas which were not displayed by the body metaphor." Radmacher, *The Nature of the Church*, p. 246.

This is an overwhelming picture of the great love and mercy Christ has for the Church, His bride. You are a very important part of the Bride, a continuing recipient of this unconditional love that should flow through you as a vehicle meeting needs in others. His love is the vehicle for your spiritual gift. Christ never stops giving. It is by this love you are united with all the rest of the parts. Note the characteristics of this love: "and walk in love, just as Christ also loved you, and gave Himself up for you, an offering and a sacrifice to God as a fragrant aroma" (Eph. 5:2).

This metaphor demonstrates unconditional unity—the fact that this relationship or betrothal is inseparable. It is binding until Christ comes for the bride. According to Jewish customs, to break the betrothal required a bill of divorcement, which according to Matthew 19:8-9, could only be given for uncleanness or as indicated in Leviticus 18, where incest was involved. The idea was that this betrothal period is permanent. In fact, He says, "I will never leave you" (Heb. 13:5). In another place He says, "And surely I am with you always, to the very end of the age" (Mat. 28:20). You are to be His bride permanently.

The picture illustrates His uncompromising position. He has given you a seal (as in an engagement ring) by the indwelling Holy Spirit (Eph: 1:13). You are in a position to receive all the privileges of a bride. Paul adds his concern for you, "For I am jealous for you with a godly jealousy; for I betrothed you to one husband, that to Christ I might present you as a pure virgin" (2 Cor. 11:2).

93

This picture we receive from the Bride metaphor is the ultimate glory. In all the passages, the ultimate goal is the great wedding that will take place at the coming of the Bridegroom for His Bride. This is a picture of the Church. We are in the betrothal, or the preparation period. The ceremony is the next event. Christ the Bridegroom will come to the home of the bride to take her to His home. The main part of the ceremony occurs when the Bridegroom takes the Bride into His house to forever be with Him. Note Radmacher's comment:

> "It will be the bride's exalted privilege to reign with the King of Kings. 'In that sense in which other citizens are subjects,' writes Chafer, 'the wife of the king is not subject of the king. As the word consort suggests, she is a co-sharer in his reign.' Finally, after the celebration of the marriage the bridegroom takes his bride to their new home. He usually prepares a place for her before the marriage supper takes place. So while the church, the bride of Christ, makes herself ready for the marriage supper, Christ, the Bridegroom, prepares a place for her." Radmacher, *The Nature of the Church*, p. 25.

His Mercy is seen in the Branch Metaphor

This metaphor emphasizes the source of fruit-bearing. Why? It is because they are vitally and organically connected to the vine. This is the figure Jesus uses to give us a picture of the vital union of the believer as the branch and Christ as the Vine. The early Church knew no members that were not connected to the Vine. John gives us this beautiful picture in Jn. 15:1-8.

A grape branch is only good for one thing and that is to bear fruit. A branch may be cut off the vine and within seconds the leaves will begin to wilt. You are a branch and you will only bear fruit as you are vitally connected to the vine. Jesus said, "I am the vine." What is the vine? Where do the vines end and the branches begin? Hudson Taylor paints a beautiful picture of the relationship between the vine and the branches.

> "Nor was this all He showed me, nor one half. As I thought of the vine and the branches, what light the blessed Spirit poured direct into my soul! How great seemed my mistake in wishing to get the sap, the fullness out of Him! I saw not only that Jesus will never leave me, but that I am a member of His body, of His flesh and of His bones. The vine in not the root merely, but all—root, stem, branches, twigs, leaves flowers, fruit. And Jesus in not that alone—He is soil and sunshine, air and showers, and ten thousand times more than we have ever dreamed, wished for or needed. Oh, the joy of seeing this truth! I so pray that the eyes of your understanding too may be enlightened, that you may know and enjoy the riches freely given us in Christ." Howard Taylor, *Hudson Taylor's Spiritual Secrets*, p. 261.

To make a practical application, the vine is the Church, and you—as part of the vine—are vitally connected to the vine as a branch. What is the branch? It is the part of the vine that bears fruit and it is the part of the vine that people see. That is what you are!

Did you ever see a grapevine struggle or have a nervous breakdown bearing fruit? No! Grapevines are just content in bearing fruit. That is their special gift, their special purpose in living—just to bear fruit. This is an overwhelming lesson in metaphor. You have a special minister of mercy, a special purpose, and God has given you a gift to accomplish this purpose and all He asks you to do is just abide in Him and let Him do the rest. For without Him you can do nothing. Note Radmacher's comments:

> "Because they are branches in the Vine, the fruit which is produced is not their fruit.
> The branches simply bear the fruit, and the fruit is the life of Christ Himself which the Holy
> Spirit will form in every member of the church who is abiding in the Vine. This life of Christ

which the Holy Spirit forms in them will be manifested in love for the brethren—the other branches of the Vine." Radmacher, *The Nature of the Church*, p. 299.

Christ's Mercy is seen in the Priesthood Metaphor

This metaphor illustrates God's mercy toward His people because Jesus is the High Priest caring and ministering to His children through His priests, which we are. He was the perfect sacrifice that provided the payment for our sins. You are very special. You have been commissioned a priest and not just an ordinary priest. You are a royal priest, not just a priest as spoken of in the Old Testament. They were concerned with the physical temple and dead sacrifices. You are a priest in a spiritual temple; one who offers up living sacrifices. The Old Testament priests' sacrifices were to atone for sin. Your sacrifice is *you*, being dedicated to function in your gifted area, challenging men and women who are in sin to be reconciled to Christ who has made atonement for their sin. But, even beyond that, you are ministering to the Body to deter the people from sinning. "Love (the vehicle for spiritual gifts.) shall cover a multitude of sin" (1 Pet. 4:8). You are God's minister of mercy.

This special privilege gives you direct access to the throne of grace. You don't need a mediator to intercede for you, because you are an intercessor and can call on Him at any time in any place. Christ, the great high priest, is our example. The responsibility of a priest is serving in the temple. Therefore, one of the basic characteristics of a priest is a servant's heart. We confirmed from 2 Tim. 3 that the scriptures were thoroughly furnished for certain things in order that the man of God may be perfected (2 Tim. 3:17). The idea here is that you are complete, able to function in a godly way.

> "Wherever they are, whoever they may be, however they may rate socially, whatever their denominational connections are, if they are true believers, they belong to this royal priesthood. All together they form a priesthood. The church is not an oligarchy where a few have authority to dictate to the many, nor is it a sacerdotal religion in which there is a class of priests with special privileges." Radmacher, *The Nature of the Church*, p. 279.

Christ is our example of a servant. He gave up all His rights to exist with God in glory in order to come into time and space as a man. I might add He became the lowest kind of man—a servant—and was obedient unto death, the death of the cross.

The characteristic mentioned is "the mind of Christ." The battle is for your mind. Wrong thinking demands a change. Paul says, "Don't be conformed to this world but be transformed by the renewing of your mind that you may prove what the will of God is" (Rom. 12:2). This whole process is a reprogramming of the mind, translating our thinking from the natural or temporal realm to the supernatural or eternal realm.

This is the battleground. The Holy Spirit desires to control your mind with the principles Christ taught when He was here. From the world, the demonic forces desire to neutralize your mind by influencing your emotions. The solution then is to resist the world forces and they will flee from you, then draw near to God (right thinking) and He will draw near to you (Ja. 4:7-10). Radmacher states the difficulty clearly:

> "The battle lines are drawn pretty tight aren't they? Satan, the god of this world system, assaults my thinking with stimuli which are designed to pull me down and make me ineffective for God, and the Holy Spirit desires to guide me into the truth—to help me to think straight about God and his will so that I may be effective as a Christian." Radmacher, *You and Your Thoughts*, p. 299.

Our mandate then, is to exercise the God given computer-like organ we call the brain. We must be diligent in the study of the whole counsel of God; in order that we may faithfully exercise or utilize those

God-given spiritual abilities as a workman who is not ashamed, always sincere in accurately handling the Word (Mind of Christ) of God. Humility is a special attitude that places us in a position to receive grace from God. Not all Christians are in a position to appropriate the grace of God, only those who humble themselves in obedience to God. James says, "God is opposed to the proud but gives grace to the humble" (Ja. 4:7). Humility is the opposite of pride. It has the idea of lowliness, to keep moving oneself back. As Jesus said, "The last shall be first" (Mat. 19:30). Such a person is one who is humble in the things of the world, but alert and active; one who is not entangled in the affairs of this world; one who is unassuming and always seeking to meet the needs of others.

Paul succinctly describes this priestly attitude. This quality is diametrically opposed to everything we have learned from the philosophy of the world. To be merciful demands a submissive spirit. The idea here is to fit into God's divine arrangement. Jesus gives us a dramatic picture in His humiliation process.

> "Let this mind be in you which was also in Christ Jesus, who being in the form of God, did not consider it robbery to be equal with God, but made Himself of no reputation, taking the form of a bondservant, *and* coming in the likeness of men. And being found in appearance as a man, He humbled Himself and became obedient to *the point of* death, even the death of the cross" (Phil. 2:5-8).

There are three things that are necessary for the submissive spirit. First, you should work through the Emptying Process (note the Beatitude chart); second, humble yourself; and third, become obedient to the way of the cross. Obedience is an integral part of faith. Faith involves knowing the facts will result in a feeling (giving confirmation to what you know), and also results in volitional acts. Without faith, it is impossible to please God (Heb. 11:6).

The product of all this is a servant leader. Christ—by His obedience and self-denial—has sovereign control over all things. He has assumed the position as Spiritual head of the Church. Because of what He has done, we too, can experience this leadership. As we develop the mind of Christ and humble ourselves in submission, He will lift us up to a position as a servant leader. Dr. Ira Tunnell, a Christian psychiatrist, in recent years who contributed his time one afternoon each week doing medical treatments for clients with severe depression and other psychiatric conditions that needed his professional care. He has the gift of helps, and never complains or grumbles about a lack of appreciation from our clients. He just faithfully continues to treat them week after week. I might add that he's not doing it for money, as he contributes his time to the counseling center. The point I want to make is that he has earned a position of authority by his humility. Everyone has high regard for him because of his love for helping people. He is involved in His priestly function, serving people.

Christ's Mercy is seen in the Flock Metaphor

His mercy is shown through the guidance and protection the shepherd provides for the flock. The flock requires two things: first, a shepherd to watch over, guide, feed and tend them and second, sheep that regularly sacrifice their wool and produce lambs. The parable of the Good Shepherd illustrates how Christ the Good Shepherd has called out His flock from the larger fold, and how it is to function under His leadership. This metaphor best illustrates the relationship of the universal church and the local church. The two ideas of the fold (αυλεν) and the flock (ποιμνε) are presented distinctly. Judaism was the fold out of which the Shepherd called His own sheep by name and led them out. Radmacher comments:

> "But Jesus declared that the Jewish sheep were not the only ones which He had; 'And other sheep I have, which are not of this fold: them also I must bring, and they shall hear my voice; and there shall be one fold (flock) and one shepherd.' (Jn. 10:16) Thus, the flock of Christ is not confined to the Jewish fold." Radmacher, *The Nature of the Church*, p. 285.

First, you need to understand the need for spiritual leadership. You can see from the above text, His flock is made up of Jews and Gentiles. The division has been broken down and He is the Good Shepherd over His flock. He is no respecter of persons; now there can be unity in the Body as you walk worthily in the sphere of His flock. God has only one flock, but they gather in local assemblies divided among many under-shepherds responsible for their care. These men are gifted men given by God to the local church for a special purpose. Paul describes the gifted men for the perfecting of the saints in Eph. 4:11-12. These men are the spiritual leaders in the local church given by Christ the Chief Shepherd. Christ has given to the flock (church) certain men as overseers or under-shepherds. These men are to give leadership to the flock, feeding, disciplining, caring, protecting, restoring, keeping them healthy or discipling them, and training them to disciple others.

The second thing you need to draw from this metaphor is that the sheep are submissive and they respond to the shepherd. Your response to those over you in the Lord should be just as you would respond to Christ. The writer of Hebrews emphasizes your responsibility:

> "Obey those who rule over you, and be submissive, for they watch out for your souls, as those who must give account. Let them do so with joy and not with grief, for that would be unprofitable for you" (Heb. 13:17).

Sheep are very responsive animals when they have proper nourishment. However, when they are not properly feeding or being fed they tend to go astray. The warning here is both to the leaders and to the members. Some churches have fallen into the world's trap. The key for both leader and member is exercise. God has given us all a certain capacity to function and to the extent that we do so; to that extent we will be fulfilled. Everyone has certain needs that can only be filled by actively participating in the Body.

Finally, this metaphor expresses His mercy through the unity He provides through His leadership and through His sensitivity and love. One thing particularly unique about sheep is that they always follow or walk along with the shepherd. They are never driven, lest they scatter in all directions and become lost. Note John's description of what happens:

> "But a hireling, he who is not the shepherd, one who does not own the sheep, sees the wolf coming and leaves the sheep and flees; and the wolf catches the sheep and scatters them" (Jn. 10:12).

Christ's Mercy is seen in the Body Metaphor

His mercy in this metaphor is manifested in the direction given by the Head to the body. The Bible has a lot to say about the body; however the predominant use is as a metaphor of the Church, the body of Christ. Some tend to take this as a plain literal statement. In fact most churches with their roots in Catholicism and most liberal churches would see it this way. They see it as an extension of the incarnation of Christ. For our purpose we will view the body metaphor as a figurative literal statement. What did it mean to the believers who were recipients of these letters, the Romans, the Corinthians, the Ephesians and the Colossians? It would seem obvious that God is revealing to man a word picture of Christ as the preeminent head and the Church as the animated submissive body representing Him in the world. The central thrust of the body metaphor is the vital connection between the head and the members of the body. It is clear in Scripture who the head is. Several passages emphasize Christ's headship.

> "And he put all things under His feet, and gave Him to be head over all things to the church, which is His body, the fullness of Him who fills all in all" (John 10:12).

> "And He is the head of the body, the church, who is the beginning, the firstborn from the dead, that in all things He may have the preeminence" (Col. 1:18).

"And not holding fast to the Head, from whom all the body, nourished and knit together by joints and ligaments, grows with the increase that is from God" (Col. 2:19).

The significance of the head is very important as it controls the whole body. The head not only controls what the body does and does not do, it is the source of all intake into the body; visual, sensual, audible, digestive, and respiratory. In other words, everything the body receives comes through the head. The head controls all systems of the body through the voluntary and involuntary nervous systems as well as the limbic system.

In your infant and childhood years you were uncoordinated and clumsy. Your nervous system had not developed and as a result, your muscular system was not coordinated, resulting in spilled milk, stumbling and other accidents. You were depending totally on your feelings and they were changing every day, resulting in awkward incidents. Intellectual development was the key which would give better control over your body: you learned to depend upon your head.

The same difficulty is experienced spiritually. You are born again as a spiritual infant and begin to grow primarily depending on your feelings. Your knowledge of God is minimal and the result is that you stumble and fall, or more specifically, you sin. At a point in your life you believed in Christ and were born again. At that moment you began to grow up in Him all functions came under the direction of the head. Whether it is a physical, psychological or spiritual function it all comes through the head.

You can now transfer these principles to the relationship of Christ to His Body, the Church. Christ never functions apart from His body and you are a part of that Body. Remember you are not all of His body, only a part; however, you are a special part, with a special function. Paul says, "For as the body is one and has many members, but all the members of that one body, being many, are one body, so also is Christ." (1 Cor. 12:12).

This metaphor demonstrates the need for interdependence on the rest of the body and complete dependence on the head. That is, you have a responsibility to all the other members of the body and they are likewise dependent upon you. This is not a Lone Ranger program; it is a shared load. God desires to work through you as a physical instrument to meet needs in the Body and to have your needs met by other members of the body. So you are important to the function of the body; in fact, it will only function at full capacity if you are operating at full capacity. You have a niche to fill and the other members are dependent upon you.

The purpose of these metaphors is to illustrate the mercy or sensitivity of Christ toward His people. This mercy is manifested by each member functioning in their gift(s), ministering to the needs of the body. Next we need to learn how to develop and manifest the same sensitivity or mercifulness Jesus demonstrated and this demands a perfecting process.

Christ's Body Being Perfected

Because of the devastating fall of Adam and Eve and our natural development under the influence of the world as descendants of Adam and Eve, our brain is controlled by all the paradigms that are stored there. In the Emptying Process we have been in the process of removing all the bitterness, guilt and un-forgiveness. In the discovery area we begin the process of filling. First we looked at hunger and thirst, or renewing our mind concerning spirituals—or a spiritual paradigm shift.

Here under *merciful*, we have looked at the nature of the Church and how the sensitivity of Christ is manifested by the use of a metaphor by the writers of Scripture. Now we will attempt to answer the question why the church is insensitive to people's needs today and why is it many Christians do not know their gift, much less function in it?

"For it has been declared to me concerning you, my brethren, by those of Chloe's household, that there are contentions among you. Now I say this, that each of you says, 'I am of Paul,' or 'I am of Apollos,' or 'I am of Cephas,' or 'I am of Christ.' Is Christ divided? Was Paul crucified for you? Or were you baptized in the name of Paul?" (1 Cor. 1:11-13).

The Bottom Line Problem

This problem was evident as early as the Church in Corinth. Paul was very troubled when he saw the division and conflicts they were experiencing, and those divisions were not unlike those experienced by most churches today, even evangelical conservatives. What is the bottom line problem? I am afraid we have lost sight of some fundamental principles regarding Christ's perfecting of His Body the Church. The Church is not a place for perfect people. It is a hospital where sick people come to get well. The late Dr. J. Vernon McGee used to say, "There is no perfect Church! If you find one don't join it. You will ruin it." The church is a place where members minister to members in their gifted abilities in order that they keep strong to reach out to those in the world who are sick and dying" (Eph. 4:11-12).

The term *pop music* alludes to whatever music is popular and what everyone is doing. I'm afraid the Church has adopted the same tactics and buys into whatever is popular. We could call it *Pop Christianity*. :

POP CHRISTIANITY

1. Divorce—for any cause.	5. Women selected as elders.
2. Partying in the Church.	6. Justification based on works.
3. Unmarried couples living together.	7. Social drinking, smoking, etc.
4. Total emphasis on justification.	

How does God look at these things in a popular culture? Are these things acceptable just because churches allow them? I'm not saying all these things are evil or wrong, but this is the subtle way the world operates. Something becomes popular in the world, and in a short time, it has penetrated the church. This happens when the saints have not been properly perfected, either by choice or by ignorance. More often than not, it's because of a lack of knowledge. This happens in many churches because they have neglected the basic leadership positions God has given to the church. Paul gave specific instructions in Eph. 4 for the leadership to prevent what is happening in churches today.

The Foundation of the Church

We noted before that the foundation of the church is made up of the apostles and prophets, and Jesus Christ is the Chief Cornerstone. The foundation or the New Testament apostles and prophets provided the resources for the superstructure to rest upon, which is the Apostles Doctrine or the Scriptures, and Jesus Christ our Savior and Sustainer.

The apostles and prophets were eyewitnesses of Christ and were taught by Him for over three years, and He appeared to them after His resurrection. They performed miracles and many signs and wonders (2 Cor. 12:11-13, Heb. 1:1-4, 2:4). They were also present at His ascension to the right hand of the Father. Since the foundation has been laid and their work is complete; there are no apostles today.

The apostles and prophets in the early Church did receive direct revelation from God and were the writers of scripture. They both foretold the future and in their lifetime, they preached the truths of Scripture. Their work is finished—the Scriptures are complete. We do not have apostles and prophets today receiving new revelation from God. However, we do have gifted men (Evangelist, Pastors and Teachers) who proclaim the Word or the Apostles' Doctrine today.

The Builders of the Church

The builders of the superstructure or the Church in the world today are the Evangelist, Pastors and Teachers. The foundation has been built now the superstructure is in the process being built upon that foundation. This is the process the Church is in today and we have the same responsibilities that were given to the early Church. God has given every church three positions as full time ministers that are absolutely necessary for the perfecting of the saints: the evangelist, the pastor, and the teacher.

We have already discussed the gifts given to believers, but now we want to see why most believers do not function as instruments of the trinity accomplishing the work of ministry. It is because there has been a breakdown in the leadership of many churches. The saints in many cases are not being perfected. Let's look at the responsibilities of these three men and how they can accomplish God's purpose in the local Church.

The Evangelist

What comes to your mind when you hear the word *evangelist*? If you are like most Christians, your answers might be an itinerant preacher, one who leads people to Christ, or who preaches at revivals. If I asked you to give me a name, you would probably say Billy Graham and he is an evangelist, but when he stands in the pulpit preaching at a crusade that is not the work of an evangelist. He is exercising his spiritual gift of preaching.

What, then, is an evangelist? The word *evangelist* (ευαγγελιστεσ) has to do with the message of good news. The responsibility of the evangelist then, is to equip the saints to do the work of evangelism. That is to train the members of the Church in their spiritually gifted area to be able to prepare a person to present the gospel in a simple, logical and persuasive way. The evangelist should be able to share his faith with the unbelieving, in fact he *must*. But that is evangelism, and we all are responsible to do that. The evangelist is responsible for motivating and training every member of the local Church to evangelize their contemporaries (2 Tim. 4:5). Like an obstetrician, he does not deliver babies. The mother delivers babies. The evangelist is like an obstetrician who teaches the mother how to have a healthy live birth. So the evangelist teaches the saints how to share their faith and lead people to Christ.

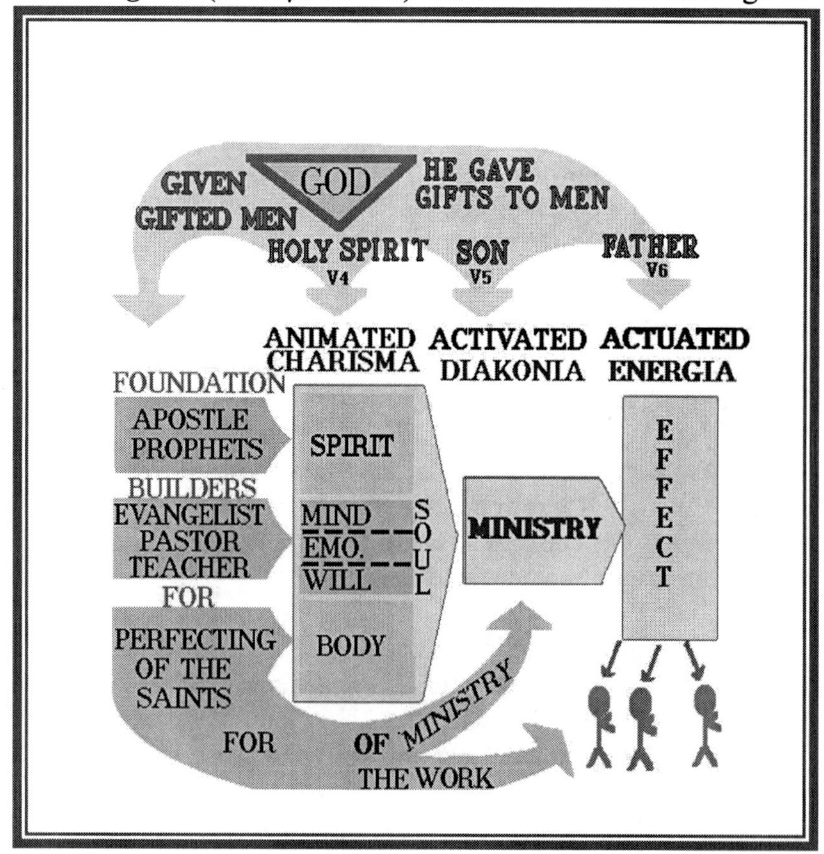

The Pastor

What do you think of when you hear the word *pastor*? Most often, we think of the one who preaches every Sunday. The word used here is ποιμεν, which translates "shepherd." The idea is one who shepherds the flock. He provides pastoral care and discipleship for the young or carnal believers in the local church. He helps them in taking care of their personal needs. When they are hungry, he may give them a fish, but also teaches them how to fish unless they are unable to do so. Then he notifies gifted ones of the body who can meet those needs. When one member is in trouble, the church rushes to the rescue. The saints (members of the body) are to be equipped to do the work of ministry. Each member, by his gift motivates other members to do the work of ministry.

The pastor then, is responsible for motivating and training each member of the body in how to disciple new believers or new members of the body, to share their gifted ability. The pastor, similar to a pediatrician, teaches in words and actions, how to care for children in a way that will produce a healthy child.

The Teacher

What comes to your mind when you hear *teacher*? We would naturally think of a Sunday School teacher or school teacher, but here it is used for a special man, called by God, for a special position in the Church. The word comes from the Greek word διδασκαλοσ, meaning "teacher," "Rabbi," or often "master." It was used by Nicodemus when he said "you are a teacher come from God" (Jn. 3:2). Jesus was the Master Teacher, a high position and great responsibility.

The word *doctrine* (διδαχη) is closely related to teacher. To put it in another way, doctrine is what the teacher teaches. He is commissioned to insure that every member of the Body has access to the teaching of the whole counsel of God. He is responsible for overseeing the education of every member of the Body in systematic theology.

The Builders of the Superstructure

These three men are given to the Church for the perfecting of the saints (Eph. 4:12). They are called men with specific responsibilities; namely Evangelism, Pastoral Care, and Education. They form a team that is designed by God to give leadership to the Body in the three most important areas of need in most churches today. There is a need for evangelism—every member trained and experienced in evangelizing. There is a need for education—every member well-balanced in systematic theology. There is a need for pastoral care—every member being discipled.

God is always the center of everything. He is the source of life and being; therefore, we picture Him as the controller of all things as the Father, Son and Holy Spirit, the trinity; each person having the same attributes but each manifested in a unique way.

Next we see the elders, who are God's overseers of the function of His physical Body in the world. The elders would include the three called men, namely the evangelist (evangelism), pastor (pastoral care), and teacher (education). They are charged with the responsibility of perfecting the saints for the work of ministry and in turn give leadership to the deacons.

The deacons are managers who affect the plans and ideas of the elders. They give guidance to the saints in implementing, or actually performing, the work of the ministry that is evangelism, pastoral care and education. The saints, or the individual members of the Body, are the ones who do the work of the ministry under the leadership of the elders and management of the deacons. They develop a ministry around their gift and are given definite tasks to perform in the area of evangelism, pastoral care, and education.

When each part of the Body is functioning in each member's calling, it will produce the sensitivity and mercifulness manifested by Christ Himself. We are His Body. How long do we keep on doing these things?

"Till we all come to the unity of the faith and the knowledge of the Son of God, to a perfect man, to the measure of the stature of the fullness of Christ; that we should no longer be children tossed to and fro and carried about by every wind of doctrine, by the trickery of men, in the cunning craftiness by which they lie in wait to deceive" (Eph. 4:13-14)

The following chart illustrates the purpose of each of these men: Note the diagram of Eph. 4:11-12.

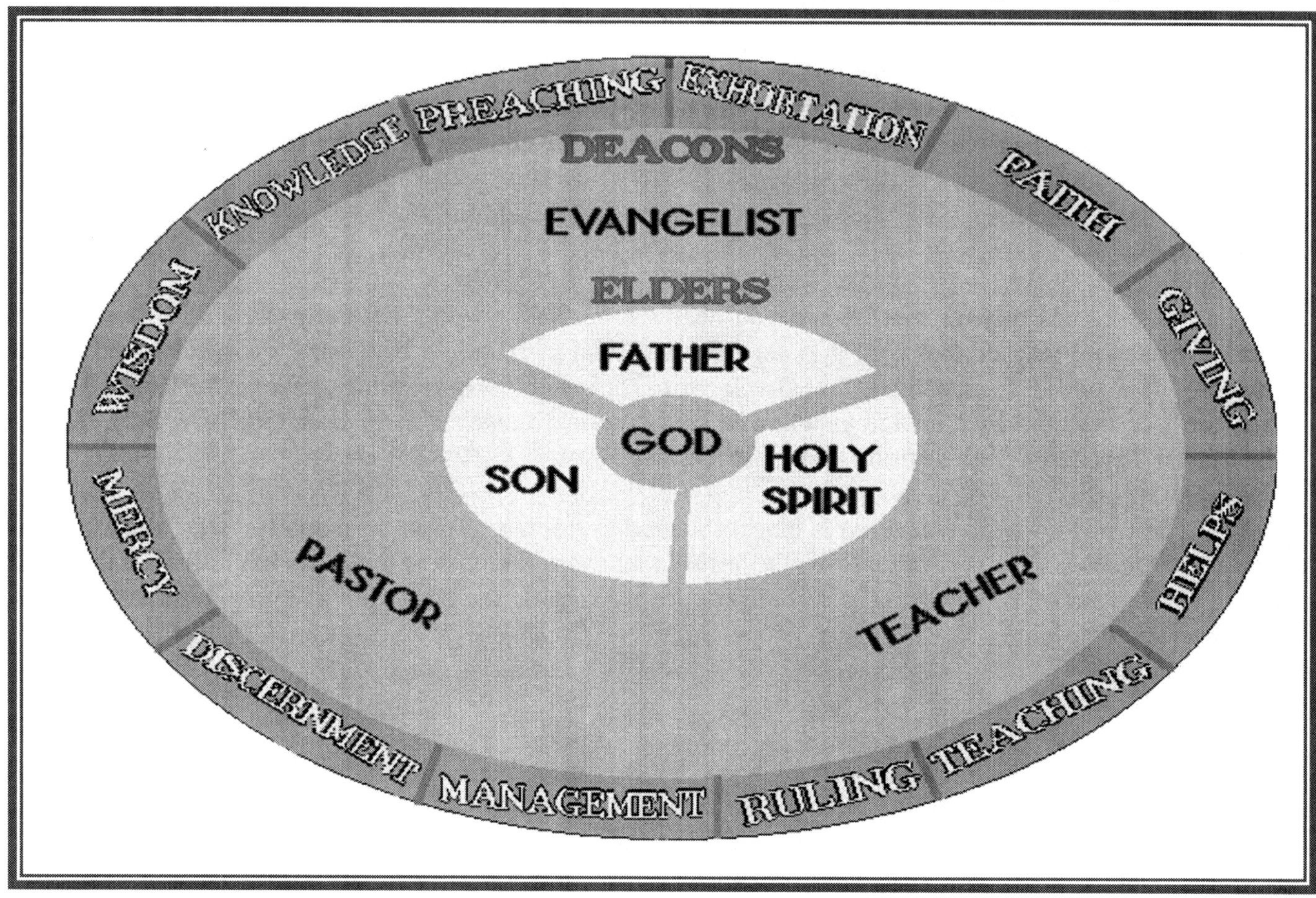

PROJECT

1. What makes up the foundation of the Church?

2. What is God's promise to the merciful?

3. What is the definition of the Church?

4. Define the nature of a servant's heart.

5. Does a Church ever come short of any of the gifts?

6. Do gifts differ from talents?

7. Who are the gifted men to the Church?

8. What is the responsibility of the evangelist?

9. What is the responsibility of the pastor?

10. What is the responsibility of the teacher?

"Blessed are the pure in heart, for they shall see God." Mat. 5:8

John was a middle-aged man with a family that was grown and gone from home; he seemingly had a good marriage—his wife related to him well. However, he was unable to keep a job and his children had rebelled against him. He did not involve himself in the ministry of his church, although he participated in several other ministries outside the church. He was severely distraught and his comments indicated that nothing was going well. After reflecting on his childhood, there remained several areas that were questionable. He had lived with his grandfather, from age four to ten, after his mother was divorced from his father. Most of his personality was developed in those years. His image of God was severely distorted by the divorce, compounded by the permissive attitude of his grandfather and then by his mother's remarriage.

Needless to say, his authority image was distorted and very confusing. Over the years, he had developed a perfectionist personality. His attitude was that this would never happen to his family, but as you might imagine, through a long chain of events, it did. I don't mean the same circumstances, but the same inner attitudes of conceit and failure to respect authority were translated down from the third and fourth generations to his children.

John had made up his mind in those early years that he was his own authority, and subsequently had real problems in relationships with his mother, step-father and others. He also had difficulty in school with regard to accepting authority (not so much outwardly, but inwardly). This problem was apparent in relationships with employers, who one after another released him, primarily for his independent spirit. He had not worked on a regular basis for over two years—he was unable to keep a job. Finally, he transferred that same image to his pastor, unwilling to accept his authority. John resigned from his position as deacon and ceased functioning in the church.

There began a search for fulfillment outside the church. He became alienated from his children, his job and his church. With his wife working and providing for the family, is it any wonder he was distraught? Well, the Lord was not finished with John. God has provided everything we need for life and godliness. So we began to examine his life through reflecting on the past. You see, although he had cleared up many conflicts in the past, he did not have a pure heart and that became apparent by his lack of activity in the church.

First, he worked through the process of clearing his conscience with those he had overlooked—his grandparents (he had already confessed to his parents and wife), his three children, four previous employers and his pastor. There perhaps would be others and the process would continue. It was interesting that the next day, after he had finished and had a clear conscience, one of his former employers called and asked him to come back to work. Amazing Grace!

Second, we began a process of developing the authority image he had not received in those early years; the personality characteristics that will insure a pure heart. Notice Paul's exhortation regarding the value of a pure heart:

> "To the pure all things are pure; but to those who are defiled and unbelieving, nothing is pure, but both their mind and their conscience are defiled. They profess to know God, but by their deeds they deny Him, being detestable and disobedient and worthless for any good deed" (Titus 1:15-16).

This was a little extreme, but John could really see how badly he had been deceived and how desperately he needed to change his mind in several areas. Paul describes the personality traits of a godly man or woman. These distinctions are given as a minimal level of development for a pure heart.

Defining the Word

The word *purity* is from the Greek word καθαροσι, from which we get the English word CARTHASIS (καθαρσιο). The idea is "to purify by cleansing or purging; to remove any impurities." This same word was used by Jesus when He said to Peter, "He who is bathed needs only to wash his feet" (Jn. 13:10). The verb *to wash* is καθαροσι. Jesus was saying to Peter that we have been born again (salvation); now we must go on dealing with sin in the present (sanctification). James uses it, "Cleanse (καθαροσ) your hands you sinners," meaning "to exhort," or "to deal with any present sin." There are other words that translate *purity*. In the above verse James says "purify (αγνιζω) your hearts you double-minded" (Ja. 4:8), which means to purify our hearts from past sins.

Manifested by Christ

Being pure in heart is another of the characteristics Christ manifested while He was here. The Psalmist portrays Christ in prophecy:

> "Who may ascend into the hill of the Lord? Or who may stand in His holy place? He
> who has clean hands and a pure heart, who has not lifted up his soul to an idol-" (Ps. 24:3-4).

The heart is synonymous with the soul. It has to do with the mind, emotions and the will, acting together with regard to moral issues. The opposite of a pure heart is a hardened (σκληροσ) heart (καρδια), a foolish heart, an evil heart or one who deceives his heart. The pure heart is highly exalted in Scripture (1 Tim. 5:22, Ja. 1:26, 3:17; 1 Tim. 1:5; and 2 Tim. 2:22; Jn. 3:3).

Purity Proclaimed by James

The disciple must develop the stability to stay above circumstances; to be able to deal with sin while it is in the mind before it becomes an action that will affect others. James gives us the source of all these principles we have buried in the old man thought patterns, controlled by the wisdom of this world that is earthly (physical), that is sensual (psychological and demonic (spiritual). Note James' development of this:

> "But if you have bitter envy and self-seeking in your hearts, do not boast and lie
> against the truth. This wisdom does not descend from above, but is earthly, sensual,
> demonic. For where envy and self-seeking exist, confusion and every evil thing are there"
> (Ja. 3:14-16).

Then he develops the source of purity. Purity is not of this world, it is a characteristic of God. It is having one's conscience cleared, and the ability to see things from God's perspective. Our old paradigms were clouded by our natural development in an impure environment. Impurity is like a dirty windshield on a car; you cannot see the road clearly and if it is bad enough you will not be able to see at all. Purity then is sourced in God. James lists it as the first in a series of characteristics of God's wisdom. "But the wisdom that is from above is first pure, then peaceable, gently, willing to yield, full of mercy and good fruits, without partiality and without hypocrisy. Now the fruit of righteousness is sown in peace by those who make peace" (Ja. 3:17-18).

The next level in developing a pure heart is to recognize the cause of impurity. We have already seen the kind of wisdom that comes from the world. It is earthly, sensual and demonic. James identifies it.

> "Where do wars and fights come from among you? Do they not come from your desires for pleasure that war in your members? You lust and do not have. You murder and covet and cannot obtain. You fight and war. Yet you do not have because you do not ask" (Ja. 4:1-2).

The disciples then learn to deal with the consequence of impurity. God always answers prayer; however, when a prayer is selfish or not within his will, He responds negatively. A faithless prayer is never within God's will. In our development years, we have been so conditioned to doing what comes naturally or flirting with the world; we don't realize how much we resist God to satisfy our own selfish pleasures. God is a jealous God, and yearns for us to believe Him or place our faith in Him. God does not take our resistance lightly. In fact, He hates the attitude of self-righteousness or personal rights. But He gives grace to those who humble themselves. Note how James illustrates this:

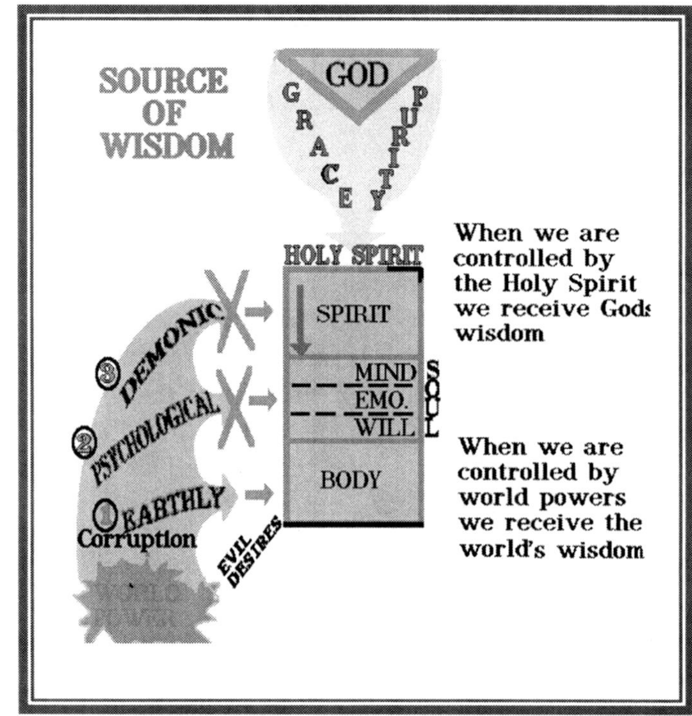

> "You ask and do not receive, because you ask amiss, that you may spend it on your pleasures. Adulterers and adulteresses! Do you not know that friendship with the world is enmity with God? Whoever therefore wants to be a friend of the world makes himself an enemy of God. Or do you think that the Scripture says in vain 'The Spirit who dwells in us yearns jealously?' But He gives more grace. Therefore He says: 'God resists the proud, But gives grace to the humble'" (Ja. 4:3-6).

That brings us to the next level—how to humble oneself. This level has to do with the cure for impurity. This process is not unlike what Jesus taught in the Beatitudes. In fact, this is another way of presenting the Emptying Process. James develops the Emptying Process for a progressive development of purity.

James has given us a distinct process for purifying the heart. This is a further amplification of the Emptying Process given in the Beatitudes by Christ. Here in Ja. 4:7-10, are ten aorist imperatives indicating the strongest commands possible. Note the words:

<u>POOR IN SPIRIT</u>
> "Therefore submit to God. Resist the devil and he will flee from you. Draw near to God and He will draw near to you. Cleanse your hands you sinners" (Ja. 4:7-8a).

<u>MOURN</u>
> "Purify your hearts you double minded. Lament and mourn and weep, let your laughter be turned to mourning and your joy to gloom" (Ja. 4:8b-9).

<u>MEEK</u>
> "Humble yourselves in the sight of the Lord, and He will lift you up" (Ja. 4: 10).

Note the strong commands in this text:

1. υποταγητε (passive)—Be aligned under God's authority.
2. αντιστητε (active)—Resist the Devil.
3. εγγισατε (active)—Draw near to God.
4. καθαρισατε (active)—Cleanse your hands.
5. αγωισατε (active)—Purify your hearts.
6. ταλαιπωρσατε (active)—Endure misery.
7. πενθησατε (active)—Mourn.
8. κλαυσατε (active)—Cry
9. μετατραπητω (passive)—Your joy turned to gloom.
10. ταπεινωθητε (passive)—Be humbled.

Our mandate is to continue the process of developing inner purity. Since most of our conflicts and broken relationships occur in our close relationships, we will look at some practical ways, given by Paul, to accomplish this task. We will start with Fathers since they are the spiritual leaders of the home or the God image to their family.

Demanded of a Husband and Father

First, we will examine the masculine distinctive, or the responsibility of a husband and father. Your first responsibility as a spiritual leader is to be sure that you and your family are worshipping in a church that is not only based on sound Biblical principles, but that this doctrine is being practiced also. You should use Titus 1: 15-16 as a checklist when you are trying to decide whether or not to become a member of a church. However, if you are already a member, be careful not to cause division in the body. In Titus 2, we find the characteristics designed for each member of the family. Paul starts in verse 1 with fathers. These are the qualities God has given for men:

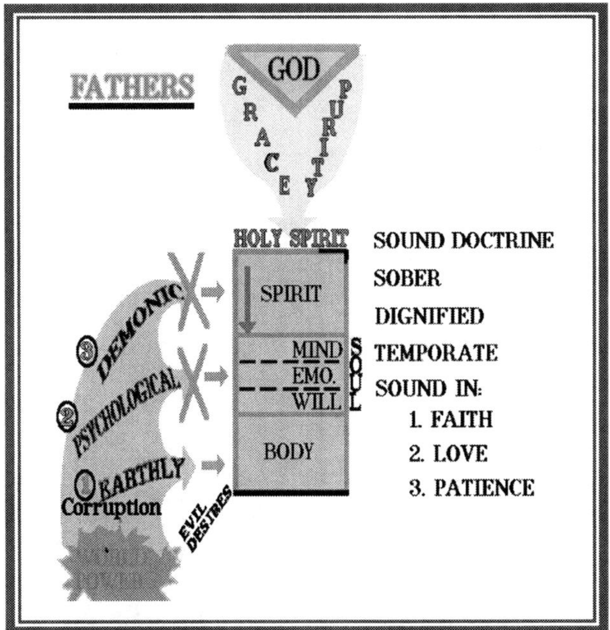

Sound Doctrine

The first quality is *sound doctrine*, from υγιαινουση διδ–ασκαλια, meaning a "sound, safe, doctrine or teaching." As a man you are—whether you like it or not—designed to be a teacher. You are a spiritual leader and one who is responsible for the guidance of others. Therefore, you must develop a system of sound doctrine. The word *sound* means "wholesome, healthy, vigorous," in contrast to being watered down, empty and diseased by the pollution of the world. The word *doctrine* (διδαχη) comes from the word *doctor* (διδασκαλοσ), and sometimes "teacher", which in this case involves the things Christ taught and did, as well as the Apostles' Doctrine (Acts 1:1, 2:42).

You then, as a man have the responsibility to continually teach sound doctrine from the Scriptures. This concept is indicated by Paul when he says the wife is sanctified "with the washing of water by the Word" (Eph. 5:26). Here the Word is used metaphorically as a spiritual cleansing agent. Paul again uses this concept regarding the husband as a sanctifying agent: "the unbelieving wife is sanctified by the husband" (1 Cor. 7:14). The indication here is that the husband has a vital roll in the development of his wife's inner purity or a pure heart.

Sober

The second quality is *sober* from νηφω, meaning "free from the influence of intoxicants." Metaphorically, it means to be alert and temperate. You are to be temperate in every area of your life. This word strongly supports sound doctrine; it demands restraints on those deep indulging desires of the flesh developed in those formative years. It involves your thinking, since you are what you think. Your thinking about the food you eat, the clothes you wear, the car you drive, the sports you play, the habits you have, the friends you make, the social life you live, etc. These things, indeed, become you.

The sober man is one who is looking at life from God's point of view. He does not see a difficulty as a problem, but translates that difficulty—designed by God—into a project and proceeds to work through it, by God's grace.

As you develop this quality, you will begin to see through the problems that come your way and be able to discern God's specific project for you. Accordingly, you will discipline yourself to the task of being God's instrument in resolving various difficulties. Not only will this be power in your own life, but as you become victorious, you will begin to see through others problems and be able to guide them into workable solutions.

Reverent

The third quality is *reverent* from σεμνουσ, meaning, "to be dignified," or sometimes "temperate." This is another unique quality of a Christian man. You are to have an obvious godly self-worth. I am not using self-worth as a secular psychologist would use it, but in a Biblical sense; in other words, seeing yourself as God sees you. In that sense, you are a very special person in a very special position, performing a very special purpose.

Reverent then, means to be of "high repute," one who has an honorable position and measures up to that position. You are a child of the King and that makes you royalty. You are in a position of demonstrating the nature of God to a world that cannot see Him (2 Pet. 1:3-4). Jesus Christ was a perfect picture of dignity throughout his life in the flesh. Now He has been resurrected from the dead, ascended on High, and has given you His dignity to go on doing the things He did.

You do have worth! You have been bought with a price. You have been purchased out of the world of sin and selfishness into a sphere of worth and that sphere of worth demands dignity. You have been raised from the dead, literally resurrected to new life to take your position among the dignified. Paul exhorts us to "walk in the manner worthy of the calling with which you have been called" (Eph. 4:1).

Temperate

The fourth quality is *temperate* (from σωφπον), meaning, "sober-minded" or "of a sound mind." It is immediately obvious that this word relates to the mind, but even more importantly, it includes the function of the mind, your thinking process. Paul says, "----not to think more highly than he ought think, but think soberly---" (Rom. 12:3b). The idea here is for you to think rightly about God, yourself, and others.

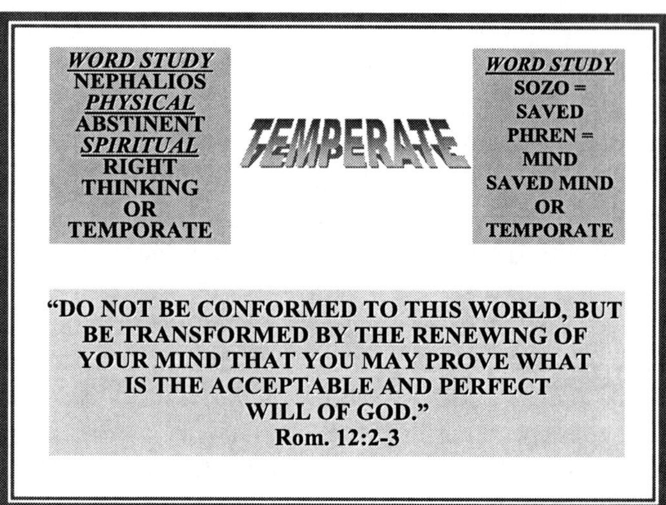

The word comes from two words in the Greek, one meaning "sound"—σωζω—and the other "mind"—φρεν. Therefore, to be sensible is too have a sound or healthy view of things, to look at life from God's point of view. The ability by faith, to rationally accept what God has said about a circumstance, even though you can't understand; to think rightly about God, about self and about relationships.

It is the process of the mind under the control of the Holy Spirit, controlling the emotions and the will, thus activating the body to function sensibly. If you are controlled by the Holy Spirit moment by moment, you will be demonstrating with your life the fruit of the Spirit.

Sound Faith

The fifth quality is *sound faith* from *sound* (υγιαινω), and *faith* (πιστει), translated "sound or healthy in faith." You are a believer and you have been persuaded or drawn by the Holy Spirit to believe supernaturally in a natural world. The participle, sound, in the Greek indicates an active voice with continuous action or a demonstration of faith by faithful living. This is a characteristic of God, manifested through you in a physical way (Tit. 2:2).

In this context Paul is saying that those men who possess these distinctions are the ones being healthy in the faith. The word healthy is in contrast to sick or unhealthy. In contrast to a faith based on temporal values, it is a faith based on things not seen. It is based on the living word: "Faith comes by hearing and hearing by the word of God" (Rom. 10:17).

Faith is the basis for all our actions and is never passive. It involves the mind, *knowing*, the emotions, *feeling*, and the will, *doing*. Sound faith, then, is knowing what you believe in such a way that you feel assured about the idea and so you confidently do it. There is no doubting; you have a sound faith.

Sound Love

The sixth quality is *sound love*, from υγιαινω τη αγαπη, meaning, "sound or healthy in love;" the unconditional love that God is. You are now solidly based in all the above qualities and by faith, they are beginning to radiate through your personality as physical actions of sound love. The word Paul uses here (*agape*) is the highest love, a love Jesus demonstrated through His life, death, burial and resurrection. That love was unconditional and was not dependent on the one being loved. It was a willful and sacrificial love. It is the ability to love the unlovable.

Today there is an extremely dangerous philosophy of "self love" penetrating our society. It has entered the church with seemingly more force than the Reformation. Man, it would appear, has discovered that the answer to most of his problems is falling in love with himself. This is not sound love it is false teaching. There is only two commands - they are: "love the Lord" and "love your neighbor", not love yourself. The phrase "as yourself" modifies the command "love your neighbor" (Mat.22:36-40).

In error, the phrase *as you love yourself* is taken as a command, when from Jesus' own words there are only two commands, not three. His commands are to love God and your neighbor as you naturally love yourself. Paul amplifies the fact that all men naturally love themselves. "So husbands ought to love their own wives as their own bodies; he who loves his wife loves himself. For no one ever hated his own flesh, but nourishes and cherishes it, just as the Lord does the church" (Eph. 5:28-29).

Sound love, then, is not a self love but allowing God to demonstrate His love through you to others. For further study on this danger, read *The Dangers of Self Love* by Dr. Paul Brownback. The love Paul is talking about in Titus 2, is an unconditional response to another person, even when he appears to be unlovable. One must not let the attitude or action of another person determine one's love for that person. A willful continuous action without being dependent on the one being loved is expected.

Sound Patience

The seventh quality is *sound in patience* (περσεϖερενχε from υγιαινω τη υπομονη), meaning an "abiding under" or "patience" which grows only through trials. Now you are able to stand. This is the quality Martin Luther demonstrated before the council when he said, "Here I stand. I shall not be moved." This is the unwavering stability that only comes from a man who is anchored in all these distinctions as a result of abiding in Christ. When everyone else has given up, he is able to patiently endure.

This word, *patience*, just as in the previous verses, is prefaced with the word healthy. This is that special quality that enables a man to stand under suffering. Note Peter's exhortation:

> "Beloved, do not be surprised at the fiery ordeal among you, which comes upon you for your testing; as though some strange thing were happening to you; but to the degree that you share the sufferings of Christ, keep on rejoicing; so that also at the revelation of His glory, you may rejoice with exultation. If you are reviled for the name of Christ, you are blessed, because the Spirit of glory and of God rests upon you. On their part He is blasphemed, but on your part He is glorified. By no means let any of you suffer as a murderer, or thief, or evildoer, or a troublesome meddler; but if anyone suffers as a Christian, let him not feel ashamed, but in that name let him glorify God" (1 Pet. 4:12-16).

This endurance is not something that comes as a result of an emotional high, but as a result of a growth process, as you allow these distinctions to become part of you.

Encouraging Young Men

Next Paul gives the qualities the father must develop in his sons: "Likewise exhort the young men to be sober-minded, in all things showing yourself to be a pattern of good works; in doctrine showing integrity, reverence, incorruptibility, sound in speech that cannot be condemned, that one who is an opponent may be ashamed, having nothing evil to say of you" (Titus 2:6-8).

It is the fathers' responsibility to disciple their sons. You have now been exposed to the masculine distinctions, and my challenge to you is to make a project of each quality that is related to you. With God's help you can develop them all.

Demanded of a Wife and Mother

The next area Paul deals with are the qualities of a wife and mother. These are special qualities that can only be accomplished one way. These abilities are totally dependent upon one's relationship with the

Lord! Any time you fail to entrust yourself to Him (the Father who judges justly, 1 Pet. 2:21-23, you will not be able to function in these special distinctions.

Reverent

The word used—*reverent* (ιεροπρεπισ)––in this text means that you are special. The first part of the word is ιρεοσ and translates "holy or sacred," meaning "set apart, different, special." The second part is πρεπετ and translates, "to be fitting, proper, or right."

The main idea, I believe, is captured in this expanded translation:

> "… the older women likewise, that they be reverent in behavior, not slanderers, not given to much wine, teachers of good things—that they admonish the young women to love their husbands, to love their children, to be discreet, chaste, homemakers, good, obedient to their own husbands, that the word of God may not be blaspheme." (Titus 2:3-5).

The first quality for the woman is reverence, from ιεροπρεπησ, meaning "holy demeanor." It is the same attitude shown by the great wise man Solomon, having reverential fear, awe and a godly deference toward God's divine arrangement. The idea in this phrase is that she is one who is fitting into God's special, divine arrangement.

In the Old Testament, Sarah—Abraham's wife—is a good illustration of this reverential attitude. Abraham asked Sarah to say she was his sister. The story continues as Sarah is taken to the Pharaoh's house. It is interesting to note that because of Sarah's reverence, the Pharaoh's officials praised her and God protected her throughout the whole ordeal (Gen. 12:20, 20:2-6).

As a woman, you have a promise from God that He'll protect you when this reverential attitude is demonstrated. This is a unique quality that is given to godly women: "the imperishable quality of a gentle and quiet spirit, which is precious in the sight of God" (1 Pet. 3:4). The word used here is *precious*, from πολυτελεσ; it's the idea of a person with great worth. If you, with these special qualities, can impress God, how much more those closely associated with you will be affected.

Not a Slanderer

The second quality for the woman is that she is not a *slanderer*, from μηιαβολοσ, meaning "not to accuse falsely" or "not to be an accuser." It would include manipulation, control, argumentation, fighting (verbal), and speaking evilly—as in one who's bent is to psychologically destroy someone through evil speaking. This attitude is in contrast to a reverent spirit.

The picture is of a person in a church or social group who is constantly finding fault with the conduct of others and/or spreading gossip or malice. This frequently seems to manifest itself in family units. When you have expectations of your husband and he fails to measure up to those expectations, rights are violated. The natural response would be to speak with anger of his attitude and actions. Instead of being a suitable helpmate, you become a hurt-mate, resulting in slandering him before your children and others.

Slander often moves from the smaller family unit to the greater family of the church. This then becomes a divisive factor, manifesting itself as carnality. This is the source of many problems in the church today but through the Emptying Process, you should be rising above this kind of attitude or action. Remember you are developing a pure heart. Note Paul's exhortation in 2 Tim.:

"But realize this, in the last days difficult times will come. For men will be lovers of money, boastful, arrogant, revilers, disobedient to parents, ungrateful, unholy, unloving, irreconcilable, malicious gossips, without self-control, brutal, haters of good, treacherous, reckless, conceited, lovers of pleasure rather than lovers of God. Holding to a form of godliness, although they have denied its power; and avoid such men as these. 'For among them are those who enter into households and … weak women weighed down with sins, led on by various lusts" (2 Tim. 3:1-6).

Not Enslaved to Wine

The third quality for the women is *not enslaved to wine*, from μηδε οινω πολλω δεδουλομενασ, meaning, "not controlled (past tense) by too much wine" or "not having your mind controlled by other things and people." This characteristic is also opposed to reverence. It is a cultural problem that has many facets in our society today. Wine in New Testament times was used in varied ways, and as a result was a common household item. It was used for medicinal, ceremonial, and sacramental purposes, as well as for purification, and a common beverage of the home. The same word is used for fermented as well as unfermented wine.

Today an overwhelming problem is that often women are under stress because of their husbands who do not respond properly to their security needs. In addition, stress from children, family, etc., are actually causing her to become physically and mentally ill. When she visits her doctor or psychiatrist, he perhaps will not have the time or understanding to seek the root problem. A tranquilizer or other drug may be given that might overshadow the root problem, giving her only temporary relief, with the root problem still unresolved.

There are also other means of controlling stress and enabling one to cope. Alcohol and drugs that are illegally procured are a common occurrence today and have fearful mind-altering consequences. This is what Paul referred to as sorcery which includes magic, spiritism, astrology, worship of spirits, visions and mind manipulation. The tendency to turn to drugs or supernatural means to sear the conscience is exploding today. So, beware.

Teaching What Is Good

The fourth quality for the woman is *teaching what is good*; καλοδιδασκαλουσ from καλοσ, meaning "good," and διδασκαλοσ, meaning "teacher." Not every woman has the spiritual gift of teaching, but that does not relieve her of the responsibility to teach because we all have that responsibility. The word *teach* is a compound word meaning an artistic ability gained by personal and spiritual development, enabling you to communicate principles to others.

You are not to teach just anything, but teach what is good. Now, what is good? There is only one good and that is what is accomplished in the power of the Holy Spirit. Paul says "there are none that do good, not even one" (Rom. 3:12). You are to be a Holy Spirit-controlled woman, that is, the inward character with the outward manifestation of functioning in your spiritual gift. The basic idea, then, is that you teach and encourage others in doing good through their spiritual functions.

Encouraging Younger Women

The fifth quality for the woman is that they may *encourage young women* ('ινα σοφρονιζωσιν νεασ, meaning "in order that they may train" save the minds of younger women in self-control). This is the missing element in parenting today and a problem in most homes. I don't think Paul is just addressing the older women of the church, although, that is the central thrust. I believe there is a great need for application of this to mothers training up their daughters. Note Paul's comments:

> "… that they may admonish the young women to love their husbands, to love their children, to be discreet, chaste, homemakers, good, obedient to their own husbands, that the Word of God may not be blasphemed" (Titus 2:4-5).

Let's look at the typical local church. How many older women do you know who have a ministry of teaching younger women? Generally, it is pastors' wives and they are usually younger than the other women. Occasionally you will see a godly older woman teaching, but that is infrequent. The reason for this is that the men of the church are not teaching the older women and therefore, they have nothing to teach.

More often than not, the basic characteristics that Paul exhorts the older women to teach are missing in their own lives. This is not because they are not interested, but because their mothers never taught them. Thus the pattern continues from generation to generation. The problem will stop when pastors and teachers equip men to teach their wives basic characteristics that they in turn teach their children.

What are the basic qualities every older woman or mother should be teaching the younger women or their daughters, in order that they might have a pure heart? They are clearly listed in this text. You need to remember that as an older woman or mother, you can only lead someone else as far as you have been yourself. These qualities are found in Titus 2:5.

Now we will look at the qualities mothers are to teach their daughters. These qualities are best taught by example. Therefore, it is necessary that mothers not only develop them but consistently demonstrate them. These are the qualities that will enable your daughter to become a godly woman (Titus 2:4-5).

1. Husband Lover—how to meet Husband's basic needs.
2. Child Lover—how to parent her children.
3. Discreet—how to think rightly about her image as a mother.
4. Chaste (Purity)—how to keep a clear conscience.
5. Homemaker—how to manage the affairs of the home.
6. Good—how to develop all her spiritual gifts and talents.
7. Submissive—how to submit to God's divine order.

Notice the warning at the end of this project. Paul says, "so that no one will malign the word of God" (Titus 2:5). This is a strong warning to the woman who has a tendency to deviate from God's divine plan. In other words, if you do stray from His plan, someone may bring the charge, "If that is a Christian, I do not desire to be one."

Demands for a Husband and Father

This Beatitude, Pure in Heart, makes an appeal to Fathers to turn their hearts to their children, and the hearts of the children to the fathers (Mal. 4:6). Just as the others, this Beatitude has two promises: first, they shall be blessed or have inner peace. This is the seventh time you have come across this word *happy* or *blessed* in the beatitudes. Remember, God is blessed. He is totally at peace. The more you experience this attribute of God, the more you are able to perceive Him.

Here is the second promise in this Beatitude: "they shall see God." The one who is in sin does not see or know God (1 Jn. 2:4), He is spiritually discerned. This describes this Beatitude in reverse. God cannot be seen, either by microscope or by telescope, even though this has been the desperate search of man since his fall. You see, a pure heart is a prerequisite to perceiving God. The heart, as you have already learned, is the mind, emotions and the will all functioning together. These elements are also the functioning parts of your conscience. The conscience is the grid through which God translates His infinite wisdom and knowledge into finite perception.

The promise to the pure in heart is, "For they shall see God" (Mat. 5:8). The verb is $\omega\rho\alpha\omega$, meaning "to see, to perceive," or "perception" in general. It is in the future tense, which indicates a continuous action. As we are cleansed, we are able to perceive God in a much greater way. The more we are purified, the more we will perceive Him until that day when we are transformed into His image (Col. 3:10. Then we shall know Him as He is. John MacArthur states it this way:

> "You comprehend Him, you realize that He is there, you see Him with the spiritual eye. Like Moses who cried, 'I pray Thee, show me Thy glory' (Exodus 33:18), the one whose heart is purified by Jesus Christ sees again and again the glory of God. To see God was the greatest thing a person in the Old Testament could dream of. Purity of heart cleanses the eyes of the soul so that God is visible." MacArthur, *Kingdom Living*, p. 133.

One thing is certain in this text—the pure in heart shall see God. The pure in heart take on this profound characteristic that Jesus demonstrated when He was here. You are now His representative in the world. You are, as a disciple, spiritually mature, and have the task of a peacemaker until He comes.

PROJECT

1. Define pure in heart.

2. What are the responsibilities of an older man? (Titus 2:1)

3. What are the responsibilities of an older woman? (Titus 2:3-4)

4. What are the responsibilities of a younger man? (Titus 2:6-7)

5. What are the basic needs of a wife? (1 Pet. 3:1-6)

6. What are the basic needs of a husband? (1 Pet. 3:7)

7. What is the only way a wife or husband can fulfill the needs of their mate? (1 Pet. 2:21-23)

8. What was John's root problem? (page 166)

CHAPTER 11 - RIGHT THINKING ABOUT SECURITY

"Blessed are the peacemakers, for they shall be called sons of God." Mat. 5:9

The ideal disciple of Christ is one who becomes a peacemaker; one who is reproducing; not just new converts, which is just a part of salvation, but taking them on through a progressive process of sanctification. This is His method of reaching out and rescuing His children from the darkness of the world. The disciple develops the skills to make other disciples reproduce themselves.

Defining the Word

The word *peacemaker* (ειρηνοποιοσ), is a compound word from ειρηνη, meaning "peace" or "harmony" in relationships, and the word ποιεω meaning "to make," signifies an action or pursuit. This word is also used by James in: "Now the fruit of righteousness is sown in peace by those who make peace" (Ja. 3:18). Note also:

> "And you, who once were alienated and enemies in your mind by wicked works, yet now He has reconciled in the body of His flesh through death, to present you holy, and blameless, and above reproach in His sight-- - (Col. 1:21-22).

It is used in this context of one that is making peace or making friends out of enemies. Jesus demonstrated it when He saved us (justification), and is now continuously saving us (sanctification) or reconciling us to Himself. Paul amplifies this:

> "Now all things are of God, who has reconciled us to Himself through Jesus Christ, and has given us the ministry of reconciliation, that is, that God was in Christ reconciling the world to Himself, not imputing their trespasses to them and committed to us the word of reconciliation. Therefore, we are ambassadors for Christ, as though God were pleading through us: "We implore you on Christ's behalf, be reconciled to God" (2 Cor. 5:18-20)

Ministry of Reconciliation

As we can see, *peacemaker* is a synonym for *reconciliation* from καταλλασσω, meaning "to reconcile" or "to make friends out of enemies." It was used of money changers changing worthless money for money used in the temple or in this case, *a change from enmity to friends*. This is our mandate as disciple s, to be God's instruments of reconciliation or peacemakers in the world. He has called us to peace. Now we must call others to peace with God. He has given us everything we need for living this life and demonstrating godliness in the world (2 Pet. 1:3). Paul clearly outlines our responsibility as peacemakers. The first level of becoming a reconciler or peacemaker is to help them understand the overall process and guide them to recognize what has happened. They now have the responsibility of reproducing themselves in others.

I have good news and bad news for Christians. First the good news—our battle is not a physical warfare and our weapons are not of this world. We have enlisted into a new army, which is an elite force empowered supernaturally by God. We are soldiers, specifically chosen by the Commander-in-Chief for a special function and we are strategically located for a specific task. We are to be peacemakers in a world where there is no peace. Peace is our profession. Not the kind of peace the world is trying to defend and certainly not a passive peace, but a peace that surpasses all human understanding. The kind of peace to which the Bible refers is peace with God. This is not a passive peace that must defend itself but an aggressive peace that penetrates the front lines of the enemy, bringing life to those who are separated from God and know no peace.

The bad news is that the unbelieving world cannot understand this new peace that we are experiencing. They will think we are peculiar and may even call us Jesus freaks, fundamentalists, holy-rollers or a long list of other names they use because they cannot understand us. Notice how Paul describes this paradox: "For the message of the cross is foolishness to those who are perishing, but to us who are being saved it is the power of God" (1 Cor. 1:18). We can now see that the lines have been drawn between those who are perishing and those who are living in the world and Paul gives us the source of our power:

> "For though we walk in the flesh, we do not war according to the flesh. For the weapons of our warfare are not carnal, but mighty in God for pulling down strong-holds, casting down arguments and every high thing that exalts itself against the knowledge of God, bringing every thought into captivity to the obedience of Christ, and being ready to punish all disobedience when your obedience is fulfilled" (2 Cor. 10:3-6).

The Message

The power of the peacemaker or reconciler is in the message. The message comes from a position of power but not a power whose source is in the world. Our weapons are not engineered by human hand, nor empowered by nuclear devices. Divine power is the source of our weapons that are designed to penetrate any defense the world can raise up. We are thoroughly equipped. Our offensive weapon is the Word. The writer of Hebrews says:

> "For the Word of God is living and powerful, and sharper than any two-edged sword, piercing even to the division of soul and spirit, and of joints and morrow, and is a discerner of the thoughts and the intents of the heart" (Heb. 4:12).

The Word is our message of peace and Christ is the living Word. When we are walking in the Spirit and are obedient to the Word, we are actually living the Word for our contemporaries to read. That is how it lives, as we participate in the divine nature, energized by the Holy Spirit who translates those Words into living actions and concepts. These concepts penetrate the depths of man's heart giving spiritual answers to the complexity of the soul. This is what gives the disciple power to perform in a supernatural way. The Holy Spirit works through our gifts and spiritual abilities to break down or penetrate the darkness caused by the evil forces of the world.

Although you are in the world, you are not of this world. You are specially designed in a new creation, and according to Paul, everyone in Christ is a whole new creation. "Therefore if any man is in Christ, he is a new creature; the old things passed away; behold, new things have come" (2 Cor. 5:17).

This passage is often misunderstood. It means we are new creatures in Christ, but that is just one small part of what has happened. You are not only a new creation, but everything else is new. The way you now perceive things is different from the way you have ever seen them. In Christ, you look at the trees differently, you see your work differently, you relate to people differently. Behold! Old things (the way you saw them before) have passed away; all things have become new (the way you perceive them now).

This is not a natural phenomenon, but comes "from God," the one who reconciled you to Himself. In other words, in this reconciliation process, He has created all things new. You are in a new sphere—a spiritual sphere—which the unbelieving world cannot understand. Paul says:

"But a natural man does not accept the things of the Spirit of God; for they are foolishness to him, and he cannot understand them, because they are spiritually appraised" (1 Cor. 2:14).

Your old friends will have a difficult time understanding your new attitude and actions, but don't let that discourage you. Just remember all things have become new; old things have passed away (2 Cor. 5:17). You are now living the Word. The verb "passed away" indicates an action that has taken place in past time (when you were regenerated) that has continuing results. You will see in this new lifestyle as old friends drop away, as old attitudes pass away, behold, there will be new ones. You will spend a whole lifetime seeing the old pass away and seeing your world taking on a new shape. This is truly an exciting life.

All of this took place when Christ reconciled you to Himself. But that is not all that happened. He has now given you the ministry of reconciliation (2 Cor. 5:18). This is a parallel ministry with that of peacemaker. Christ came into the world to make peace with you, His enemy. The process of His making that peace is called reconciliation. That is what Christ has done for you and now He gives you that same responsibility in the divine encounters that He places in your path.

The Ministry

You and all other believers are His special agents in the world for the purpose of heralding the good news about the Kingdom. He has not only given us the ministry of reconciliation or peacemaking, He has also given us the message, "He has committed to us the word of reconciliation" (2 Cor. 5:19c). That is the message as it is revealed in the Scriptures. In order for you to carry out that responsibility, you have been especially appointed as an ambassador for Christ and you are speaking on behalf of the King.

The Commission of the Peacemaker

Since you are a special agent with a strategic ministry and a specific message, you need to develop them to the best of your ability. First, you must understand the basics; the attitude, the authority, the action and the assurance of the messenger. The Lord Himself gives us our marching orders in the classic passage that we call the "Great Commission."

"Then the eleven disciples went away into Galilee, to the mountain that Jesus had appointed for them. When they saw Him, they worshiped Him; but some doubted. And Jesus came and spoke to them, saying: 'All authority has been given to Me in heaven and on earth. Go therefore and make disciples of all the nations, baptizing them in the name of the Father and the Son and of the Holy Spirit, teaching them to observe all things that I have commanded you; and lo, I am with you always, even to the end of the age'" (Mat. 28:16-17).

After Jesus was resurrected from the dead, this important meeting with the disciples took place. In a few days Christ would ascend into glory with the Father, and this was the commissioning service that would empower the disciples to reach out and change the world. In fact, as a result of this meeting, you have been made a disciple. This commission is now also *your* mandate.

The Attitude of a Disciple

First we will look at the attitudes of a disciple. It is important that you see the three very significant attitudes of a disciple. These three attitudes noted in these verses are 1) obedience, 2) worship and 3) doubt. Then the eleven disciples went away into Galilee, to the mountain which Jesus had appointed for them. When they saw Him, they worshipped Him; "----but some doubted" (Mat. 28:19-20).

Obedience

This was a fulfillment of Christ's direction to them, but after He was resurrected they were obedient. They left their nets, their tax collecting and other responsibilities and proceeded to Galilee because Christ specifically directed or commanded them to go. Christ has not directed us to go to Galilee, but there are other commands He has given us. One thing He expects of us is to be obedient when He does give direction. Like the early disciples, when He speaks to an issue, we are directed to respond.

Worship

The second attitude is they worshipped Him. There was majesty about Him that commanded their full attention. Notice the immediacy and urgency in the words "when they saw (immediacy) Him, they worshipped (urgency) Him." This was not a natural happening. Can you imagine going across the desert to meet a man who has been raised from the dead? There must have been extreme anticipation and overwhelming expectations as they traveled and then, finally, He was there in their presence and they fell down, prostrating themselves and worshipping Him. These two attitudes should represent our response to God. Obedience is to serve Him and worship is to praise or glorify Him. However, there is a third attitude that is negative. That should be a warning to us.

Doubt

The third attitude is negative—"some doubted." This was a traumatic experience for all the disciples. They were being asked to give up a lifetime of service to Israel, to their system of religion and to respond to a new way of thinking. So naturally some questioned this supernatural event. They were questioning His resurrection; they were saying someone had stolen His body as the guards indicated and even His actual death.

We too, are vulnerable to this same doubting attitude any time we are not thinking rightly or are not in obedience to Him. To doubt is to negate our effectiveness spiritually. Any time you are confused (remember God is not a God of confusion) or lacking wisdom (God is a God of wisdom). Stop! Don't doubt. Humble yourself before Him and ask for wisdom (Ja. 1:5-8).

The Authority of a Disciple

Secondly we will look at the authority of a disciple. What is the authority behind this commission? We can be sure there is no higher authority in the physical world or in spiritual realms. Can you just visualize this scene? The disciples come very reverently into His presence and fall down to worship Him, evidently from some distance away. The scripture says, "And Jesus came and spoke to them, saying, 'All authority has been given to Me in heaven and on earth'" (Mat. 28:18). Jesus came before them in all His majesty and glory, with no hesitancy or indication that He was anything less than God, yet the same person that had walked with them for over three years.

Notice the sphere of authority in His first word "all." I would venture to say that leaves nothing out. The word He uses here for authority is εξουσια. Jesus is saying literally, "all rights belong to Me" or, paraphrased, "I own everything and the deed of trust is in My Name." (Mat. 28:18).

To give you a little glimpse of the sphere of this authority, Jesus is speaking of all human authority, world leaders, national leaders as well as local. In other words, there are no human authorities that escape His control. But, it is not just the physical earth or world He controls. He is the authority over the heavenly—or spiritual world. Notice Paul's exhortation:

"Yet in all these things we are more than conquerors through Him who loved us. For I am persuaded that neither death nor life, nor angels nor principalities nor powers, nor things present nor things to come, nor height nor depth, nor any other created thing, shall be able to separate us from the love of God which is in Christ Jesus our Lord" (Rom. 8:37-39).

You see, the authority is all-inclusive: the truth is that this authority, this all-knowing, all-powerful force lives in you. We now have the same power (εξουσια) that Christ demonstrated when we are living the Word or controlled by the Holy Spirit. Our potential is unlimited. This great commission that Jesus is about to give is supported in full by this authority. There is no other power, no army, no weapon strong enough to hinder you in fulfilling this special commission.

The Action of a Disciple

Thirdly, we will look at the action of a disciple. What is my commission and how do I go about accomplishing it? Here, then, are those long-awaited marching orders. Here is your task with no limitations. You are free to perform—under any circumstances—this great commission. This is probably one of the most misunderstood verses in the Bible. Therefore, I want you to be careful not to take my word for the truth, but meditate on these verses to know the truth. I believe the reason for this misunderstanding is a result of translations. Note the following diagram:

The Imperative

The problem is not so much that it is a wrong translation, but a mixing of participles and verbs. If we translate the wrong word for the verb, then it changes the whole concept. In this case the verb is in the "imperative mood," meaning a direct command from God Himself. This suddenly changes the whole emphasis of the commission. It is not something that we can take or leave—it is a necessity. It demands an immediate action. It is the strongest form of the imperative mood.

The Modifiers

The commission is not *to go*. The word *to go* is a participle that only modifies the verb. It is a means of accomplishing the great commission that is directed by the main verb "make disciples." Now don't misunderstand. The going is important; it is a part of the command. It should read something like this: "As you go, wherever you go, make disciples." And I might add, we are always going, whether next door, to work, to school, or by telephone across the country.

The commission is not to evangelize the world, although that is the ultimate result. It is to "make disciples." To make a disciple is to draw a person's interest, by exposing them to the Word, to the extent they want to follow or they want to hear more about this. In other words, as you live and speak the Word, His Spirit will draw those who are seeking and they shall find." The idea, then, is to present the good news in a relevant way to those who are in darkness. The Word and the Holy Spirit bring about a new birth and a disciple is born. The Good News is the *Gospel*. The Gospel is the part of scripture that reveals the life, death, burial, and resurrection of Christ. Paul reveals the nature of the Gospel:

"Moreover, brethren, I declare to you the gospel which I preached to you, which also you received and in which you stand, by which also you are saved, if you hold fast that word which I preached to you—unless you believed in vain. For I delivered to you first of all that which I also received: that Christ died for our sins according to the Scriptures, and that He was buried, and that He rose again the third day according to the Scriptures" (1 Cor. 15:1-4).

Presenting the Gospel

The initial task in making a disciple, then, is to present the Gospel in a clear and understandable way. Remember, you now are commissioned as a peacemaker with the ministry of reconciliation. You are now a peacemaker making peace with the enemies of God. In order for you to do this, you must establish a good rapport and gain their confidence. This is accomplished by demonstrating—with your life and lips—the things that Jesus did when He was here.

Once you have gained their confidence, you can proceed with the simple Good News or Gospel. Christ's message was "repent for the Kingdom of heaven is at hand" (Mat. 4:17). The message of repentance starts with changing their mind about God or salvation. To change their mind about God, we must find out their spiritual condition. James Kennedy has designed two questions that are very effective in discerning their spiritual position: "Do you think you have come to the spiritual place where you know—or have the assurance—that if you died tonight, you would go to be with Christ?"

This question requires a "yes" or "no" answer. Someone may say, "I did not know we could know that!" That's a good sign that they don't know; or they may just answer "No." The next step is to present the plan of salvation. If they say yes, then move on to the next question. "Suppose you were to die tonight and went to heaven and as you approached heaven God should say to you, why should I let you into my heaven?"

The Plan: "God So Loved"

Let's assume they said "no" to the first question. Then we would present the plan of salvation. We must realize we are God's instruments of reconciliation. That demands repentance.—or that they change their mind about God. Jesus explained this change in His discussion with Nicodemus. He said, "except one be born again he cannot enter the Kingdom of Heaven" (Jn. 3:3). Then in Jn. 3:16, He gives the process for entrance into the kingdom. The first phrase is "God so loved." This is His Plan for man's existence in the world.

He designed man in a way that He could express His love to and through man. Man is a unique creation, in God's image and likeness. God's desire is that we experience that love and be able to express that love to others.

God loves you and has a special plan for your life. In fact, if you were the only person in the world, He would have done all He did just for you. He created man basically for three reasons. First, to have dominion over his circumstances in the world. God wants you to be above circumstances, to have dominion over them. Second, He created man to fellowship with Him and walk and talk with God in the garden. Third, God created man to express His love to and through him. Man is God's instrument of expressing His love to those he comes into contact.

The Problem: "The World"

But something happened. Man sinned and was separated from God. God took him out of the garden and placed him in the darkness of the World. Man had the opportunity to obey God, but because of the influence of the world power, man disobeyed God by eating of the fruit that had been forbidden. As a result of that sin, man was separated from God and under judgment in the darkness of the world. Unfortunately, Adam and Eve reproduced after their kind, and as a result, we all come into the world separated from God. We face the same problem today.   We all came into the world separated from God, under the influence of the

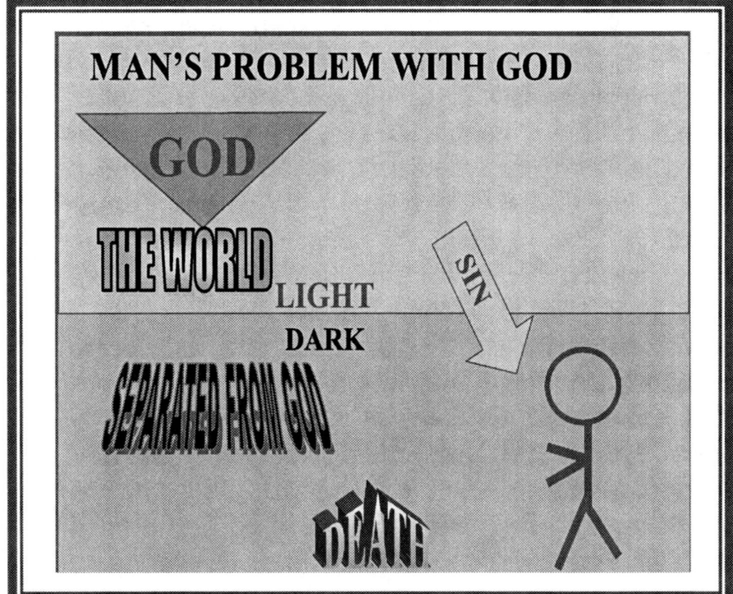

world system. Paul says, "Who were dead in trespasses and sin." Like the rest of the world, we were under the influence of the world system, doing what comes naturally.

That is not what God desires for us. There must be more to life. God gave Adam dominion over the world and Adam sold out. Now we have the same problem—we have lost our dominion; we allow people and things to control us.

The Provision: "He Gave His Only Begotten Son"

God does not want anyone or anything controlling us, only Him, and He has made a provision for man. John says; "God so loved the world that He gave His only begotten Son" (Jn. 3:16). God saw man in darkness, and because of His great mercy, He sent His only begotten Son into the world to show man the way to live. Jesus demonstrated this life for 33 years and then paid the penalty for man's sin by dying on the cross. He was buried in a tomb sealed by Caesar, and on the third day, God raised Him from the dead. He returned to the right hand of God where He now offers His life, eternal life to those in darkness. But

man is still under judgment. Paul spells out the dilemma that faces those who will not believe:

"And you He made alive who were dead in trespasses and sins, in which you once walked according to the course of this world, according to the prince of the power of the air, the spirit who now works in the sons of disobedience, among whom also we all once conducted ourselves in the lust of the flesh, fulfilling the desires of the flesh and of the mind, and were by nature children of wrath, just as the others" (Eph. 2:1-3).

121

The Promise: Whosoever Believes… Shall Have Eternal Life"

"Whosoever believes… shall have eternal life." God does not leave us without hope. He gives us the promise that if we will believe we will never perish but have eternal life (Jn. 3:16). It is in the word "believe" that man has a problem. It is not just a head knowledge. There are three elements in the word *believe*. First, the intellectual element—believing that Christ was lifted up (death) and we are looking to Him for eternal life and that He really is who He says He is. Second, knowledge causes the emotions to respond which is the emotional element that stimulates a need inside to experience more in life. This is the Holy Spirit ministering to your spirit, giving authority to what you know intellectually. But that is not all. Third, the mind and emotions activate the will or the volitional element, which is an act of your own free will

believing in Jesus Christ for eternal life. Then you are saved or have received eternal life. The next response is:

Baptism: Identification with His Body

First participle is baptizing. When a person believes, he is baptized by the Holy Spirit. But that does not make one an obedient disciple, one only becomes an obedient disciple when they follow the Lord in water baptism, this is only an outward demonstration of one who has surrendered to God's divine order.

To be dipped or immersed into water is a physical symbol of identification with the life, death, burial, and resurrection of Christ. It is a sign of submission to what one is identified with and an outward demonstration of one who has surrendered his will to a higher authority, acknowledging God's sovereignty and control over one's life.

Remember the attitude for learning is a submissive spirit. So because of this submissive act of identification, a disciple becomes much more teachable. The idea is that no one can learn unless they have a teachable spirit. This is all demonstrated in baptism. In other words when we are identified with Christ the result is a teachable spirit. Through baptism, we are identified with the body of Christ.

Notice the authority of baptism is clearly placed in the hands of the Father, the Son, and the Holy Spirit. This leaves no question with whom we are being identified—their names are listed, and this cannot be taken lightly.

Teaching them all things I have commanded

The second participle is teaching. This is another almost forgotten art. Most new Christians at this point are just left to grow on their own. You should be careful never to allow this to happen to a new disciple. The reasoning would be like a father taking a newborn child out into the forest and leaving him to grow up on his own. This is the most important growth period in the life of a new Christian.

Another point to consider is that many Christians do not really understand what it means to submit himself or herself to a teacher or leader. You see, babies do not respond very well to leadership. First, they must go through a process of physical and mental growth, and it is the same with new Christians. That is why the process you have been going through is so important. You are a spiritual parent with a child to train up in the way they should go.

We will find many Christians who have been baptized but have never grown because they have not been taught Biblical doctrine. They need someone who is willing to guide them through the levels of discipleship.

Jesus goes on to tell us what to teach. This is the Master Teacher who has spent three years teaching the disciples—who ultimately wrote the rest of the Bible after the Gospels. You see, the world could not contain all the things Jesus did and said (for further development of this see Jn. 21; 25). Notice your responsibility as a teacher: "teaching them to observe what I command you; and lo, I am with you always, even to the end of the age" (Mat. 28:2).

You have a great responsibility to those you are discipling. You can only teach someone what you have learned yourself. Therefore, you must follow Paul's exhortation, "Be diligent to present yourself approved to God as a workman who does not need to be ashamed, handling accurately the word of truth" (2 Tim. 2:15).

Would you teach a baby to feed himself and then never give him any food? The task of making disciples is to teach them how to feed on the Word and then giving the Word as a regular diet (teaching). It is very dangerous to teach a newborn baby only a few principles. Remember this when you make a disciple: you become a spiritual parent to that person. Therefore, we have the responsibility of bringing those whom we disciple to maturity.

The Assurance of a Disciple

Next we will look at the assurance of a disciple. You have the greatest security in your position in Christ. Not only has He saved you from your old self, the world, and the devil, but Jesus says, "Lo, I am with you always, even to the end of the age" (Mat. 28:20). You are experiencing the personal presence of Christ in your life. Even when you do not acknowledge Him, He is still there. That is why Christians are so frustrated and miserable when they are not in obedience to Him.

The text makes the extent of his presence very clear. "I am with you always" (Mat. 28:20). This is His ministry. Just as He guided the early disciples, He now promises His personal presence, power, and peace to be with you, supernaturally enabling you to accomplish the commission He has given you.

You are now ready to make disciples as you go, and wherever you go. But be alert, for there are many dangers and you are in a battle. You are on the front lines, but He does not wish for you to be hurt.

The promise to those who become peacemakers is "they shall be called sons of God" (Mat. 5:9). When we have become poor in spirit, have mourned over sin, have yielded our self-righteousness to meekness, are hungering and thirsting after His righteousness, demonstrating mercy and purity (truly perceiving God), and functioning as peacemakers, people will see us differently. They will see God in us, and will acknowledge us as children of God. Like the disciples in Antioch, because of their likeness to Christ, they were called Christians (Acts 11:26).

The word *called* here comes from the root καλ, meaning "to call, to acknowledge, to identify, or to name." Those who are doing these things shall be acknowledged as sons of God. In other words, when we participate in His divine nature, people will see the radiance of Christ in us. We will be manifesting the character of a son of God. It also has a future fulfillment, for in glory, we are called sons of God. Dr. Dillow also speaks to this issue in his book.

"Who are the Sons of God? Christians can be 'sons of God' in two senses in the New Testament. It is, of course, true that all Christians are sons of God by faith in Christ. We are all part of his family. But it is also true that the word υιοι (sons) can take a different emphasis depending on the context. In Matthew 5:45 we are to do the work of loving our enemies in order that we may become sons, and in Matthew 5:9 we need to be peacemakers before we can be called sons of God. In the book of Revelation we are told, 'He who overcomes will inherit these things, and I will be his God and he will be My son' (Rev. 21:7). Now obviously these are not conditions for becoming sons of God in the sense of being saved. In fact, the Sermon was directed to the disciples so that the disciples could become sons of God. It is possible for those who are already sons, according to these three verses, to 'become sons.' Is it not obvious that the Lord's meaning in Matthew is something like 'sons indeed.' In other words, if we love our enemies and function as peacemakers, we are not only sons in fact but we act like it and are therefore called sons. When we become a peacemaker and are doing the things Jesus did when He was here, we can be sure the world will persecute us. We need to understand how to stand under persecution." Dillow, *Reign of the Servant Kings*, 346-347.

PROJECT

1. What is a peacemaker?

2. What does Jesus promise those who make peace?

3. List the four elements of the Gospel. 1 (Cor. 15:3-4)

4. What is the main verb in Mat. 28:19?

5. What are the four P's?

6. What are the three tenses in salvation?

7. What is the only way to eternal life?

8. Draw the diagrams for the Plan, Problem, Provision, and Promise.

<table>
<tr><td>PLAN</td><td>PROBLEM</td></tr>
<tr><td>PROVISION</td><td>PROMISE</td></tr>
</table>

CHAPTER 12 - RIGHT THINKING ABOUT SUFFERING

**"Blessed are those who are persecuted, for righteousness' sake,
for theirs is the kingdom of heaven." Mat. 5:10**

Sometime ago Jesse came into my office and said, "Bill, you are not going to believe what I'm about to say. In fact, three months ago I would have been in jail for murder. Last night I went by my house to see the children. I thought it was strange that the lights were off, so I went in quietly and first checked the children and they were in bed. Then I went into the bedroom, and my wife was there in bed with another man."

Let me explain the circumstances. Jesse and his wife were having real marital difficulties. She had asked him to leave home and initiated divorce action. Jesse had come in for counseling and realized how wrong he had been in so many ways. He had been through the processes of mourning, meekness, hunger and thirsting, merciful, pure in heart and peacemaker.

His final words in our last session were, "I think I can handle things now." Little did he know how severe the circumstances would become! Jesse continued, "Bill, I was amazed at my response. I still cannot believe it. I was so calm. I understood a little bit of how Jesus must have felt when we flirt with the world. I had such a love for her. I could not get angry at her personally, although I did have a godly wrath toward what they were doing." Jesse continued with tears of joy. "I told him to get out and never to come into my house again. I calmly told her I was disappointed and could not accept what she was doing to herself, but I really loved her and nothing she could do could ever change that love."

I believe that is what Jesus meant when He said, "Satisfied are those who are persecuted for the sake of righteousness" (Mat. 5:10). Even in a seemingly impossible situation, with God's point of view, you can stand. However, I'm sure as you were reading Jesse's experience, you probably wondered "How could he do that?" But even greater the question, "How in the world could *I* handle something like that?"

Let us consider the significance of the process of spiritual development. For so long Christians have confused humility before God with humility before the world. The definition of humility is obedience to God. Therefore we are not to humble ourselves to the world. You are in a war with the world; you are in enemy territory; the battle is fierce; you are in God's army and you are a select soldier. The question is, will you bow down to the world or will you bow down to God? A popular author has written a book that implies that Satan is alive and well. I have news for you, he is alive, but he is not well. He has been stricken a fatal blow, although he is very active, pursuing every avenue of deceit and using many cunning devices.

This Beatitude, like all the Scripture, it is the opposite of what the world says. The world is desperately searching for peace where there is no peace. This world is under the control of Satan, the father of lies, and His forces. He has deceived the unbelieving world to believe that peace can come through humanistic effort. The author of the book *Aquarian Conspiracy* reveals how deeply this transpersonal teaching is ingrained in our schools all across our country:

> "Transpersonal education can happen anywhere. It doesn't need schools, but its adherents believe that schools need it. Because of its power for social healing and awakening, they conspire to bring the philosophy into the classroom, in every grade, in colleges and universities, for job training and adult education." Ferguson, *Aquarian Conspiracy*, p. 28.

It's amazing how many Christians have bought into the big lie being proclaimed around the world by these new age philosophers. Liberalism is rampant in the church; apathy to the Word is common place. We are the enemy and the lines are being drawn. We are in a battle with the world system, which is empowered by demonic forces and, I might add, it is spiritual warfare. This warfare has been going on since Adam, the first man, sold out his dominion over the world (Gen. 3). It is part of God's redemption program. He is going to bring this battle to an end when He takes His place on the throne of David. In the meantime, we are His soldiers in this world, persecuted as we continue in training for reigning with Him in the future, and rescuing His children from the enemy. The persecution has always been there for those who have been partakers with Him. Jesus warned us:

> "If the world hates you, you know that it hated Me before it hated you. If you were of the world, the world would love its own. Yet because you are not of the world, but I chose you out of the world, therefore the world hates you. Remember the word that I said to you, 'a servant is not greater than his master.' If they persecuted Me, they will also persecute you. If they kept My word, they will keep yours also" (Jn. 15:18-20).

It sounded somewhat strange when Jesus said "happy are the poor in spirit," and a little stranger when He said "happy are those who mourn." However, this has to be the strangest one of all: "happy are the persecuted" (Mat. 5:10). James echoes this same principle when he says, "count it all joy when you fall into various trials" (Ja. 1:2-6). Consider Paul's persecutions in Antioch, Iconium, and Lystra, and how the Lord delivered Him through all of them. Then he noted, "Yes, and all who desire to live godly in Christ Jesus will suffer persecution, but evil men and impostors will grow worse and worse, deceiving and being deceived" (2 Tim. 3:12-13).

Defining the Word

The word *persecute* comes from the Greek word διοκο which means "to put to flight, to drive away, to pursue." In this context, the latter seems to fit —"to pursue with the motive of persecuting. The verb used is a passive, perfect participle that expresses an action that has continuous results and comes from an outside force. The persecuted willingly stand as faithful servants.

He then gives the cause….. for righteousness sake. Unfortunately, most of us are persecuted for our own wrongdoing. That is not what He is talking about here. We notice He says "for righteousness sake," for standing in His righteousness. Peter warns us, "Don't think these things that are happening to us as something strange." In other words, the persecution will always be there, so be aware.

The persecution is there because not only are we manifesting His transferable attributes, but we are doing the same things (gifts) Jesus did when He was here. These things are diametrically opposed to the world system. We must be strong in our confrontations with the world, never resisting persecution but in His power, welcoming it. Lenski says:

> "This passive perfect may be regarded as permissive; 'who have allowed themselves to be persecuted,' or: 'have endured persecution.' The idea is that they did not flee from it when it came to them. Thus the perfect tense is explained; they held out under persecution and are now people of this kind, martyrs who have stood firm in just trials." Lenski, *Interpretation of St. Matthew's Gospel*, p. 194-195.

Unlike the other Beatitudes, he repeats the word *persecute* three times in verses 10, 11, and 12. However, in verse 11, he adds the word ονειδιζο, which means, "to heap insults, to defame, to revile or reproach." The *they* is referring to the enemies of Christ who desire to tear down all that Christ is doing and manipulate what we say to make us look bad and say all kinds of evil about us.

In verse 12, He is very encouraging: He says, "rejoice and be glad" (Mat. 5:12). Both words are durative imperatives, indicating that rejoicing will continue even though we are persecuted and reviled. We all, to some extent, will be persecuted and reviled if we go on functioning in His righteousness. Note how the Disciples experienced severe persecution: "So they departed from the presence of the council, rejoicing that they were counted worthy to suffer shame for His name" (Acts 5:41).

Most of the principles we developed in those early formative years and most of your education has been designed to serve the world. That is why you need to understand the Biblical principles of renewing your mind and reprogramming your personality to prepare you for the persecution that will come as you follow Christ.

The Scriptures never teach that the Christian life will be without difficulty. On the contrary, God allows these difficulties for the perfecting of our character or our spiritual growth. The Bible teaches that we will be persecuted and we will suffer. He does not necessarily remove the difficulty but He gives the grace necessary to handle it. Notice the exhortation from Peter and Paul and James:

> "For to this you were called, because Christ also suffered for us, leaving us an example, that you should follow His steps: 'Who committed no sin, Nor was deceit found in His mouth;' who, when He was reviled, did not revile in return; when He suffered, He did not threaten, but committed Himself to Him who judges righteously" (1 Pet. 2:21-23).

> "You therefore must endure hardship as a good soldier of Jesus Christ. No one engaged in warfare entangles himself with the affairs of this life, that he may please him who enlisted him as a soldier" (2 Tim. 2:3-4).

> "My brethren, count it all joy when you fall into various trials, knowing that the testing of your faith produces patience" (Ja. 1:2-3).

The point here is that persecution for doing what is Godly should never be taken personally. However, if you are attacked for your own wrong doing, you will experience personal persecution. When people attack you for doing the right thing, they are attacking Christ in you, and you are His front line soldier so whatever you do, stand firm in His power.

> "See then that you walk circumspectly, not as fools but as wise, redeeming the time, because the days are evil. Therefore, do not be unwise, but understand what the will of the Lord. And do not be drunk with wine in which is dissipation, but be filled with the Spirit" (Eph. 5:15-18).

However, when we are walking in the spirit, the world system cannot touch us except it is within God's purpose. Persecution will always be there, but "He who is in you is greater than he who is in the world" (1 Jn. 4:4).

Called to Stand

The responsibility now is yours. You are probably thinking that you do want God's best, but just don't know if you can stand. You can! Paul says; "I can do all things through Christ who strengthens me" (Phil. 4:13). Do you realize that as a Christian, you can never again say "I can't" to a difficulty in God's program for you without implying that God is a liar? Because He has given you an ability to face any circumstance, and the grace to enable you to stand firm, you can bear up under any circumstance.

How do we stand firm? You only can stand firm in the power of God. This battle is spiritual and your enemies are not merely physical beings; they are physical beings, manipulated by the spirit world. They can either be possessed (the unbelievers) or influenced (the believers) by the powers of this world known as Satan and his cohorts, the demons. These are real created beings that are of the spirit world. Paul gives a strong emphatic warning regarding this spiritual warfare when he says, "Finally, be strong in the Lord, and in the strength of His might" (Eph. 6:10). You are assured of access to the greatest source of power.

The Power to Stand

This is the only way we can stand. I have talked a lot about spiritual abilities, gifts, and a servant's heart, but now we are confronted with a strong passive imperative ενδυναμουσθε, from εν meaning "in," and δυναμαι, meaning "power." This is translated as "to be empowered." Your response to this, then, is to acknowledge who you are in your relationship with the all-powerful God. You are vitally connected to a power source that is boundless, and He is more than sufficient in every circumstance. You will be able to exercise the strength of His might and function supernaturally in the spirit world. "Put on the full armor of God, that you may be able to stand against the schemes of the devil" (Eph. 6:11).

The Need for Armor

God has not left you without protection in this world. In verse 11, Paul uses a strong command ενδυω—"to put on." The tense (aorist) of the verb indicates durative action—to put it on and keep it on. Why? Because it gives protection beyond any force the world offers. This was demonstrated through Christ's life. From the day He was born, enemies tried to kill Him physically, and persuade Him to commit spiritual suicide by yielding to Satan's tactics, but He stood firm. He was never touched, though they tried to kill Him from birth. Paul says, "For our struggle is not against flesh and blood, but against the powers, against the world forces of this darkness, against the spiritual forces of wickedness in the heavenly places" (Eph. 6:12).

That same armor is available to you, enabling you to face the overwhelming wickedness rampant in the world today. You can see in verse 12 the far-reaching effect of the powers of this world. Paul gives us four word pictures of the demonic forces in the sphere of this world (fallen angels), each one describing different aspects of these powers rampant in the world.

Principalities

The word *principalities* is from the word αρχη and is translated "principalities" or "rulers." It has the idea of beginning, first in line, first place, or headship. Paul describes the demon world as principalities. The idea is that there are multitudes of them in the world, and each one has his place or domain where he has first place or authority. These are spirit beings or fallen angels, and they have a specific boundary of rule. The dictionary states the meaning of *principality* as "the rank, dignity, or jurisdiction of a prince," "a territory ruled by a prince," or "a country with which a prince's title is identified." This concept will help you understand why evil is suppressed somewhat in a country where Christians are in great numbers. Demonic forces are powerful in the world, but "---He who is in you is greater than he who is in the world" (1 Jn. 4:4).

You possess supernatural power over these beings, and God has raised you up in your specific area of influence for a reason. You are strategically located to do battle against the forces of this world. This illustrates there are geographical boundaries in the spirit world.

Authorities

The word *authorities* is from the root word εξουσια and is the same word we have used for "rights." It is translated here as "authority," but it has depth of meaning. It comes from the word εξεστι meaning "beginnings," "government," or "rule," indicating they are organized. In this context, it refers to spiritual powers. These are the same powers mentioned above but from another perspective. The same powers that implanted this εξουσια nature in man continue to this day manipulating those who are possessed or oppressed by these authorities. (Note 2 Cor.11: 13-15).

These words describe a basis from which these powers rule, but in this context the idea is more of influence or manipulation. The warning here is that if you are not obedient, if you are standing in your own authority system rather than God's, you will be influenced by enemy forces. Since Satan is the ruler of this world, all of his cohorts are authorities exerting influence. This word picture illustrates the nature of these powers.

Rulers of Darkness

The next group is the rulers of the darkness of this age. The word *rulers* come from the word κοσμοσκρατωρ, which is a compound word from κοσμοσ, meaning "world" and κρατοσ meaning "power" or "dominion." This is a lower level of power. They are tyrants in this world, hidden in darkness. The concept of darkness is that they are hidden and cannot be seen by you and me, but they are not hidden from God. The main idea is that they are in direct opposition to the light which is God. This is the reason you need the whole armor of God to protect you from them. The root of the word *darkness* is σκα, meaning "to cover." Thus, only the glorious light of Christ will expose them. This concept illustrates the wide unseen sphere of th Eph. 4:13-14
eir operation.

Spiritual Hosts

Then finally, a lower echelon of demons is called spiritual hosts of wickedness in heavenly places. This phrase πνευματικα της πονηρις translates "evil spiritual ones."   The emphasis in this picture is on the results of their spiritual influence. the word *spiritual* is the same word used by Paul: "Brethren I would not have you ignorant concerning spirituals" (1Cor. 12:1). Paul then gives you a test to enable you to discern between these wicked spirits and the work of the Spirit of God (1 Cor. 12:3).

Note the following chart. On the left are those who believe and are controlled by the Holy Spirit. On the right are those controlled by the world system in the middle is the area of doubt those who are ignorant of the Word or immature will find them-selves in doubt. We all have been caught in a state of doubt. Paul's explanation of his dilemma.

"We are hard-pressed on every side, yet not crushed, we are perplexed, but not in despair, persecuted, but not forsaken, struck down, but not destroyed--- always carrying about in the body the dying of the Lord Jesus, that the life of Jesus also may be manifested in our body. For we who live are always delivered to death for Jesus sake, that the life of Jesus also may be manifested in our mortal flesh. So then death is working in us, but life in you" (1 Cor. 4:8-12).

This is our calling, this is our ministry and God is preparing us through discipleship to stand in the midst of suffering and persecution and having done all stand in our giftedness against the evil forces of the world. We stand together as the Body of Christ with the whole armor of God giving us the stability and ability to die for Him. Remember the old hymn "faith is the victory." Like Martin Luther said, "Here I stand. I shall not be moved."

Although they are spirit beings and wicked, they are not omnipotent, omniscient, or omnipresent. They are limited by the permissive will of God. However, they do not have power over the believer's will when it is yielded to Him. You do have power over these spirits of wickedness. This metaphor of spiritual hosts shows the overwhelming need for the Christian to put on the whole armor of God. Doubt places us in an uncontrolled position and we all have these times of doubt. Like Paul in 2 Cor. 4, He was attacked from every side, but he never lost control. He always yielded to the Holy Spirit. You see, Paul, in his knowledge of God and his training, had put on the whole armor of God. He knew God intimately, understood scripture, was well acquainted with his spiritual gifts, was aware of the world powers, and as a result he could stand against the wiles of the devil. You have the same power. As you empty the old man thought patterns, get to know Him intimately, discover your gift, and become a partaker in His Kingdom, you will be able to stand. These pieces of armor give us a better understanding of the extremes of the battle. The intervention of these powers in the affairs of men go far beyond what you could ever think or imagine. These powers actually participated in Satan's sin. They are unique agents of the god of this world, the father of lies. We have already described their craftiness. Note how Paul describes them as they work through a human being:

> "For such are false apostles, deceitful workers, transforming themselves into apostles of Christ. And no wonder! For Satan himself transforms himself into an angel of light. Therefore it is not great if his ministers also transform themselves into ministers of righteousness, whose end will be according to their work" (2 Cor. 11:13-15).

I would caution you. There is a danger in becoming preoccupied with these spiritual powers. Volumes could be written about what is not known but all that God wants you to know has been revealed, and we are not to go beyond what is written. I only mention them because the Scripture does (1 Cor. 4:6). You must concentrate on the positive. One of the most subtle tactics of these powers is to arouse the emotional nature of believers to exaggerate the revealed truth about demonic forces.

The other extreme is to ignore Biblical principles that warn us of the enemy's tactics and deception. You need to be aware of what the Scriptures teach in regard to world powers and how they possess the bodies of those who have rejected Christ. The following are some passages for further study:

1. The results of demonic forces—Jn. 8:44.

2. Satan's deceptive nature—2 Cor. 11:14.

3. Satan's strong will—2 Tim. 2:26.

4. Satan's intellectual strategies—2 Cor. 11:3.

5. Christ's victory over Satan in the wilderness—Mat. 4:1-11.

6. Effects on the world—2 Tim. 3:1-9 and 4:3-4.

You are probably wondering "What in the world is my defense, then?" You must remember who you are. Your identity is in Christ Jesus. You are a child of the King of Kings and Lord of Lords. God has promised He will never desert you, nor will He ever forsake you (Heb. 13:5). You have been submerged into His body and there you are protected. However, there are some things you need to do. Here is His strategy for His soldiers on the front line.

Understanding the Armor

"Therefore, take up the full armor of God, that you may be able to resist in the evil day, and having done everything, to stand firm" (Eph. 6:13). Because of the overwhelming dangers of these spiritual forces, you are to "take up". This is from αναλαμβανω, the tense of the verb again indicates durative action and it is one of those strong imperatives in Scripture that does not leave you a choice. Even the words "take up" are emphatic (Eph. 6:13). These words were used by the Roman Army in the final preparation for battle and always demanded an immediate response.

Making your final preparations is the immediate responsibility. Every soldier has a certain amount of equipment issued for his mission. The idea in the command is that you not only make sure you have the equipment but be certain it is in working condition. In other words, like a pilot who, before take-off, checks a list to insure that all the systems are functioning. Even in the process of take off, the pilot and the crew continue with their checklist. In fact, they never cease checking until the plane is returned to the ground, completely shut down, and the passengers and cargo are off-loaded. That is the idea in this command.

Next there are special reasons why you need armor. We have already established from Scripture that the days are evil and are becoming more wicked as time goes on. So your purpose in these times is to have the power of the armor to resist. Each piece of armor gives you special supernatural or spiritual power (δυναμισ). This is the Greek word from which our word dynamite is translated, i.e., a strong explosive force.

What you have been doing throughout this process is putting off the old ways and putting on the new strategies. Now we must understand each piece of armor in order to take it up (Eph. 6:13). These weapons are spiritual and we can only describe spiritual things in physical terms. You must understand your equipment. There is no question whether you have it or not. Peter said, "His power has given us everything we need for life and godliness" (2 Pet. 1:3). We have it now and Paul gives six metaphors as our checklist.

Belt of Truth

First, we must put on the belt of truth: "Having girded your loins with truth" (Eph. 6:14). The word used for gird in the culture of that day signified a soldier with a long robe. In order for him to be ready for battle, he would draw the robe up around his hips and put on a wide breech-like leather belt, not only to enable him to maneuver better, but also to protect vital organs in the abdomen. It was sometimes a belt with an apron like flap that protected the genital area. The Roman soldier always put on this belt first before taking up the other items of armor.

"I believe that being girded with truth primarily has to do with the self-discipline of total commitment. It is the committed Christian, just as it is the committed soldier and the committed athlete, who is prepared. Winning in war and in sports is often said to be the direct result of desire that leads to careful preparation and maximum effort. It is the army or the team who wants most to win who is most likely to do so even against great odds." MacArthur, *Ephesians: New Testament Commentary*, p. 350.

The spiritual application is—after having given up your rights and anything that would hinder you— that you should purpose to put on the truth to become a part of you, literally binding yourself up with it. The truth is what Christ is (Jn.14:6). This demands that you know the truth and you are able to demonstrate the truth with your life and He promises "the truth will set you free" (Jn. 8:32).

Just as the belt of the Roman soldier gave him freedom to maneuver, it freed him also from injury to vital organs. Jesus says, "The truth will set you free" (Jn. 8:32). Again He says, "If therefore, the Son shall make you free, you shall be free indeed" (Jn. 8:36). You—having put on the belt of truth—are free indeed. This enables you to participate in the divine nature of God, although there is more. The thrust of this metaphor is to know the truth and the truth will set you free.

Breastplate of Righteousness

The second metaphor concerns the breastplate of righteousness: "Put on the breastplate of righteousness" (Eph. 6:14b). In the Roman world, this was a piece of armor that protected one from the shoulders down to the hips, even a secondary protection to the abdominal area. It was sometimes a steel plate, and other times a chain mail (a flexible metal piece that surrounded the body from shoulders down to hips), used to protect the vital organs. Note Rienecker's comments:

> "The word denotes a piece of armor that can mean everything that was worn at different periods to protect the body between the shoulders and the loins. The average Roman soldier wore a piece of metal, but those who could afford it used the very best available: a scale or chain mail that covered chest and hips." Rienecker, *Linguistic Key to the New Testament*, Vol 2, p. 195.

Spiritually applied, having girded up with the truth, you will begin to demonstrate with your life and your lips, righteousness—the same righteousness Jesus demonstrated when He walked on this earth. Righteousness, then, is living the truth. Paul tells us that we not only are justified as results of His act of righteousness, but we now also have the privilege of participating in His righteousness. "And do not present your members as instruments of unrighteousness to sin, but present yourselves to God as being alive from the dead, and your members as instruments of righteousness" (Rom. 6:13). "Do you not know that when you present yourselves to someone as slaves for obedience, you are slaves of the one whom you obey, either of sin resulting in death, or of obedience resulting in righteousness?" (Rom. 6:16).

This righteousness is the same protection Jesus had in His lifetime here on earth, and His wilderness experience vividly illustrates the power of His righteousness. Satan tried every deceitful tactic, but Jesus, being girded up with the truth (He is the truth, and answered Satan with the truth), stood firmly in His righteousness.

Try to understand that we do not stand in our own righteousness, but we stand in His righteousness. "But seek first His kingdom and His righteousness; and all these things shall be added to you" (Mat 6:33).

To put on the breastplate of righteousness, then, means that we must put off our breastplate of self-righteousness or self defense. Such an example might be a runner in the Olympics who goes into strict training, giving up leisure time for exercise, candy bars for a nutritional diet, late nights for reading and studying, and giving up the right to confront the trainer but have a humble and responsive spirit.

Applying this spiritually means you must give up a self-righteous tendency to do things your own way and allow truth to control your mind and guide you in God's principles for life. You must give up feelings that cause you to be easily offended, and instead, take a strong objective stand to allow truth to filter through your mind to control your feelings. As your feelings are controlled by the truth, you will be free from the stimulus that comes from the world powers. Ultimately, as your will is surrendered to His will, your body is activated and you will demonstrate the righteousness of Christ.

Feet Shod With the Gospel of Peace

Third, we must have our "feet shod with the preparation of the gospel of peace" (Eph. 6:15). The words here are very descriptive. The Roman soldiers' shoes were strapped on and they were heavy, sturdy and studded with hobnails. This was another important part of the armor. The word *preparation* is significant, in that it has a much deeper meaning than you would think. The idea is more of readiness, and even has further meaning—that of firmness. It expresses the need for solidity, firmness, and a good foundation.

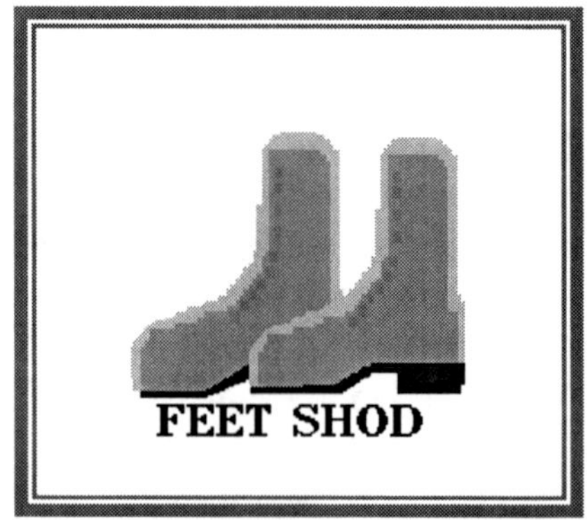

This is your *going power*. Jesus introduced His commission with the participle "as you go" (Mat. 28:19). We must always have our spiritual shoes on, ready to go, always firmly founded and prepared. Just as the Roman soldier would go into battle with his necessary shoes, we, too, must go fully prepared with the gospel of peace. The word *Gospel* comes from two words ευ, which translates "good" and αγγελοσ, which translates "messenger." Put them together and you have "good news" and the word *peace*—the Good News of peace.

Here is your weapon in a world that has no peace. Man is searching for peace in every direction and the world offers all kinds of counterfeits. You now have the real thing—the message of the peacemaker Himself. As a good soldier, as you go—wherever you go—give the good news of peace. Note Peter's exhortation regarding this responsibility: "but sanctify Christ as Lord in your hearts, always being ready to make a defense to everyone who asks you to give an account for the hope that is in you, yet with gentleness and reverence" (1 Pet. 3:15).

Shield of Faith

Fourth, we must put on the shield of faith: "above all, taking up the shield of faith" (Eph. 6:16). The shield was a very important part of the soldier's armor, as it was the first line of defense. There were many weapons to be hurled at a soldier and it was necessary to have a movable defense. The Roman shield was a large, wooden, door-shaped shield that was framed with metal and covered with several layers of leather, then centered with a piece of metal in front. This shield could ward off any known weapons.

Faith, then, is your shield and as such, you have been given a measure to enable you to stand firm under any circumstances. You are vulnerable in so many areas, for the world is firing arrows from different directions. Your only defense is exercising your faith. Remember the definition of faith. That faith gives substance or reality to things that you cannot see. The weapons of the world are not physical, and they cannot be seen. It is by faith alone that these things can be discerned and that you then will be able to stand, "in addition to all, taking up the shield of faith with which you will be able to extinguish all the flaming missiles of the evil one" (Eph. 6:16b).

The indication in this verse is that the weapons are fierce. The participle "flaming" indicates the arrows or spears were dipped in pitch, set on fire, and were burning. Translating that into the spiritual sphere, there is only one way to be in combat and that is by faith. Peter states it clearly:

> "Now for this very reason also, applying all diligence, in your faith supply moral
> excellence, and in your moral excellence, knowledge; and in your knowledge, self-control,

and in your self-control, perseverance, and in your perseverance, godliness; and in your godliness, brotherly kindness, and in your brotherly kindness, love" (2 Pet. 1:5-7).

You do not need *more* faith; you must apply or exercise what you have already. Having shod your feet with the truth, put on the breastplate of righteousness, and now, having taken up the shield of faith, you are ready for the next piece of armor. Note Paul's exhortation regarding faith: "For in it the righteousness of God is revealed from faith to faith, as it is written, that the righteous man shall live by faith" (Rom. 1:17).

Helmet of Salvation

Fifth, we must put on the helmet of salvation: "And take the helmet of salvation" (Eph. 6:17). The Roman soldier was distinguished by his headgear, which was an elaborate, decorative bronze helmet, usually very expensive. It was heavy and required a soft liner to make it bearable; only a sharp ax or hammer could penetrate it. The value of this helmet was to prevent an injury to the head with subsequent death or debilitation.

Now to translate that into the spiritual sphere, it would indicate a need for armor to protect our knowledge of God. That is why Paul calls it the helmet of salvation. This is the armor that gives you security to stand under any circumstance the world powers can bring against you. One of Satan's great tools is to plant doubts in your mind in order to blind your eyes or sense of perception. If you really know God and understand who you are in Him, then you will be secure in your helmet of salvation.

The writer of Hebrews poses a question that will alert you to some grave dangers, particularly to those who are insecure. This salvation is the most important thing that has ever happened to you, therefore to neglect it brings grave consequences. In this passage, the writer is speaking to us as believers when he uses the personal pronoun *we*. If the Old Testament law—that is, the message spoken by angels—was binding, how much more the warnings of the New Covenant? Notice Peter's instructions: "And so we have the prophetic word made more sure, to which you do well to pay attention as to a lamp shining in a dark place, until the day dawns and the morning star arises in your hearts" (2 Pet. 1:19).

"For if the word spoken through angels proved steadfast, and every transgression and disobedience received a just reward, how shall we escape if we neglect so great a salvation, which at the first began to be spoken by the Lord, and was confirmed to us by those who heard Him" (Heb. 2:2-3).

So the question presented is how shall we escape if we neglect so great a salvation? The answer is "we will not." It's very obvious he is not indicating that you can lose your salvation, because the writer spends the rest of the book explaining the overwhelming losses to the believer who neglects salvation. Briefly those things are:

1. They will not enter His rest—Heb. 3:11.

2. They will not bear fruit, only frustrating works—Heb. 6:7-11.

3. Premature physical death—Heb. 9:l0- 26 (also 1 Jn. 5:16; Ja. 5:l9-20).

4. Loss of eternal rewards—Heb. l2:25-29, 1 Cor. 3:11-15.

How do we neglect this great salvation? We are guilty of neglect when we do not respond to the truth given to us through salvation, and do not get to know Him as the sovereign God that called us out of darkness into light. This further leads to an ignorance of His righteousness that He wants to demonstrate through our gifts and abilities. Subsequently, there is a failure in sharing the God News of peace, resulting in a lack of faith that is unshielded to the tactics of the devil and to losing our security in Him.

Because of your helmet of salvation, you can really experience Him and actually participate in His divine nature. This security is amplified by Paul: "And we know that God causes all things to work together for good to those who love God, to those who are called according to His purpose" (Rom. 8:28).

Sword of the Spirit

Finally, we must take the sword of the Spirit, "And the sword of the Spirit, which is the Word of God" (Eph. 6:17). The final piece of armor is the sword. In the time of Paul, the sword was the most effective weapon known to man. The reference here is to a Roman sword that was short, double-edged, sharp, and the most destructive of all swords. This is the final metaphor, and is the only offensive weapon mentioned. This is the weapon of the Holy Spirit, who was sent into the world to magnify the *Word*, and to aggressively pursue the enemy with this special weapon.

The Scriptures are alive, active, and living. The writer uses the same word used by Jesus, "I am the way, the truth, and the life" (Jn. 14:6). It is always used for eternal life, and is the principle of life. It is the life the Father has in Himself that He gave to His Son, who in His incarnation became the Living Word (Heb. 4:12), in the midst of man in order that man might see God.

The Word, then, is the Holy Spirit's offensive weapon. You are the physical body (means) through which the Spirit brings to life the Word, which contains the same principles by which Jesus lived and ministered. In a real sense then, as you are controlled by the Spirit and obeying God's principles, men and women see the Word living in you.

You are God's chosen instrument in translating His message into a living manifestation of Godliness. As you minister this message (The Word), it is powerful, and penetrates even to the dividing of the soul and spirit, separating out the psychological problems mankind faces and giving spiritual answers to those in otherwise impossible situations. The Word discerns our thoughts and intentions (Heb.4:13).

Salt of the Earth

You are now His soldier with the sword of the Spirit in your hand. What in the world are you going to do with it? The final words of the Beatitudes illustrate your ministry in the world: "You are the salt of the earth" (Mat. 5:13). Salt is a special mineral with unique qualities and that is why Christ uses it to describe the character of a Christian. First, salt is found throughout the earth. It is made up of many granules, and is a crystalline compound commonly called sodium chloride; its potential is wide and varied. I want you to see the beauty of these potentials applied to the spiritual life.

It is a condiment for <u>seasoning</u> that keeps things from being as bad as they could be, or helps them be as good as they could be. You are a seasoning for the world in that you keep it from being as bad as it could be. On the other hand, you—in obedience to Christ—are the instrument that He will use to make those around you as good as they can be.

Second, like salt, we are capable of <u>preserving</u>. When I was a boy, my Dad would butcher a pig and preserve it with salt. We are, by exercising our saltiness, preserving the actual lives of those who would die in their sins. You are a preserver.

Third, salt was used in <u>accompaniment with a sacrifice</u>. The Old Covenant demanded salt as a seal presented with the dead sacrifice. In the New Covenant, Christ demands a living sacrifice that is our selves, and our saltiness is a seal of that covenant (Mat. 5:13).

Fourth, it was used in <u>medicinal bathing</u>. Salt was used for bathing, especially newborns, who were bathed in salt water and rubbed with it. Even today, we use it for soaking sprained ankles or to soothe a sore throat. Spiritually, we are salt; and newborn babes in Christ need to be treated gently and carefully with our special gifts and abilities. However, even the mature saints need you. You are a special medication.

Salt is essential because it <u>causes thirst</u>. It is a mineral that is used by the body to control the fluid balance, and is the vehicle for many intravenous medications. It has much to do with body temperature. When the body systems are functioning correctly and salt is taken in, it will cause the person to become thirsty. When your saltiness is right, everyone with whom you come in contact will become thirsty. They will desire to know more about the one you represent. You will cause thirst to those around you.

It has the <u>highest osmotic pressure</u> of any mineral. Normal saline in the circulatory system allows the nutrients and many of the cellular needs to penetrate the membranes of the body cells by osmotic pressure. Thus, the cells are healthy and the person functions normally. You are salt in Christ's circulatory system, with supernatural gifts and abilities to penetrate the psychological front put up by people, reaching in and meeting spiritual nutritional needs of which they are unaware. You are God's special nutritional agent, meeting spiritual needs in His children.   I could go on with the many applications of salt, but I believe you understand that it is special. There is a warning, however. Notice how Matthew says it:

> "You are the salt of the earth; but if the salt loses its flavor, how shall it be seasoned?
> It is then good for nothing but to be thrown out and trampled underfoot by men" (Mat. 5:13).

Light of the World

"You are the light of the world" (Mat. 5:14). Light is what God is, and as a result of all that has been said, you become a reflector of the Light. Light is superior to darkness, for where there is light there is no darkness. However, when a river enters an ocean, it is difficult to tell where the river stops and the ocean begins. That, too, is the problem in the world.

We all come into the world in darkness, actually loving darkness more than light, but when we believed in Christ, we passed from darkness into light. At that point, we became reflectors of His light. As newborns, the light reflected through us dimly, because our reflectors were clouded with immaturity— we didn't understand all the principles He had given us. The more mature we become, the more brilliant will be our reflection of His light.

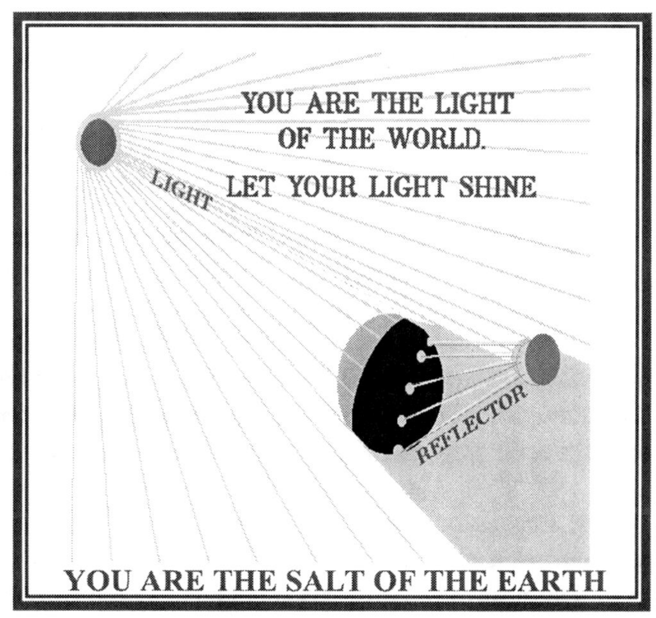

Finally, He says don't hide your light, but let it shine. No matter how smudged your reflector, keep on polishing but never stop shining. Matthew tells it well in the following verses:

> "You are the light of the world. A city set on a hill cannot be hidden. Nor do men
> light a lamp, and put it under the peck-measure, but on the lamp stand; and it gives light to all

who are in the house. Let your light shine before men in such a way that they may see your good works, and glorify your Father who is in heaven" (Mat. 5:14-16).

It is very clear that we cannot do all that Jesus did, since He had all the gifts. However, each disciple has needs for preaching, teaching, exhortation, knowledge, wisdom, mercy, helps, giving, faith, administration, ruling, and discernment of spirits. The work of the Spirit, through the believer, is the armor for the church. It is also clear that Jesus exercised all the spiritual gifts in the making of His disciples, because they had needs that demanded fulfillment.

No one has all the gifts; therefore it would be inconsistent with scripture to expect an individual to make a disciple. Each member needs all the other members. Paul amplifies this need:

"... from whom the whole body, joined and knit together by what every joint supplies, according to the effective working by which every part does its share, causes growth of the body for the edifying of itself in love" (Eph. 4:16).

"For as the body is one and has many members, but all the members of that one body, being many, are one body, so also is Christ. For by one Spirit we were all baptized into one body—whether Jews or Greeks, whether slaves or free—and have all been made to drink into one Spirit. For in fact the body is not one member but many" (1 Cor. 12:12-14).

Every part has a function in the development of each member. I am convinced this is the root of most divisions in churches today. God not only allows needs in the body; He has given sufficient assistance to meet those needs. Most believers don't know they have a gift, much less know how to develop it and use it to protect the Body. Then people get frustrated, which results in conflicts and divisions.

"As you therefore have received Christ Jesus the Lord, so walk in Him, rooted and built up in Him and established in the faith, as you have been taught, abounding in it with thanksgiving. Beware lest anyone cheat you through philosophy and empty deceit, according to the tradition of men, according to the basic principles of the world, and not according to Christ" (Col. 2:6-8).

"In this passage the exhortation is given to walk consistent with the faith that introduced them into the body of Christ. Again, the passage points to the fact that a proper 'walk' in Christ is not guaranteed, but something worth the exhortation for the believer to pursue." Lybrand, *Back to Faith: Reclaiming Gospel Clarity in an Age of Incongruence,*

All believers are subject to disobey. We all are subject to the old nature, and actually follow it to our downfall, any time we allow the old man thought patterns, and deviate from the faith that saved us. That is why Paul warns us to walk the walk that is consistent with our salvation. In other words, it is possible for us to walk according to the traditions of men, rather than God.

I believe many evangelical churches are doing these three things; evangelism, baptism and application centered instruction, but it is not working. There must be that pastoral caring that Christ demonstrated in making His disciples. One-on-one confrontation is necessary as indicated in the Emptying Process of the Beatitude Model and amplified by Peter in the virtues (2 Pet. 1:1-10). We cannot loose sight of how Christ made disciples. I agree that we cannot do all that Jesus did, as an individual but as His Body, with all the spiritual gifts, and His Spirit controlling, we can.

The Church is the Body of Christ, and it was to the Body He gave the great commission to go on making disciples. Each member has a function that will contribute to this task. This first phase generally involves the Speaking Gifts. The gifts were given to the Body to keep us alert to wrong-doing and to minister to the weak areas of the Body. The strong protecting the weak, and nurturing them to full strength. Paul encourages this body function:

> "... but our presentable parts have no need. But God composed the body, having given greater honor to that part which lacks it, that there should be no schism in the body, but that the members should have the same care for one another" (1 Cor. 12:24-25).

The Emptying part of the process demands one-on-one confrontation. We need to help the disciple detect any guilt, bitterness, an unforgiving spirit, bad habits, or undesirable traits in his life. Since this is the first part of discipling, most new Christians never experience this vital emptying. As a result, all the psychological garbage is buried and forgotten. The result is that few are being discipled adequately. As the Church moves from year to year, the problem is compounded until we have a situation we are seeing in many churches today.

PROJECT

1. What is the promise for those who are persecuted for righteousness?

2. What are the results of enduring or participating in righteousness now? (2 Tim. 2:11-13)

3. What should be the believer's attitude be toward suffering? (1 Pet. 4:12-13)

4. How does a believer stand against the devil? (Eph. 6:13)

5. How does Satan manifest himself in the world? (2 Cor. 11:13)

6. How did Jesus resist Satan in the wilderness? (Mat. 4:1-11)

7. What is the source of our weaponry against world powers? (2 Cor. 10:3-6)

8. List each piece of armor and describe it. (Eph. 6:13-18)

9. Now that we have discovered and developed our life ministry, and are participating in that ministry on a regular basis, what will be our rewards here on earth, and in glory?

CHAPTER 13 - RIGHT THINKING ABOUT REWARDS

"Blessed are you when they revile and persecute you, and say all kinds of evil against you falsely for My sake. Rejoice and be exceedingly glad, for great is your reward in heaven, for so they persecuted the prophets who were before you." Mat. 5:11-12

Introduction

This is the first time rewards are mentioned in the New Testament. Matthew has introduced the virgin birth and childhood of Christ, John the Baptist, Christ's baptism, and the calling of the disciples. Now in the introduction to the Sermon on the Mount, a great promise is revealed to those who are reviled and suffer for His sake: "great is your reward in heaven" (Mat. 5:12). Matthew is the first to discuss this almost forgotten doctrine that in reality is one of the great blessings God has promised His people. This concept of rewards is not just a temporal thing but has an eternal completion. Dillow comments on rewards:

> "When Jesus promised us treasures in heaven, there is no reason for excluding actual material treasures from His words. Indeed we are specifically told that we will have the wealth of five or ten cities and that in this age we will receive up to a hundred fold return on our efforts. Christ is said to be preparing a place for us to live. Perhaps the treasures in heaven refer in part at least to literal wealth such as enhanced eternal dwellings and greater number of cities over which to rule." Dillow, *Reign of the Servant Kings*, p. 571.

The Word

The word used here for reward is $\mu\iota\sigma\theta\sigma\varsigma$, the primary meaning is "wages," "hire," or "to reward." It is used for rewards received in this lifetime (Mat. 5:46, 6:2, 5, 16; Rom. 4:4; and 1 Cor. 9:17-18). It is used several times for rewards to be received in glory (Mat. 10:41; Mk. 9:41; Lk. 6:23, 35; 1 Cor. 3:8, 14; 2 Jn. 8; and Rev. 11:18, 22:12). Rewards, then, are a reality in this present age, as well as in the future when we go to "be with Lord " (1 Thes. 4:14-17). The writer of Hebrews says: "But without faith it is impossible to please Him, for He who comes to God must believe that He is, and that He is a 'rewarder' of those who diligently seek Him" (Heb. 11:6).

The Rewarder

In this passage, the writer uses a compound form of this word $\mu\iota\sigma\theta\alpha\pi\sigma\delta\sigma\tau\eta\varsigma$, translated "rewarder" of those who seek after Him. The word *seek* is also a compound word from $\varepsilon\kappa\zeta\alpha\tau\varepsilon\omega$. When the preposition $\varepsilon\kappa$ is compounded with $\zeta\eta\tau\varepsilon\omega$, it always seems to denote that the seeker "finds," or at least exhausts, his powers of seeking (Heb. 11:6). There is power in seeking; it is a demonstration of faith. Jesus said, "seek, and you will find" (Mat. 7:7). The words looking, seeking and drinking are often used as synonyms for believing (Num. 21:8-9). The idea in these texts, and all those relating to rewards, indicates the seeker is actively involved in the kingdom now. It involves participating in the gifts and abilities with which He has entrusted us. We are partakers now, in preparation for future reigning with Him. We are partakers or participators ($\mu\varepsilon\tau\sigma\chi\sigma\iota$ – *metochoi*) with Him in this present age (Heb. 3:14). Dillow speaks to this:

> "What then is necessary to become one of Christ's metochoi? In its most general statement the requirement is to hold fast the beginning of our assurance firm until the end (Heb. 3:14). Those who have actively kept on believing and trusting God to the end of life are included in this company. Lest anyone think, is that all? It seems that Jerry Bridges was certainly correct when he said, 'it often seems more difficult to trust God than to obey Him.' The moral will of God given to us in the Bible is rational and reasonable. The circumstances in which we must trust God often appear irrational and inexplicable. The Hebrews were not

troubled with problems of disobedience so much as trust. It was the seeming distance of God in the midst of their troubles, His lack of apparent involvement in their difficulties which caused them to doubt. It is for this reason that the writer sets before their vision the great heroes of faith in Chapter 11, who 'died in faith, without receiving his promises' (Heb. 11:13). It is difficult to 'trust God when it hurts.' While ultimately the life of faith cannot be separated from the life of obedience, God seems to particularly exalt the man who persist in faith: 'And without faith it is impossible to please Him, for he who comes to God must believe that He is, and that He is a rewarder of those who seek Him' (Heb. 11:6). When the storm was over and the sea had been stilled, Jesus was still greatly troubled. 'How is it that you have no faith?' He asked His disciples. It was the development of their faith that seems to have been most important to Jesus." Dillow, *Reign of the Servant Kings*, p. 587.

The Prerequisite

We must realize there is a Man now sitting at the right hand of God who has experienced the pain of participating or partaking, in the kingdom here on this earth. He has set the pace and is our example (1 Pet. 2:21). He was faithful as a partaker to the end. He died and was raised from the dead, in order that we, too, might participate (Heb. 2:14-18). Partaking and rewards go together; one without the other would be non-Biblical.

There is another essential element that often accompanies partaking and rewards. That element is inheritance. This word is also a compound word from *κληροσ,* meaning "a part or allotment" and *νεμο,* an old verb, indicating a legal document, but a legal allotment or an inheritance. In almost all the uses of this word it is accompanied with some form of, either works or a character quality. Inheritance then, is a reward, or a treasure laid up in heaven, and the prerequisite is that one be a partaker by cooperation or obedience to the owner or rewarder. Dillow develops this idea:

"Also like their Old Testament counterparts the words for inheritance in the New Testament often involve spiritual obedience (i.e. faith plus works) as a condition of obtaining the inheritance. Becoming an heir (κλερονομοσ) can occur through filial relationship, through faith, or through some kind of works of obedience. The acquisition of the inheritance (κλερονομοσ) includes, contextually, either the presence or absence of some work or character quality as a condition or forfeiting the possession. In view of the fact that works are associated with the acquisition of the inheritance, it is prima facie doubtful that the inheritance could be equated with entrance into heaven as is so often done. Yet in order to sustain the idea of perseverance in holiness, Experimental Predestinarians interpret the passages as descriptions of all true Christians. Theological exegesis is thus brought in to make every one of these texts say something that they do not only do not say but that is in fact contradictory to the rest of the New Testament." Dillow, *Reign of the Servant Kings*, p. 63-64.

Our inheritance, then, is a reward we will receive in the future, not like Esau, in the Old Testament, who sold his birthright—or inheritance—for a bowl of porridge (Gen. 25:32-34). Since we are commissioned to serve in a way that we might win the prize, we must diligently serve Him (1 Cor. 9:24). God's desire is that we not be like Esau, but that we press on toward the goal. Note Paul's exhortation:

"Not that I have already attained, or am already perfected; but I press on, that I may lay hold of that for which Christ Jesus has also laid hold of me. Brethren, I do not count myself to have apprehended; but one thing I do, forgetting those things which are behind and reaching forward to those things which are ahead, I press toward the goal for the prize of the upward call of God in Christ Jesus" (Phil. 3:12-14).

Qualifications for Rewards

Do you get the idea that the Lord is saying there is a work that needs to be done and we are His agents for continuing the work Christ began to do? In other words, we are His body functioning in the world, continuing to do the work and the suffering that He experienced here on earth as a man (yet God). Note again Paul's exhortation:

> "But we have this treasure in earthen vessels that the excellence of the power may be of God and not of us. We are hard pressed on every side, yet not crushed; we are perplexed, but not in despair; persecuted, but not forsaken; struck down, but not destroyed—always carrying about in the body the dying of the Lord Jesus, that the life of Jesus also might be manifested in our body. For we who live are always delivered to death for Jesus sake, that the life of Jesus also may be manifested in our mortal bodies. So then death is working in us, but life in you" (2 Cor. 4:7-12).

Demands Sacrifice

We are His body, living His life, dying the death, suffering for Him (1 Cor. 4:7-18). Someone has said, "if you are not suffering; there is something missing in your service." Jesus promised when He was here that He sent us as sheep among the wolves and that persecution was imminent (Mat. 10:16-28). In another place Jesus says, "If they persecuted me they will also persecute you" (Jn. 15:18-25). Peter says, "Do not think it strange concerning the fiery trial which is to try you, as though some strange thing happened to you" (1 Pet. 4:12). Persecution does not come to those who are not doing anything. Persecution comes when we are functioning supernaturally in a natural world. The writer of Hebrews makes it clear how Jesus, the God Man, learned obedience (Heb. 5:7-10). We are His body; therefore, what they did to Him they will do to us (Mat. 15:20).

In a class I was teaching recently, I had a student ask; "What? Do you think there will be different levels of rewards in heaven?" This is a subject that has been neglected in most Christian education programs. I have found that if you teach this subject, you should be prepared to field a lot of questions. The Bible has much to say about the subject as in this Beatitude (Mat. 5:11-12). It was by His work or obedience that God the father highly exalted Him. Note Paul's comments:

> "Let this mind be in you which was also in Christ Jesus, who, being in the form of God, did not consider it robbery to be equal with God, but made Himself of no reputation. Taking the form of a servant, and coming in the likeness of man. And being found in appearance as a man, He humbled Himself and became obedient to the point of death, even the death of the cross. Therefore God also has highly exalted Him and given Him the name which is above every name, that at the name of Jesus every knee should bow, of those in heaven, and of those on earth, and of those under the earth and that every tongue should confess that Jesus Christ is Lord, to the glory of God the Father" (Phil. 2:5-11).

In all the passages we have mentioned there is always a condition for receiving a reward, such as obedience, suffering, service, or persecution. However, we must remember we are not talking about justification or being born again. Justification comes by grace through faith alone. Jesus is talking about sanctification, the process of being conformed to His image. Remember justification is a free gift; sanctification is an obedience by faith.

Here in this text Jesus is talking about those who participate in His suffering, who are insulted, persecuted and have all kinds of evil things said about them for His sake. Jesus is implying that this is the ultimate in presenting one's body as a living sacrifice. (Rom. 12:1). Notice the future rewards for:

those who become poor in spirit—"Blessed are the poor in spirit for theirs is the kingdom of heaven" (Mat. 5:3);

those who are meek—"Blessed are the meek, for they shall inherit the earth" (Mat. 5:5);

and those who are persecuted—"Blessed are those who are persecuted for righteousness' sake, for theirs is the kingdom of heaven" (Mat. 5:10).

These are rewards for service in this present age, to be given at the Judgment Seat of Christ or often referred to as the BEMA Seat.

Two Kinds of Rewards

There will be rewards specifically for Churches. Robert Cook lists the rewards for the seven churches in Asia Minor for the overcomers or those who persevere to the end.

Ephesus	The privilege of eating of the tree of life (Rev. 2:7)
Smyrna	Will not be hurt by the second death (Rev. 2:11)
Pergamum	Rewarded with hidden manna and with a new name on a white stone, which name will be known by none but the recipient (Rev. 2:17)
Thyatira	Will rule the nations with a rod of iron (Rev. 2:26-28).
Sardis	Will be clothed in white garments and Christ will not erased his name from the book of life (Rev. 3:5)
Philadelphia	I will make him a pillar in the temple of my God and I will write on him the name of my God and the name of the city of my God (Rev. 3:12)
Laodicean	I will grant to sit with Me on My throne (Rev. Rev. 3:21)

W. Robert Cook, *The Theology of John*, p. 173-181.

These are rewards offered to actual churches of Asia Minor. These rewards will be distributed to all churches so characterized in the Church Age. We will be part of those Churches and will benefit by those rewards. But the more important rewards to the individual believer will be those received for the works done here in the temporal system. Notice Paul's exhortation:

For we are God's fellow workers (partakers); you are God's field, you are God's building. According to the grace of God which was given to me, as a wise master builder I have laid the foundation, and another builds on it. But let each one *take* heed how he builds on it. For no other foundation can anyone lay than that which is laid, which is Jesus Christ" (1 Cor. 3:9-11).

Partakers in the Building Process

We are God's fellow workers partaking in His business in the world. We are gifted, as I tell my students, to the extent that we function in our life ministry built around our gift, to that extent the church will prosper. We are in the field, training for future service; therefore we must be wise builders, building in people, first, the foundation and that foundation is Christ (1Cor. 3:11). Then on that foundation, we build the superstructure—which are the things He did and said when He was here, and the Apostles' Doctrine. Paul continues His exhortation:

"Now if anyone builds on this foundation with gold, silver, precious stones, wood, hay, straw, each one's work will become manifest, for the day will declare it, because it will be revealed by fire; and the fire will test each one's work of what sort it is. If anyone's work which he has built on it endures, he will receive a reward" (1 Cor. 3:12-14).

The Building Material

The quality of the building is determined by the materials used. Here Paul gives six types of building materials. We are vitally connected to the foundation; which is Jesus Christ the Chief Cornerstone. The apostles and prophets are the foundation stones joined to the Cornerstone; we are being built upon this solid foundation (Eph. 2:20). We are living stones (1 Pet. 2:4-5), being shaped to fit a special niche in the building, which no other stone can fill. We are responsible for the character of the building materials used to fill this niche. Paul amplifies the result of faulty or inadequate materials:

"If anyone's work is burned, he will suffer loss, but he himself will be saved, yet so as through fire. Do you not know that you are the temple of God and that the Spirit of God dwells in you?" (1 Cor. 3:15-16).

Paul is exhorting us to use the potential God has given us. If we use that potential, then we will receive rewards for faithful service. We must remember that rewards are not just for the eternal state. There are many rewards promised for the present time, such as inner peace and joy for those who will follow His directions. Cook develops the substance of our rewards:

"The substance of the reward is described in Revelation 21:1-7. It is stated (v. 7) that the 'overcomer' will inherit certain things, and the items enumerated in the context include a dwelling place with God, tearless eyes, deathless years, the absence of sorrow and pain, spiritual satisfaction without cost, and a sort of miscellaneous category that encompasses everything stated and unstated: all things made new... Finally, there is a sense in which reward may be diminished or even lost (2 Jn. 8). By a failure to 'watch' oneself, that is, by careless living and ministry, one may lose what he has accomplished and not receive his full reward. While each man's praise will come to him from God (1 Cor. 4:5), some will receive less praise than others." Cook, *The Theology of John*, p. 234.

The Potential for Loss

But if we do not use the opportunities He provides we will suffer loss. Note the results if we do not use or function in our potential. It will be a sad experience to come before Christ and reflect on what we did with what He gave us and come to the realization that we have failed to develop the skills and abilities He gave us, much less not to use them. Jesus will not have to say anything. We will be so regretful, that we will probably turn our head and walk away, reflecting on what we could have done with all that He gave us.

Inheritance Related to Rewards

It really does matter how we build our lives and utilize our God given abilities. The result will be our inheritance, our reigning with Him as kings. This is an awesome responsibility on our part. What is the prerequisite to our inheritance? We have already developed the idea of meekness in Chapter 6. But here it is important to understand the promise, "they shall inherit the earth." This is a promised reward to those who actively pursue meekness in this life time.

Two Kinds of Inheritance

There are two kinds of inheritance we can have. The first is our inheritance of God and heaven. Every believer inherits God when they believe, and they will go to heaven. There is no work required for this inheritance it is only by grace through faith in the Lord Jesus Christ for eternal life. Jesus said; "Blessed are the poor in spirit, for theirs is the kingdom of heaven" (Mat. 5:3). They will go to heaven but that is not all. This brings us to the second inheritance.

The second inheritance is different. This inheritance is a possession, and just like the Israelites inheriting the Promised Land, they were required to possess it. It was not enough to just enter the land, they must possess it. Those who crossed the Red Sea were believers but did not enter the Promised Land, because they would not trust God. They did their own thing, and as a result died in the wilderness (1 Cor. 10:1-6). Many of the Israelites who *did* enter did not inherit the land because of unbelief. They were apathetic in their participation (Heb.4:16-19). Dillow comments on this:

> "The Israelites, as a nation, seemed to reveal their regenerate condition when they promised, 'We will do everything the Lord has said' (Ex. 19:8). They had 'bowed down and worshipped' and trusted in the blood of the Passover lamb (Ex. 12:27-28), had by faith crossed the Red Sea, and had drunk (i.e., 'trusted in,' John 4:13-14; John 6:53-56) that spiritual rock which was Christ, yet they never obtained Canaan, their inheritance, because of their unbelief and disobedience. Here two categories of Old Testament regenerate saints are presented: those who inherited the land and those who did not. The inheritance (possession) was dependent upon their obedience. Not all who entered were obedient, just as not all who left Egypt were regenerate, but the nation as a whole was obedient. The Old Testament writers, as is well established, thought in corporate terms." Dillow, *The Reign of the Servant Kings*, p. 55.

Partakers Receive the Rewards

Now it is also true of the New Testament saints: we must be actively possessing or participating in our calling, our life ministry. Just as the Israelites were called out of Egypt to possess the Promised Land, we have been called out for a special ministry in this lifetime. We are in a training status in preparation for reigning with Him in the future.

Peter exhorts, "Therefore, brethren, be even more diligent to make your call and election sure; for if you do these things, you will never stumble" (2 Pet. 1:10). Your calling is the ministry God has given you, built around your giftedness (Eph. 4:1-2) and your election is having participated in His kingdom here on earth, will result in being chosen or elected for a great reward at the judgment seat of Christ (1 Cor. 3:9-15; 2 Tim. 2:11-13; 2 Pet.1:11, Rev. 20:4, Dan. 7:9).

> "This is a faithful saying: For if we died with Him, we shall also live with Him. If we endure, we shall also reign with Him. If we deny Him, He also will deny us. If we are faithless, He remains faithful; He cannot deny Himself" (2 Tim. 2:11-13).

However, our mandate here is to υπομεϖω, "to endure," "to bear up under suffering," or "to abide under." Without a doubt, this person is one who is participating in the ministry. The Bible is filled with exhortations to endure to persevere. But it has nothing to do with salvation in a justification sense. It has everything to do with salvation in the sense of sanctification. This endurance is a part of sanctification, and produces salvation in regard to the present tense or laying up treasures in heaven (Mat. 6:19-21).

Those who endure are laying up treasures in heaven. Remember, justification is a free gift—it costs one nothing; all that is required is "to believe." But sanctification is costly; it demands participation or partaking in the kingdom *now*. It has to do with what we do with what He has entrusted to us here on earth. We are preparing now for what we will be doing when we reign with Him.

Partakers Destined for a Throne

Reigning is a special reward to those faithful in their ministry now. This idea of rewards is often referred to as "crowns." Crowns allude to royalty. Jesus very clearly states of those who are participating in the kingdom now, will receive rewards and will reign with Him in His future Kingdom here on earth:

> "But you are those who have continued with me in my trials. And I bestow upon you a kingdom, just as my father bestowed one upon me. That you may eat and drink at my table in my kingdom, and sit on thrones judging the twelve tribes of Israel" (Lk. 22:28-30).

These are amazing concepts that we hear so very little teachings of in churches today. If we could realize the overwhelming supreme blessing this will be, we would fall on our face and worship Him. In fact that will be, as best I can discern from Scripture, the most humiliating and at the same time the most joyous experience we could ever imagine. We get somewhat of a glimpse of this humility and joy from John:

> "Whenever the living creatures give glory and honor and thanks to him who sits on the throne, who lives forever and ever, the twenty-four elders fall down before Him who sits on the throne and worship Him who lives forever and ever, and cast their crowns before the throne, saying: 'You are worthy, O Lord, to receive glory and honor and power; for You created all things, and by Your will they exist and were created" (Rev. 4:9-11).

What a privilege to look forward to this glorious experience when Jesus says, "Well done, good and faithful servant, enter into the joy of the Lord" (Mat. 25:21). We will fall on our face and praise Him. However, this is sort of like telling a three year old in March, "I'll get you a tricycle for Christmas." Ten minutes later that child has lost sight of the tricycle completely. We often read these passages, or hear someone talk about them, but as soon as the sound of the words have died out, we've either forgotten or minimized them. This idea of rewards is a serious matter.

Great Reminder

This is so important, that Peter says he will keep on reminding us, even after he is dead. He is speaking concerning our participating in the divine nature of God, and the effects of it in our lives here on earth and in the eternal state. He states it like this:

> "Therefore I will not be negligent to remind you always of these things, though you know *them*, and are established in the present truth. Yes, I think it is right, as long as I am in this tent, to stir you up by reminding *you*, knowing that shortly I *must* put off my tent, just as our Lord Jesus Christ showed me. Moreover I will be careful to ensure that you always have a reminder of these things after my decease" (2 Pet. 1:12-13).

Knowledge is the Source of His Power. How easy it is for us to minimize even so great a fact as an eternal reward. The verb he uses here is from $\mu\varepsilon\lambda\lambda\omega$, meaning, "to be about to do something." The idea is to be always ready, always partaking. Here with the infinitive, it indicates that these are some very important facts and he will keep on reminding us. This word is used again in verses 13 and 15. Without going into great exegetical detail, it's obvious Peter is deeply concerned about us remembering these principles. But what principles? His power has given every believer everything they need to live this life psychologically and physically and to manifest godliness with their body. When we are born again, Christ implants within our spirit His life; that animates our soul, giving spiritual answers to psychological problems. The soul then, energizes the body that will manifest virtue (God's transferable concepts). We, in our physical body, will demonstrate godly character. Next, He gives us the source of that power; "through our knowledge of Him". In an earlier chapter we discussed the fact that eternal life is for us, "that they may know Him" (Jn. 17:3). He is the same who called us out of darkness. This was accomplished by two of His attributes—His Glory and His Goodness. It is by these same attributes He has given us these great and precious promises (2 Pet. 1:2-4).

Partakers and Escapers

There is deep meaning in the words "precious promises" (2 Pet. 1:3). The word *promises* relates to the Scriptures, and *precious* relates to the value of Scripture. Then He explains the purpose of giving us His Word, "In order that we might be partakers of the divine nature" (2 Pet. 2:4). That is, our physical bodies in the natural world may demonstrate or manifest His character to those we minister to. The verb here *may be* is in the future tense, indicating something that will happen as we work through this process. We will become partakers. Note the following chart.

Next he gives the result of becoming a partaker. We will escape the corruption of this world. We will be better able to detect those old man thought patterns that allow the demonic world to manipulate us through our psychological makeup. This brings us to the characteristics of a partaker.

Character of a Partaker

The first characteristic of a partaker is *faith* (2 Pet. 1:5a). It was by grace, through faith, that we were made alive (Eph. 2:5-6). Faith is not something we add, it is something we exercise. When we were born again, God gave us the ability to make right decisions sufficient to accomplish all the things He has called us to do. That is why He can say He'll never give us more than we can handle (1 Cor. 10:13). Faith has to do with the mind—it translates us from a resister to a partaker (2 Pet. 1:3-4).

The next characteristic of a partaker is *goodness* (2 Pet. 1:5b). Goodness is what God is. Everything He does is Good; He can do no evil. Since we come into this world naturally, we have developed a lot of wrong principles, and we have a lot of badness that allows the world system to keep us in bondage (2 Pet. 1:4, 5, 9). By faith, we are able to deal with all those bad attitudes and actions that separate us from God, and we are able to manifest godliness.

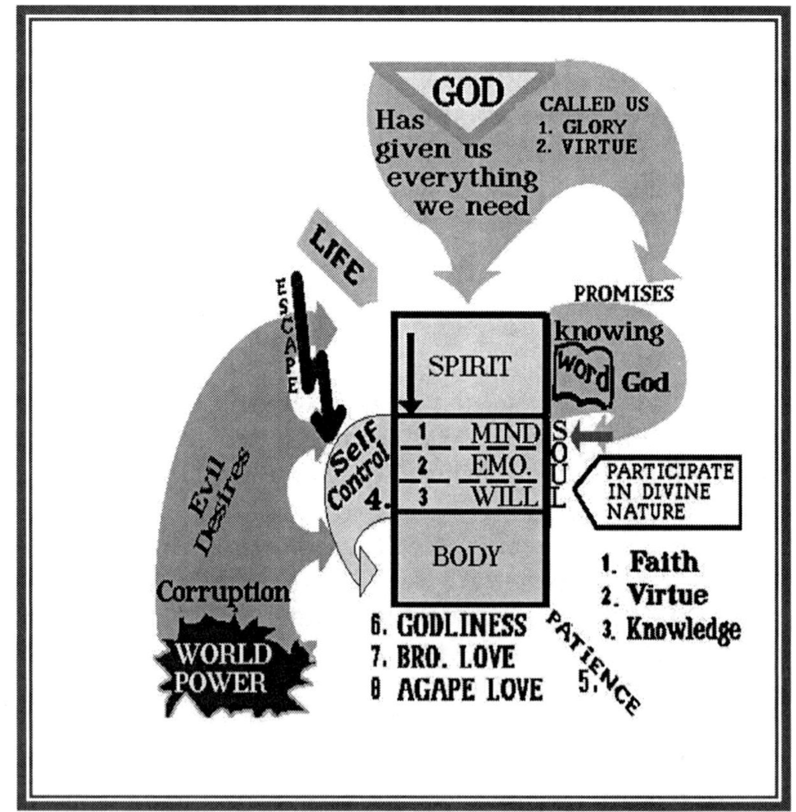

The third characteristic of a partaker is *knowledge* (2 Pet. 1:5b). When our minds are renewed and we are able to radiate His goodness, then we can submit our wills to His will. The more knowledge we have of Him, the more our ways become His ways. This demands that we yield our will to His righteousness.

The fourth characteristic of a partaker is *self-control* (2 Pet. 1:6). Having transformed our minds, purified our hearts, and yielded our self-righteousness, we can now—through self control—get a handle on the flesh. To do what I ought to do, rather than what I want to do.

The fifth characteristic of a partaker is *patience.* I am now able to get out of myself and reach out to others, always thinking more highly of others than I think of myself (Phil. 2:3-4). This is a characteristic of God. It enables us to hang in there with others, ministering in love to the unlovable.

The sixth characteristic of a partaker is *godliness* (2 Pet. 1:7a). Now we are able to partake in the divine nature, doing what God would have3 us do. We are truly His representatives in the world where people are blinded. We are His radiant lights.

The seventh characteristic of a partaker is *brotherly love* (2 Pet. 1:7b). This enables us to reach out to those around us. We are now God's peacemakers, His reconcilers, His ambassadors. We are His agents, calling out to the lost, "be reconciled to God" (2 Cor. 5:20).

The eighth characteristic of a partaker is *love* ($\alpha\gamma\alpha\pi\eta$) 2 Pet. 1:7c. This is the higher love; this is what God is. This is that ability Jesus demonstrated, unconditional love, in His becoming sin for us (2 Cor. 5:21). It is the kind of love that enabled God to give His only son that we might be saved.

Results of Doing These Things

Then Peter amplifies the significance of these character building qualities with two promises, one positive and one negative. First, he promises that if we will do these things in a continually increasing way, we will not be ineffective or unproductive, but we will be effective and productive in everything we do. That is the positive reward we will receive in this lifetime, but there is more as we go on making investments in eternity

But with the positive next comes the a negative (2 Pet. 1:9). Here Peter warns us to be alert. If we do not do these things, we will become nearsighted, blinded, and will have forgotten that we have been forgiven of our past sins. In other words, all the old man thought patterns will return with the guilt, bitterness, and general wrong thinking. Note the following chart.

Assurance and Stability

The solution to all this is in verse 10. First, make sure of your calling; be sure you are looking to Jesus for your salvation. Secondly, make sure of your election. We make sure of our election as we go, adding to our faith the godly qualities of 2 Pet. 1:7-8, in an increasing measure. Our eternal security is confirmed as we function as partakers. When we are resisting God's way (wrong thinking) we are implying that Christ's death was not sufficient for our sins. All those old thought patterns will re-surface and we will become "nearsighted, blinded and will have forgotten that our sins have been forgiven." As a result we will not have the confidence we experienced when we were thinking rightly or obedient. Our thinking will be distorted by guilt, and the effort to make atonement for our sins. This is a discipline from the Lord in this lifetime.

Finally, the great promise is imminent; the culmination of all this. The training program is over for those who have done these things, who have served faithfully as partakers, and there will be a special honor. Our crowns or rewards will be appropriate for what we have done with what He has entrusted us with in this lifetime (Mat: 25:14-30, Rev. 22:12). Paul says; "I have fought the good fight, I have finished the race" (2 Tim. 4:7).

Peter makes it clear that all the passages we have studied are now confirmed by this great promise: "For so an entrance will be supplied to you abundantly into the everlasting Kingdom of our Lord and savior Jesus Christ" (2 Pet 1:11). Jesus Himself will welcome you with those special words, "Well done good and faithful servant" (Mat. 25:22-23). It's no wonder Peter says, "I'm going to keep on reminding you of these things even though you already know them" (2 Pet. 1:12-15). We must keep on learning, always alert, anxious to partake in His ministry here and now. Dillow gives a strong challenge:

> "We believe the great neglect of Western Christianity is not that our pulpits have failed to warn people who claim the name of Christ that they are perishing. Our neglect is that we have not sufficiently explained the future joy of sharing in the coming messianic partnership and the danger of forfeiting this inheritance. If such a vision were consistently held before our congregations, the love and fear of God would be greatly increased. Surely many of those fifty million reported by the Gallup poll who claim to be born again would begin to act like it." Dillow, *Reign of the Servant Kings*, p. 605.

The writer of Hebrews states it this way: "How shall we escape if we neglect so great a salvation?" (Heb. 2:3). The sad truth is we will not escape if we go on neglecting this great salvation; we will suffer loss and experience discipline in this lifetime and the loss of rewards in the future. The following chart amplifies the results of neglecting our great salvation (Heb. chapters 2, 3-4, 5-6, 10, 12-13).

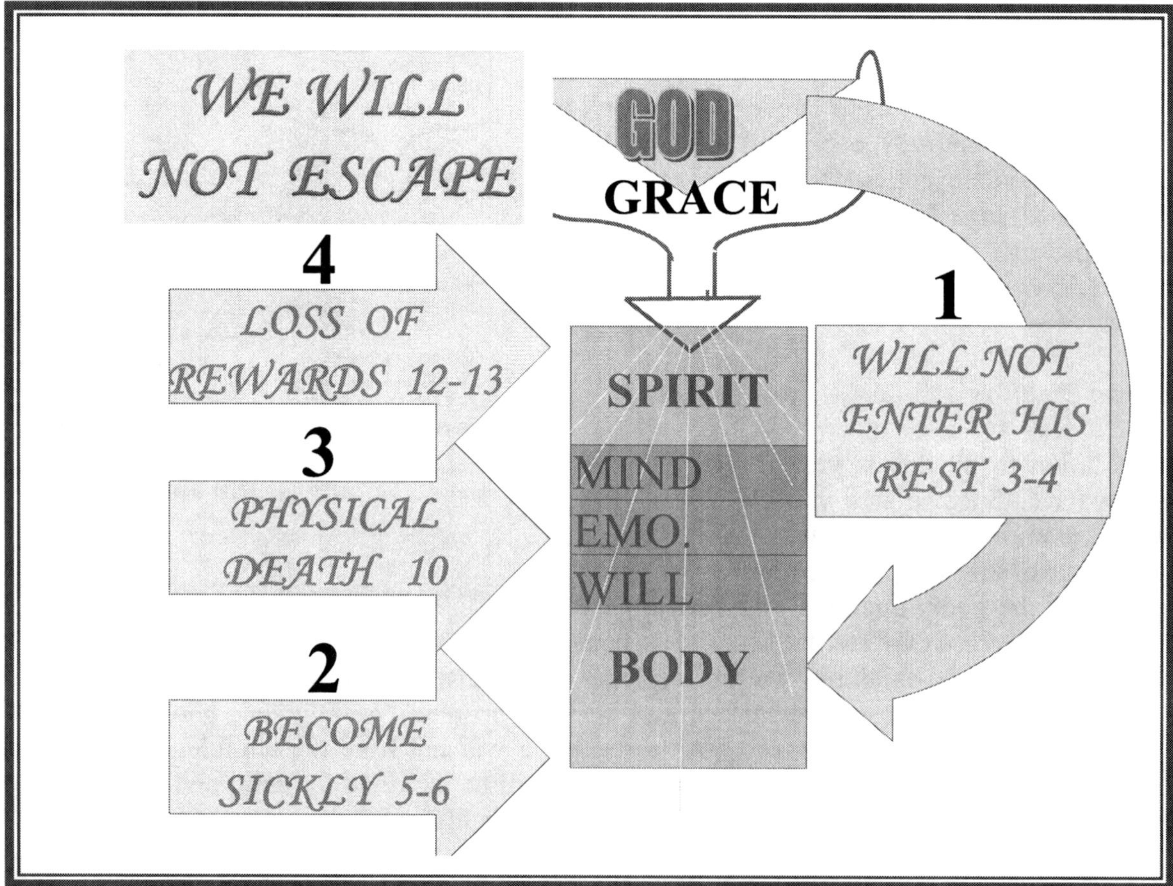

Conclusion

We are the partakers. We are the salt of the earth, the light of the world (Mat. 5:13-6) we are the parts of the Body that keep things from being as bad as they could be. We are His light reflectors, exposing sin in the dark world. What are you doing with what He has given you? Remember, a person's work will be revealed by fire. The quality of that work, whether good (work done in the Spirit) or bad (work done in the flesh), will determine whether we receive a reward or suffer loss (1 Cor. 3:12-15). If our saltiness has been watered down by apathy, and our light is smudged by the flesh, then there will be no reward. In the Beatitudes, Jesus has given us a formula for experiencing happiness or blessedness here on earth and rewards for eternity. What will you do with what He has entrusted to you? You have been given a special niche to fill as a stone in the building of His Body, the Church.

PROJECT

1. What is the nature of the reward for participating in His kingdom now? (Mat. 5:12; 2 Pet. 1:11)

2. What is the condition for rewards? (Heb. 11:6, 3:14)

3. Will there be any rewards for those who do not participate? (Heb. 2:1-3, 2 Tim. 2:11-13)

4. What are the two kinds of rewards? (Page 162)

5. Name the different building materials. (1 Cor. 3:12-13)

a. __________________		d. __________________	
b. __________________		e. __________________	
c. __________________		f. __________________	

6. What are the two kinds of inheritance? (page 98-99)

7. What are the promises to the participator in this lifetime? (2 Pet. 1:4)

8. Read; <u>Majestic Destiny,</u> by Curtis Tucker

BIBLIOGRAPHY

Adams, Jay Edward, *A Call to Discernment*, Stanley NC: Timeless Texts, 1999.

Bing, Charles C., *Journal of the Grace Evangelical Society* article, "Coming to Terms With Discipleship," Vol. 5:1, Spring 1992.

Cook, W. Robert, *Systematic Theology, Vol. II*, Portland, OR: Western Conservative Baptist Seminary, 1970.

-------, *The Theology of John,* Chicago, IL: Moody Press, 1979.

Currah, Galen, *Spiritual Gifts, Designed and Described*, Masters thesis, Western Conservative Baptist Seminary, Portland, Oregon.

Dillow, Joseph C., *Reign of the Servant Kings*, Hayesville, NC: Schoettle Publishing Co., Inc., 1992.

Ferguson, Marilyn, *Aquarian Conspiracy*, Los Angeles, CA: J. P. Tarcher, Inc. 1987.

Hodges, Zane Clark, *Grace in Eclipse, A Study on Eternal Rewards*, Dallas, TX: Redención Viva, 1985.

-------, *The Epistle of James*, Irving, TX: Grace Evangelical Society, 1994.

Hull, Bill, *Jesus Christ Disciple-Maker*, Colorado Springs, CO: Nav Press Publishing, 1984.

Ironside, H.A., *1 Corinthans*, Neptune, NJ: Loizeaux Brothers, 1983.

Kennedy, D. James, *Evangelism Explosion: Equipping Churches for Friendship, Evangelism, Discipleship, and Healthy Growth*, Wheaton, IL: Tyndale House Publishers, Inc., 1966.

Lenski, R.C.H., *Interpretation of St. Matthew's Gospel*, Minneapolis, MN: Augsburg Publishing House, 1961.
Lybrand, Fred R, *Back to Faith,* Xulon Press, 2009

MacArthur, John F., *Ephesians: New Testament Commentary*, Chicago, IL: Moody Press, 1986.

-------, *First Corinthians: New Testament Commentary*, Chicago, IL: Moody Press, 1984.

-------, *Kingdom Living, Here and Now*, Chicago, IL: Moody Press, 1995.

McMillen, S.I., *None of These Diseases*, New York, NY: Jove Publications, 1982.

Miller, Wendell E., *Forgiveness: The Power and the Puzzles*, Warsaw, IN: ClearBrook*Publishers*, 1994.

Nee, Watchman, *The Body of Christ*, Anaheim, CA: Living Stream Ministry, 2001.

Tucker, Curtis H. *Majestic Destiny,* Portland OR, Last Chapter Publishing LLC, 2011

Allen, Ronald B. *The Majesty of Man*, Multnomah Press, Portland, OR, 1984

RESOURCES - "YOU CAN BE SURE!"

By Dr. Bob Wilkin, used by permission from the
Grace Evangelical Society

Do you know for *sure* that you are going to heaven? If you're like most people, you're a little afraid to say "Yes." You think it sounds a little presumptuous. I mean, can anyone really be *sure*? Well, the Bible has good news for you. You *can* be sure. In fact, God *wants* you to be sure. And it's not as complicated as you might think.

Let's look at what God says in His Word.

God says...

There is none righteous, no, not one.
The Letter of Paul to the Romans, Chapter 3, Verse 10

For all have sinned and fall short of the glory of God.
The Letter of Paul to the Romans, Chapter 3, Verse 23

For God so loved the world that He gave His only begotten Son, that whoever believes in Him should not perish but have everlasting life.
The Gospel of John, Chapter 3, Verse 16

You were not redeemed with corruptible things, like silver or gold… but with the precious blood of Christ, as of a lamb without blemish and without spot. The First Letter of Peter, Chapter 1, Verses 18-19

Jesus Gives Eternal Life to Those Who Believe in Him.

God clearly explains in His Word that we are all sinners. "All have sinned." None of us is good enough to get into heaven on his or her own merits to spend eternity with God. There is none righteous, no, not one." But God loves us so much that He provided a way. That way is through His Son, the Lord Jesus. By dying on the Cross, Jesus paid the full and complete price for our sins so that we don't have to.

Because He shed His blood and died for us, Jesus Christ is able to fulfill His promise to freely give believers eternal life.

But what is eternal life?
God says...

I am the way, the truth, and the life. No one comes to the Father except through Me. The Gospel of John, Chapter 14, Verse 6

He who believes in Me has everlasting life.
The Gospel of John, Chapter 6, Verse 47

The life was manifested, and we have seen, and bear witness, and declare to you that eternal life which was with the Father and was manifested to us.
The First Letter of John, Chapter 1, Verse 2

That means...

In one sense, eternal life is what its name suggests: unending life. After all, if *eternal* life could be lost, then it is misnamed, because it wouldn't really be eternal. All who have eternal life will live forever in God's kingdom. No one who has come to faith in Christ will ever go to hell. Once you believe in Christ, your eternal destiny in God's kingdom is guaranteed.

In another sense, eternal life is not merely unending life. It is the life of God. Indeed, John refers to Jesus Christ Himself as eternal life. Eternal life is God's kind of life. It is life that comes from God. Thus a person who has eternal life has God's life within him.

It is obvious from what we have just said that eternal life doesn't begin when we die. Jesus said, "He who believes in Me *has* [present tense] everlasting life." He didn't say that the one who believes in Him *will have* (future tense) everlasting life. He said that he *has* eternal life—from that very first moment of faith. Thus a brand-new believer has God's life, which is unending and full of potential.

But I already believe that Jesus is God, that He lived a sinless life, and that He died and rose again.

God says...

Jesus said to her [Martha], *"I am the resurrection and the life. He who believes in Me, though he may die, he shall live. And whoever lives and believes in Me shall never die. Do you believe this?" She said to Him, "Yes, Lord, I believe that You are the Christ, the Son of God, who is to come into the world."*
The Gospel of John, Chapter 11, Verses 25-27

That means...

Just believing in Jesus' deity, without sin, death, and resurrection won't give you assurance that you have eternal life. Millions of people believe those things and yet lack assurance. The reason is because it is sadly possible to believe that Jesus died and rose again, and yet not believe His promise to give eternal life freely to all who believe in Him. Multitudes of people believe that Jesus' death and resurrection was *necessary* for their salvation, but that it wasn't *enough.* They believe that their commitment, obedience, and good works are *also* necessary for them to go to heaven.

To be sure you are saved, you must believe that Jesus Christ has given you eternal life as He said He would if you believed in Him. It's simply a matter of taking God at His word. Martha did, and she *knew* she had eternal life. So can you.

Is it really that simple?

God says...

Jesus said to her [Martha], "I am the resurrection and the life. He who believes in Me, though he may die, he shall live. And whoever lives and believes in Me shall never die. Do you believe this?" She said to Him, "Yes, Lord, I believe that you are the Christ, the Son of God, who is to come into the world."
The Gospel of John, Chapter 11, Verses 25-27

That means...

Yes, it really is that simple.   Take a second look at how Martha responded to the Lord's question, "Do you believe this?"

She was definite and assured. Martha didn't hesitate to say, "Yes, Lord I believe." She believed that Jesus was the Christ, the Messiah, the Son of God, the One whom the Old Testament prophets had foretold. She knew that the Messiah gives eternal life to all who believe in Him. There was no doubt in her mind.

Like Martha, you too can be sure you have eternal life. The Bible says that you must believe in Christ for eternal life. Have you done that? If you have, then you are saved! It really is that simple!

BUT... aren't good works necessary for assurance?

God says...

By grace you have been saved through faith, and that not of yourselves, it is the gift of God, not of works, lest anyone should boast.
Letter of Paul to the Ephesians, Chapter 2, Verses 8-9

That means...

Knowing you have eternal life is dependent on believing Christ's promise, not on the works you do. Since the possession of eternal life is based on believing God's promise and on nothing else, how could works ever be necessary for assurance?

As we've already noted, many people think they gain eternal life by believing in Christ *and* by doing good works. Yet the Bible says that salvation is "the gift of God" and that it is "not of works, lest anyone should boast." Only by believing in Christ can you be sure you have eternal life.

Until you come to the place where you stop depending on your own good works, you won't have eternal life. To be saved you must believe in Christ, not in your works. And, once you believe in Christ, you will be sure you are saved because your salvation is dependent on your belief in God's promise, not on your works.

BUT... I thought I could lose my salvation.

God says...

Most assuredly, I say to you, he who hears My word and believes in Him who sent Me has everlasting life, and shall not come into judgment, but has passed from death into life.
The Gospel of John, Chapter 5, Verse 24

And Jesus said to them, "I am the bread of life. He who comes to Me shall never hunger, and he who believes in Me shall never thirst... All that the Father has given Me will come to Me, and the one who comes to Me I will by no means cast out. For I have come down from heaven, not to do My own will, but the will of Him who sent Me. This is the will of the Father who sent Me, that of all He has given Me I should lose nothing, but should raise it up on the last day."

The Gospel of John, Chapter 6, Verses 35, 37-39

That means...

There is no way salvation can be lost. Jesus said that the person who believes in Him shall not come into judgment. That's a promise. If a person who had everlasting life ever "came into judgment," then Jesus would not be true to His word. Yet it is impossible for God to lie.

Many people think that staying saved is a matter of *their* doing God's will. However, Jesus Christ said that it is really a matter of *His* doing God's will! Jesus promised that whoever believes in Him will *never* hunger or thirst. Never. He promised that He will by no means cast out anyone who comes to Him and that He won't lose even one person who has believed in Him.

If anyone who came to faith in Christ ever lost his or her salvation, then Jesus would have failed to fulfill His promise and to do the will of the Father. Christ's eternal gift can never fail for any reason. He guarantees it.

Can assurance be lost?

God says...

I marvel that you are turning away so soon from Him who called you in the grace of Christ, to a different gospel, which is not another; but there are some who trouble you and want to pervert the gospel of Christ.
The Letter of Paul to the Galatians, Chapter 1, Verses 6-7

Stand fast therefore in the liberty by which Christ has made us free, and do not be entangled again with the yoke of bondage.
The Letter of Paul to the Galatians, Chapter 5, Verse 1

That means...

Yes, assurance can be lost. While eternal life can't be lost, assurance can. Whenever a believer stops looking to Christ for assurance, he will lose assurance of his salvation. The believers in Galatia were confronted by false teachers. The false teachers told them that they had to keep the Law of Moses in order to be saved. The result was that some of the believers in Galatia lost the assurance that they were saved.

A person is saved the very moment he believes in Christ for eternal life. At that moment, he knows for sure that he has eternal life and that he can never lose it. However, that does not mean that all Christians always have assurance of salvation. If a Christian takes his eyes off Christ, then he will lose his assurance. Each day you must believe Christ's promise to you in order to stay sure that you have eternal life.

If you lose your faith, you will also lose your assurance. Therefore you need to cultivate your faith in order to keep your assurance. "Avoid truth decay: Read your Bible every day" is a slogan that is true of all aspects of the Christian life, including assurance of salvation.

Shouldn't I feel happy all the time if I'm really saved?
God says...

Now we exhort you, brethren, warn those who are unruly, comfort the fainthearted, uphold the weak, be patient with all.
The First Letter of Paul to the Thessalonians, Chapter 5, Verse 14,

Therefore, when Jesus saw her weeping, and the Jews who came with her weeping, He groaned in the spirit and was troubled. And He said, "Where have you laid him?" They said to Him, "Lord, come and see." Jesus wept. Then the Jews said, "See how He loved him!"
The Gospel of John, Chapter 11, Verses 33-36

"In the world you have tribulation..."
The Gospel of John, Chapter 16, Verse 33

"And God will wipe away every tear from their eyes; there shall be no more death, nor sorrow, nor crying. There shall be no more pain, for the former things have passed away."
The Revelation of Jesus Christ, Chapter 21, Verse 4

That means...

No. You won't experience unbroken happiness until you go to be with the Lord. Only then will He wipe away all your tears. Only then will all your sorrows and pains cease.

Many people mistakenly think that once they receive eternal life all of their problems are behind them. Yet that just isn't true. Even the Lord Jesus Himself groaned and wept over the death of his friend Lazarus. Christians experience tribulation in this life. Grief, depression, family problems, illnesses, injuries, financial problems and chronic pain are just some of the things Christians have to deal with in their lives.

Feelings are like thermometers. They fluctuate. Sometimes you feel great. Sometimes you feel "lousy." Christians can be bold and strong or fainthearted and weak. Feelings come and go. Just as your knowledge of your earthly citizenship is not based on how you feel ("I'm really discouraged today; I wonder if I'm *really* an American"), so neither is your knowledge of your *heavenly* citizenship.

God promised you eternal life if you believed in Christ for it. God doesn't lie. The Gospel is true. If you have believed in Christ for eternal life, then you have it, even if you're in great physical or emotional pain. You can depend on His promise regardless of how you feel.

But... if I were really saved, wouldn't my circumstances be better?

God says...

From the Jews five times I [Paul] received forty stripes minus one. Three times I was beaten with rods; once I was shipwrecked; a night and a day I have been in the deep; in journeys often, in perils of waters, in perils of robbers, in perils of my own countrymen, in perils of the Gentiles, in perils of the city, in perils in the wilderness, in perils in the sea, in perils among false brethren, in weariness and toil, in sleeplessness often, in hunger and thirst, in fastings often, in cold and nakedness—beside the other things, what comes upon me daily: my deep concern for all the churches.
The Second Letter of Paul to the Corinthians, Chapter 11, Verses 24-28

That means...

It's easy to think that if I'm truly a child of God, then nothing bad could ever happen to me. Yet bad things *do* happen to God's children. As the quotation above shows the apostle Paul experienced several lifetimes' worth of trouble in his service for Christ

Circumstances are fickle. Sometimes you're on top of the world. Sometimes the world is on top of you! Until you are in heaven, you can't look to your circumstances to see whether or not you're saved.

But... I already made the decision to follow Jesus and to serve Him.

God says...

Not by works of righteousness which we have done, but according to His mercy He saved us, through the washing of regeneration and renewing of the Holy Spirit.
The Letter of Paul to Titus, Chapter 3, Verse 5

For the love of Christ compels us, because we judge thus: that if One died for all, then all died; and He died for all, that those who live should live no longer for themselves, but for Him who died for them and rose again.
The Second Letter of Paul to the Corinthians, Chapter 5, Verses 14-15

I beseech you therefore, brethren, by the mercies of God, that you present your bodies a living sacrifice, holy, acceptable to God, which is your reasonable service. And do not be conformed to this world, but be transformed by the renewing of your mind, that you may prove what is that good and acceptable and perfect will of God.
The Letter of Paul to the Romans, Chapter 12, Verses 1-2

That means...

You've made a wonderful decision. That's a noble goal. However, it has nothing to do with obtaining eternal life or assurance. Following and serving the Lord are not the issue in salvation. The only issue in salvation is faith. Of course, serving Christ is something that you as a growing Christian should do. The love of Christ should move you to serve Him. Serving Him *is* reasonable.

However, you should serve Him because you know you have eternal life, not in order to try to gain it. If you think you need to serve Christ in order to have eternal life, then you don't believe His promise.

Believing in Christ assures you that you are saved. Then, by all means, *do* follow Him!

You mean I really can be sure?

God says...

If we receive the witness of men, the witness of God is greater; for this is the witness of God which He has testified of His Son. He who believes in the Son of God has the witness in himself; he who does not believe God has made Him a liar, because he has not believed the testimony that God has given of His Son. And this is the testimony: that God has given us eternal life, and this life is in His Son. He who has the Son has life; he who does not have the Son does not have life. These things I have written to you who believe in the name of the Son of God, that you may know that you have eternal life, and that you may continue to believe in the name of the Son of God.
The First Letter of John, Chapter 5, Verses 9-13

That means...

Yes, you can *really know* that you have eternal life. God didn't say that you could *guess* or *hope* or *think* that you have eternal life. He said you could *know*.

In fact, if you don't know that you're saved, then you aren't focusing on the truth of God's testimony. All you need to do to be sure you have eternal life is to believe God's promise. Don't look within yourself. Introspection is a bottomless pit. Look instead to God's promise. He guarantees eternal life to all who believe on Him for it. How simple!

Let's review: Neither your good works, nor your circumstances, nor your feelings will give you assurance. Those things are all changeable and undependable. Only one thing will give you assurance: believing God's testimony concerning His Son. God guarantees that all who believe on His Son for eternal life have it and will never perish. If you believe in Christ for eternal life, then you are sure that you're saved. It's that simple.

Now what?

God says...

I am the vine, you are the branches. He who abides in Me, and I in him, bears much fruit; for without Me you can do nothing.
The Gospel of John, Chapter 15, Verse 5

As the Father has loved Me, I also have loved you; abide in My love. If you keep My commandments, you will abide in My love, just as I have kept My Father's commandments and abide in His love. These things I have spoken to you, that My joy may remain in you, and that your joy may be full.
The Gospel of John, Chapter 15, Verses 9-11

That means...

Knowing you have eternal life is just the beginning. You have before you a door of opportunity which is wide open to something magnificent and wonderful: fellowship with the Lord Jesus Christ. He not only wants you to live with Him forever in His kingdom, He also wants you to enjoy fellowship with Him here and now.

A life of meaning and purpose is to be found in fellowship with Christ. If you walk in fellowship with Him, your life will have *eternal* value and significance. Also, you will experience God's love and joy.

Growth in Christ, like the physical growth of children, takes time. Spend time daily in prayer and in God's Word, the Bible. The Gospel of John is a good place to start. Find and regularly attend a church where Christ is honored and where the Bible and the Gospel are clearly taught. Seek out an older, mature Christian who is willing to mentor you in the faith.

Remember one thing: Jesus Christ guarantees eternal life to all who believe in Him for it. Assurance of salvation is something which is, and always will be, vital to your walk with Christ. Keep looking up! As long as you look to Him and His promise to you, you will know you have eternal life.

WHAT IS THE GRACE EVANGELICAL SOCIETY?

Grace Evangelical Society (GES), founded in 1986, seeks to focus worldwide attention on the distinction between the freeness of eternal life and the costliness of eternal rewards. GES provides many ways to help you grow in your faith:

A free bimonthly newsletter which deals with important questions and key passages of Scripture
A semiannual journal providing more in-depth analysis of questions and passages
Commentaries on books of the New Testament
Tapes of sermons dealing with important passages and issues
Seminars and conferences

If you are interested in further information about GES, or if you would like to receive a free subscription to our newsletter, you can contact us at:

GES
100 WEST OAK ST. SUITE G
DENTON TX 76201-4144

Phone: 940-565-0000
Fax: 972-255-3884
E-mail: www.ges@faithalone.org
Website: www.faithalone.org

CPSIA information can be obtained at www.ICGtesting.com
Printed in the USA
LVOW031531160912

298992LV00001B/38/P